ENGLISH PLACE-NAMES EXPLAINED

—— Charles Whynne-Hammond ——

COUNTRYSIDE BOOKS
NEWBURY BERKSHIRE

Contents

PREFACE   6

SECTION A – THE HERITAGE AND EVOLUTION
    OF PLACE-NAMES   7

1   THE STUDY OF PLACE-NAMES: RESEARCH &
UNDERSTANDING   8
    Introduction   8
    Undertaking Research   12
    Sources   15
    Linguistic Developments   17
    Interpreting Source Material   18
       (a) *The Formation of Names*   19
       (b) *Compound Names*   20
       (c) *Misleading Names*   21
       (d) *Misleading Spellings*   22

2   THE BLENDING OF LANGUAGES: MIGRATION &
CONSOLIDATION   24
    Introduction   24
    The Mixing of Tongues   28
    The Celtic Fringe   29
    The Saxon Kingdoms   30
    Danelaw   33
    The Development of Shires   33
    The Consolidation of Counties   36
    County Sub-Divisions   37

3 COMMUNICATION: TRACKS, WAYS & ROADS   41
      Ancient Trackways   41
      Roman Roads   44
      Trading Routes   48
      Non-Trading Routes   50
      Turnpikes and Toll Roads   52

4 THE NATURAL WORLD: LANDSCAPE & NATURE   54
      Topographical Features   54
      Directional Names   56
      Climatic Names   58
      Rivers and Estuaries   59
      Coastal Areas   60
      Forest Names   63
      Tree and Plant Names   67
      Animal Names   68

5 THE NATURE OF SOCIETY: CULTURE & BELIEF   70
      Folk and Tribal Names   70
      Personal Names   72
      Group Names   73
      Pagan Names   78
      Christian Names   80
      Death and Burial Names   83
      Folklore and Legend Names   84

6   THE NEEDS OF SOCIETY: CO-OPERATION & PROTECTION   87
     The Spread of Agriculture   88
     Enclosure Names   90
     Estate Names   91
     Fortified Settlement Names   93
     Colonisation Names   97
     Bastide Towns   101

7   THE WEALTH OF SOCIETY: INDUSTRY & TRADE   102
     Transport Names   102
     Market Names   104
     Mineral Names   104
     Industrial Revolution Names   106
     Resort Names   111
     Urban Names   112

8   NAMES WITHIN TOWNS AND VILLAGES   117
     Street Names   117
     House Names   123
     Pub Names   124
     Theatre and Cinema Names   133

SECTION B – COUNTY GAZETTEER   137

COMMON PLACE-NAME ELEMENTS   244

INDEX   248

Preface

I wrote *Tracing the History of Place-Names* (published 1992) as an academic introduction to the study of geographical etymology: how and why the names we see about us evolved. Since my university days I have travelled and researched widely, this subject still holding a fascination. The landscapes around us, both natural and man-made, tell us their pasts – their evolving character, structural history and culture. And the understanding of the place-names within those landscapes strengthens our sense of place and deepens the ties with our national roots.

The book was well received. Now I have revised, expanded and restyled it under the title *English Place-Names Explained*, extra material being added and photographs introduced. It has been a worthwhile and interesting undertaking which I hope will bring this subject to a wider public.

I should like to thank my wife Glenys for her constant support and advice and my brothers Alec and Peter for their additional research. I should also like to thank Lynn Whyte, Trevor Jones and Marian and Ian Douglas for their extra information and photographic material. I must, in addition, thank Nicholas Battle and Paula Leigh (at Countryside Books) for their enthusiasm for this project.

Charles Whynne-Hammond

SECTION
A

THE HERITAGE AND EVOLUTION OF PLACE-NAMES

———••◄∞►••———

The Study Of Place-Names: Research & Understanding

·•◦∞◦•·

▦ INTRODUCTION

E very name, like every word, has an origin. Whether it be a name of an object, a person or a place, it will have a derivation based upon a past development of sounds and meanings. It will have connections with other names, and correlations with other words from similar cultural or linguistic backgrounds. It will be the product of a distillation of the oral traditions and written customs experienced within historic landscapes and societies. The study of such name and word developments is called 'etymology'.

Finding out more about the names all around us can be fun. Whether we enjoy walking or driving in the countryside, reading guidebooks or maps, looking around our villages and towns, going to a pub or football match, even just shopping, we can increase our enjoyment by understanding more about the names we see. Everywhere there are names, and everywhere there is a place-name story to be told.

Even the names of the clothes we wear can have origins in place-names. Our woollen jerseys are named after Jersey, balaclava helmets after Balaclava (where the Crimean war battle was fought and the famous Charge of the Light Brigade took place) and our riding jodhpurs after Jodhpur in India. The 'jeans' we wear derive their name from 'Janne' the old French name for the town of Genoa where the twilled cotton cloth used in their manufacture was originally made. Today jeans are made of 'denim', a word we get from 'de Nimes' – Nimes being a town in southern France. And talking of material, 'nylon', it is thought, is so-called because it was invented and developed simultaneously at two places, New York and London.

Westward Ho!, Devon

In place-names, too, life can imitate art. Westward Ho! is a book by Charles Kingsley (published 1855) and Jamaica Inn was written by Daphne du Maurier (published 1936). The north Devon town Westward Ho! was actually named after the novel, built as a tourist resort and commemorating the famous local author whose statue stands in nearby Bideford. The isolated pub on Bodmin Moor was called Jamaica Inn long before the novel, the name going back to the mid-18th century. It was not so called because of any link with smuggling, even though rum was indeed a popular contraband. It was, in fact, named in honour of the local landowners of the time, the Trelawney family. Two of its members, Edward and William, were Governors of Jamaica during the 18th century.

Jamaica Inn, Cornwall

Place-names also crop up in our everyday speech. Not just when giving directions or relating travels, of course, but indirectly in our phrases and daily conversation. Taking 'coals to Newcastle' is of little help when one remembers that Tyneside was a centre for solid fuel long before coal was mined, coastal sea-coal having been collected there since medieval times. And being 'sent to Coventry' was certainly no fun during the Civil War when Royalist prisoners-of-war were despatched to that very pro-Roundhead city in the Midlands. No wonder the saying has stuck.

Place-names can be curious like 'High Easter' and 'Christmas Common', or courteous like 'Pleasley' and 'Thankerton'. They can be amusing like 'Knotty Ash' or murderous like 'Bloodybush Edge'. They can be euphonic, 'Iwerne Courtney', or the opposite, 'Ugly'. Some place-names even sound as though they might be human – 'Edith Weston', 'Hartley Wintney', 'Barton Seagrave'. Such are surely a rich source of personal names for writers of fiction.

Who could not be distracted by the fascination of names? For the pure enjoyment of knowledge alone the study of place-names would be worthwhile. Names make up a large part of our vocabulary and are, everywhere, a large part of our lives. They are used to distinguish, locate and describe the places about us and therefore reflect our own human characteristics. They help to distinguish, locate and describe ourselves. A general interest in their origins is therefore both understandable and natural.

But the study of place-names can be more than just informative and pleasurable. It can be central to our very real need to learn about ourselves and our past, about the world as a whole and our rôle in the evolution of life.

Place-names have both a linguistic derivation and an interpretative one. They derive from past languages, ancient Greek, Latin, Saxon and so on, and from past meanings, telling us something of the topography, climate, society and philosophy of different places and periods in history. Hence, the study of place-names not only complements studies in other spheres of knowledge but can also actually enhance and explain those studies.

Briefly, place-names can be used within other subjects in the following ways:

ARCHAEOLOGY. Place-name evidence can give supplementary information about known antiquities and new information about possible new sites for archaeological excavation. For example, names containing the Saxon element 'straet' may indicate the existence of a Roman road and the names containing an element meaning 'fort' might suggest a Roman camp. Archaeologists often study place-names before carrying out a dig.

HISTORY. The study of the linguistic origins of place-names, and the mapping of linguistic elements within place-names, can indicate early population movements, cycles of invasion and settlement, tribal distributions and ethnic settlement patterns. Scandinavian place-names in Britain, for instance, show the progress of Viking invasion down Eastern England, in the North-west and across into Ireland.

GEOGRAPHY. Study of place-name meanings can tell us the character of landscapes at the time of initial habitation. Where a river flowed, or where a lake existed might be important information to a geographer, especially if a date can be given. Such knowledge could indicate speeds of erosion or deposition, the nature of weathering, the action of wind and rain, or the extent of landform construction. Similarly, place-name meanings might tell the geographer about former climatic or weather patterns, vegetation cover or animal life. The comparison of meanings may also indicate the ways in which early peoples changed the countryside, by clearing the woodlands, draining the marshes and cultivating the hills.

THE NATURE OF SOCIETY. Place-names give us a great wealth of evidence regarding the way people lived in centuries past: how they thought, how they were organised, what they did. Some of the earliest names include pagan gods, telling us about pre-Christian beliefs, and names from ancient legends telling us, perhaps, about old superstitions. Later names indicate customs, institutions and land ownership, thus telling us the way class systems were organised and authority was wielded. Place-names which include the names of tribal leaders, for example, suggest societies divided into groups and hierarchies; place-names which refer to meeting places ('moots') suggest ordered societies in which rules were both made and obeyed. Place-names referring to particular occupations or commodities, like fishing, hunting, milling on the one hand and salt, sheep, wheat on the other, tell us about early economic life. Some place-names even tell us about the sports and pastimes of the past, bear baiting and horse-racing for instance.

LINGUISTICS. The way some place-names have been formed can help language students decide how early tongues were spoken. Inflexions and verbal stresses can be worked out, meanings can be cross-checked with known alternatives. Links between different old languages and indeed, between old and modern languages can be assessed. Saxon and Viking tongues had certain similarities, for example, and the structure of Saxon is related to that of modern German. Some place-names actually use elements not found in other records, thus helping to extend the known vocabulary of past languages. For example, the Saxon word 'beos' (for a bush) is not found elsewhere but does correspond to Low German 'bese'. Place-names also help in the study of dialects. For instance, the modern spellings and distributions of the names 'Stratford' and 'Stretford' (both from 'straet' meaning 'street') indicate that the Angles and the Saxons had different accents.

NOMENCLATURE. Finally, but no less important, is the fact that place-names have played a large part in the development of human names. Not a few of the surnames used in Britain today are derived directly or indirectly from the places where those surnames originated. Go down any list of surnames in the telephone directory, in a classroom, in an office and trace their derivations. Some will be descriptive, like Brown or White. Some will be familial, like Richardson. Some will be trade-linked, like Smith. But many will be from place-names: Burton, Crawford, Davenport, Fenton.

▓ UNDERTAKING RESEARCH

Studying the origin of place-names goes back almost as far as place-names themselves. It can be found in the Bible and, as one might have imagined, the Greeks had a word for it. 'Etymology' derives from the ancient Greek 'etymos' – truth: the science of truth. The Roman poet and writer Virgil, in the first century BC, considered names in both his verses and in his most famous work the *Aeneid*, and Caesar touched upon the subject in his memoirs.

In Britain, the Venerable Bede had more than a passing interest in place-names. He was a monk, theologian and historian who lived during the 8th century AD, mostly at Jarrow in North-east England. In his *Ecclesiastical History of the English People*, completed in AD 731, he noted the Saxon and Viking invasions and their establishment of settlements. Rendlesham in Suffolk, he said, was 'Mansio Rendili', the 'home of Rendil', and Ely in Cambridgeshire was so-called because it was an island surrounded by rivers and marshes where eels could be caught.

Today, place-name study has become a more professional and scientific activity. Academics specialise in it, university students concentrate on it. A wide range of expertise is brought to it. Yet some of the most interesting work done is that undertaken by the amateur and enthusiast – the local historian.

But before embarking upon a course of investigation the local historian should be aware of certain methods and certain approaches. In particular, certain points should be noted regarding research, source material and the

Using the Internet

There is no doubt that the worldwide web has provided access to information on an unprecedented scale. At the proverbial touch of a button all kinds of knowledge can be obtained on almost every conceivable topic. In researching place-names, both individually (such as the particular names of towns and villages) and generically (such as the linguistic or topographical roots of names) the internet can be of enormous help. The experienced student or researcher will not need guidance here but some general suggestions can be offered to the casual user.

● Search engines vary in ease of use and cross-referencing. Try entering the same search enquiry into several of them and see which you get on with best.

● There is little point typing in just the name of a place, Mousehole or Wolverhampton for instance, since this will bring forth thousands perhaps millions, of references. Try adding the words 'origin', 'history', 'derivation' and 'place-name' to the name of your location. For a large settlement this might bring the number of references down to a few thousand, for a small settlement to, perhaps, a few

dozen. Immediately research becomes more manageable.

● A fairly unrefined generic search will produce thousands of references but some of these should be pursued – they may be of immediate and relevant interest. For example, the English Place-Name Society will crop up early and frequently, and this source is especially useful to the researcher.

● There is likely to be a lot of extraneous matter and the order of information given may seem bizarre – but with a little time, effort and patience results may be achieved. Scrolling down and clicking on possibilities, you should find some interesting material.

● Given the diversity and depth of information on the web, the internet is most likely to be of value to those seeking a detailed investigation for academic purposes. It is also liable to promote discussion, and even disagreement, over particular place-name derivations, their linguistic roots, historic meanings and regional characteristics. Indeed, the place-name debate generated by the web could be endless!

nature of linguistic development. Over the years various professionals have drawn up recommended courses of action for the budding place-name researcher. One of the first was W. W. Skeat who listed an order of enquiry and categorised the main problems to be overcome. Later writers, notably P. H. Reaney, Kenneth Cameron and Eilert Ekwall, expanded the main points Skeat made and added to the list of considerations. Below is a summary of all the suggestions they made:

1 Collect as many early forms of a place-name as possible, from as many sources, and list them in chronological order.

2 Compare these spellings with those of similar place-names elsewhere, cross-referencing sources and identifying possible errors. Old records and documents were hand-written and therefore contain mistakes, illegible handwriting and, often, damaged or stained surfaces. Generally, a place-name element found in many other place-names will derive from a relatively common root; an element found nowhere else will be unique – probably derived from a personal name.

3 Find the original meaning of a place-name usually, but not always, from the earliest spellings. This will require a certain knowledge of various old languages, together with an understanding of grammatical inflexions and the history of pronunciation. It should be remembered that most English place-names were already in existence by the time of the Domesday Book in 1086, and some of these had origins going back a thousand years or more even then. Many Saxon names had Celtic roots.

4 Study should bear in mind the phonetic laws governing place-name development which are not the same laws governing ordinary word development. Ordinary words in our vocabulary had to retain their essential meanings even if their spellings and pronunciations changed. But place-names did not. They were used only as a means of identification and so their meanings often disappeared.

5 Study should also bear in mind the evidence on the ground. The assumed meaning of a place-name should be compared with geographical or archaeological evidence. A name indicating a

marsh or a pond is unlikely to be accurate if the site itself has no such evidence or possesses landscape not conducive to such features, steep slopes for instance. Of course, the researcher should be aware not just of present landscape conditions but past ones, since rivers do change their courses and lakes do dry up.

▓ SOURCES

For most place-name researchers and student etymologists, the starting point will be the various sources of evidence. These vary in scope, detail and extent. Some, like the writings of Tacitus, Ptolemy and Caesar, may give the merest hint of a place-name origin; others will be surprising in their exactness, and here the Domesday Book is a prime example. Sometimes the originals must be consulted but normally good copies will be sufficient.

The following is a simplified list of the principal sources available. These can be studied either at the British Museum (for major, national documents) or at the various County Record Offices run by local councils. Church authorities also hold many useful documents and researchers should not forget the humble, but extremely helpful, reference departments in our public libraries.

ROMANO-BRITISH PERIOD: Sad to say the available evidence giving pre-Saxon place-names is not abundant. Some Celtic names can be found on inscriptions – on old tombs, altars, milestones and the like – and researchers may find it useful to look at surviving place-names in Scotland, Wales, the Isle of Man, Cornwall and, to some extent, Brittany as well. In these areas the ancient Celtic tongues have been preserved to a considerable degree, if not in the spoken form then in documents. Contemporary written evidence of Celtic names can be gained from Ptolemy's *Geography* and the *Antonine Itinerary* both of which, although written in Latin and mainly dealing with Roman settlements, have some important and interesting references. It should be remembered that many Roman place-names and, indeed, many Saxon place-names too have Celtic elements.

POST ROMAN PERIOD: The introduction of Anglo-Saxon and Scandinavian place-names into Britain has been well documented in the two great works of the period: *The Anglo-Saxon Chronicle* and Bede's *Ecclesiastical History of the English People*. The former gives a yearly account of England's history from the birth of Christ onwards. It dates from the 9th century but contains material from earlier writings, lost documents and oral tradition. The latter chronicles the various Saxon and Viking invasions which took place from the 6th to the 8th centuries. In addition to these two books there are various charters, wills and land documents which, though dating from the 11th and 12th centuries and written in Latin, refer to pre-Norman times.

MEDIEVAL PERIOD: A positive plethora of documentary evidence now greets the place-name researcher. First and foremost and the starting point for many a study is the Domesday Book of 1086. This is an exhaustive survey of England, written in abbreviated Latin, categorising the settlements, farming and land-ownership patterns in William I's newly conquered realm.

In addition there are numerous 'roll' documents which, together, give us a clear view of life and landscape in medieval England:

1   Pipe rolls dealing with tax collections and fees paid to sheriffs.
2   Charter rolls dealing with royal grants.
3   Close rolls dealing with private royal business transactions.
4   Patent rolls dealing with royal public notices and announcements.
5   Assize rolls dealing with the court cases held by travelling judges.
6   Coroners' rolls dealing with judicial cases relating to the Crown.

On a more local level there are records and charters dealing with manorial, monastic and private estates. Some of these are manorial court-rolls, rental lists and ground surveys; some are 'Terrier' documents relating to the boundaries and acreage of private and church estates; some are 'Parish Perambulations'. Many are unpublished and only to be found at the British Museum or at the National Archives or County Record Office. Some are held by university or college libraries, cathedrals and parish churches and by stately homes, notably Belvoir Castle and Chatsworth House, both of which have famous collections of local records.

Since Tudor times there have also been various charts and maps drawn which researchers can now use in their studies. Between Christopher Saxton's maps of 1574 and the first edition Ordnance Survey maps published towards the end of the 19th century literally hundreds of maps appeared, showing counties, towns, estates and routeways. In the 17th and 18th centuries estate plans were commonly drawn for both private landowners and the church and these can be set against enclosure award documents and tithe accounts of the same period.

Finally, place-name researchers should not forget the more unusual sources. Early tour accounts, for example, can be a fund of useful information. Of these perhaps the best known are:

Daniel Defoe *A Tour through the Whole Island of Great Britain* (1724).
Celia Fiennes *My Great Journey to Newcastle and to Cornwall* (1698).
William Cobbett *Rural Rides* (1830).
George Borrow *Wild Wales* (1862).

FURTHER READING: There are numerous books on place-names now available. The most detailed, and therefore the best for researchers, are those which specialise in origins and derivations. The English Place-Name Society has produced a whole series which deals with names on a pre 1974 county by county basis and this cannot be too strongly recommended. More concise books, covering the whole country, also exist and here Ekwall's *Oxford Dictionary of English Place-Names* stands out.

Some authors have spent their academic careers especially considering place-names and therefore any book by them would be worth reading. Kenneth Cameron, John Field, P. H. Reaney, G. J. Copley, M. Gelling and W. F. H. Nicolaisen are names that come to mind.

One last point worth mentioning is that, in all the works mentioned above, the original counties of Britain are used in regional sub-division. The source material will be so organised and researchers are advised to bear in mind the pre 1974 county map.

▓ LINGUISTIC DEVELOPMENTS

When gathering together source material, and collecting early place-name spellings, the researcher should bear in mind that languages, dialects, accents, pronunciations and phonetics have their own special way of evolving. Recorded spellings often reflect this evolution. The development of place-names is further complicated by the fact that Britain was subjected to more than one linguistic influence. Not only did we have Celtic, Latin, Saxon, Danish and French speakers, each superimposing their own tongue upon the place-name map, but also we had different groups with different verbal abilities. Rather like modern French-speakers finding the English 'TH' difficult to pronounce, and conversely English-speakers finding the rolled French 'R' difficult, so the early peoples of Britain had difficulties in getting their tongues around the place-names of other groups.

Some of the main linguistic developments are summarised below.

SAXON PRONUNCIATION: As far as experts can tell the Saxons pronounced all their consonants, even when they were written together, as with NG, HL and WR. With this said, however, it is thought they sounded their consonants in the same general way that we do today. The exceptions, perhaps, were 'C' which was pronounced 'CH' or 'K' 'CG' which was pronounced 'J', 'SC' which was pronounced 'SH', 'F' which was pronounced 'V'.

In addition there were two letters now lost: the 'thorn' and the 'eth'. Both were pronounced 'TH'. (Incidentally, throughout this book 'TH' is used instead of the 'thorn' and 'eth' for the sake of convenience and clarity).

Saxon vowels, like modern vowels, had two sounds, each: a long and a short. Thus 'a' was pronounced either as 'tap' or 'father'; 'e' as 'bet' or 'be'; 'i' as 'bit' or 'ravine'; 'o' as 'hot' or 'low' and 'u' as 'pull' or 'rule'. In addition to these five there was the Æ dipthong pronounced 'air' (as in aeroplane) and the 'y' pronounced 'yoo' (as in the French pronoun 'tu').

Thus, the Saxon 'hus' would have been pronounced 'hoose' (house), 'cild' would have been chilled' (child) and 'stan' would have been 'starn' (stone).

LETTER EXCHANGES: Even without the complications caused by the succession of different languages, place-name spellings tend to change in time. In particular, certain letters tend to alter as a result of oral developments. The most common exchanges include 'T' to 'D', 'K' to 'G', 'B' to 'V' and 'D' to 'TH'. An example of the first would be 'Tun' and 'Ton' becoming 'Dun' and 'Don'; an example of the last would be the modern words father and mother (from 'faeder' and 'modor'). Similarly, 'NK' often became 'NG', 'RT' became 'RD' and 'G' became 'GH'.

The Scandinavians found certain Saxon letters difficult to pronounce (J and V, for example, which became Y and W) but it was the Normans who were especially guilty of letter exchange. The scribes who wrote documents for William I and his heirs, like those who wrote the Domesday Book, were constantly altering spellings to suit their own method of speech. Their French tongues led, for example, to 'TUN' becoming 'TON', 'Y' becoming 'E', 'V' becoming 'F' and 'GR' becoming 'C'. Thus 'GRANTANBRYCGE' in AD 925 become 'CANTEBRIGIE' in 1086 (now Cambridge).

▓ INTERPRETING SOURCE MATERIAL

After the source material has been used, and reference books consulted, the place-names researcher will be ready and able to start the long process of interpretation. But cataloguing different spellings, identifying different linguistic roots and, perhaps also, deducing different meanings are not always as straightforward as may be thought. Fully and accurately to interpret place-names a researcher must understand how and why place-names evolved, the manner in which they were formed and the reasons behind their present formation. The researcher must also become aware of the many problems and dangers inherent in this place-name interpretation.

(a) The Formation of Names
In the very beginning, place-names must have been very simple. Primitive societies, isolated farmers, insular tribes and unsophisticated economic systems had little need for long differentiating place-names. 'The hill', 'the river', 'the marsh' would have been sufficient for topographical features, 'the farm', the village' for human features. No one would have asked which hill or which village since, in their closed world, there was only one.

But such a situation did not last. By the Bronze Age, and certainly by the Iron Age, society had developed and proper place-names had evolved. Tribal groups were spreading and travelling, people were intermingling, trade was growing. The need for identifying place-tags had begun.

Generally these first place-names can be divided into two groups: geographically and habitative. The first group were those names applied to physical features – hills, valleys, rivers and so on and the second group were those names applied to human features – farms, enclosures, hamlets and the like. Adjectives were used to distinguish between different, but similar, features. Thus, there developed names like 'Black Hill', 'Round Hill', 'Foaming River' and 'Stone Farm'. Plants, animals, gods, personal or tribal names were often used for these adjectives, producing 'Ash Hill', 'Woden's River' or 'Beric's Farm'.

In due course, transference took place. Geographical feature names were used in habitation place-names and, to a certain extent, vice versa. The result was an amalgam of names: some wholly topographical, some wholly habitative and some a compound of the two.

By the time of the Roman occupation, British place-names were well established. They were largely Celtic in origin (except for those with elements going back to even earlier times) and largely descriptive in character.

For the next thousand years or more, however, those place-names were subjected to adaptation, alteration and obliteration by a succession of different and alien languages. The Romans brought Latin, the Anglo-Saxons brought a Germanic tongue (called Saxon or Old English), the

Vikings brought Norwegian and Danish, the Normans brought French. Each wave changed the existing place-names. Sometimes the existing name was altered, sometimes it was merely added to, with an extra prefix or suffix. Often it was removed totally, to be replaced by an entirely new name.

The Romans, Vikings and Normans tended just to adapt existing names. The Saxons more often replaced them. But to what extent we still do not know for sure. Many place-names previously thought to be wholly Saxon are now thought to contain Celtic elements. How many other Celtic roots await discovery? Perhaps we should remember, when studying place-names, the dictum by W. G. Hoskins when writing about villages in more general terms: 'everything is older than we think'.

(b) Compound Names

Most place-names are made up of a number of different parts or elements. Within a single word there might be a first element, a prefix, and a last element, a suffix, and perhaps also one or maybe two middle elements. The skill of the place-name researcher is in the identification of these elements. This is not always that easy.

Through evolution elements have a habit of shrinking. This is especially true in names which are naturally long: centuries of oral use tend to contract words and sounds. The place-name of 'Abram', for example started out as 'Eadburgeham' in Saxon times. It became 'Abburgham' in 1246 and 'Abraham' in 1372. When this happens central elements are apt to disappear altogether. The prefixes in Shiplake, Hadleigh and Sudbury derive from 'sheep', 'health' and 'south' respectively. The importance of studying early place-name spellings becomes glaringly apparent.

Some elements do not mean anything as such – are not tribal or personal names, geographical features or terms for enclosures or hamlets – but are simply prepositions used to link other elements. Occasionally these have survived almost intact to the present day (as in 'Weston-super-Mare', 'Havering-atte-Bower' and 'Chapel-en-le-Frith') but most often they have been lost amongst the other letters of a name, surviving merely as an 'a', an 'up' or an 'e'.

The most common Saxon prepositions found in place-names include 'atten' (at the), 'binnan' (inside), 'under' (below), 'uppan' (above) and 'in' (inside). The Normans took to the habit of Latinising prepositions and so introduced 'juxta' (next to), 'sub' (under), 'super' (on the) and 'cum' (with). The preposition 'en' was the French version of 'in'.

Another feature of compound place-names stems from the fact that all the languages introduced into England were inflective languages. In other words, they were languages in which the spelling of each word varied according to its use – according to what part of the sentence it was in. Latin was inflective with different genders, tenses and cases, and so was Saxon (similar, in respect, to modern German). Thus, a single element found in a place-name would not simply be a word with a meaning but could be the dative form of a word with a meaning. Depending on circumstances a single element might have various spellings according to case and gender: accusative, dative, masculine, feminine, singular, plural and so on. Thus, place-names with common elements might have totally different spellings.

Finally, compound place-names may often have extra names tacked on separately, thus producing a two-word, or even a three-word name. Such additions are called 'affixes' and may be quite a recent phenomenon. Before a name we might have 'New' (as in 'New Winchelsea') and after a name we might have a family name as in 'Marston Trussell'. Such affixes were common during medieval times and have continued to be added ever since, as found in Bognor Regis. Here the 'Regis' dates from 1929.

(c) Misleading Names

Teddington, it has been said, is a name derived from 'tide end town', Certainly it is true that the tide running upstream along the Thames really does end at this particular Middlesex town, but that is not why the place has its present name. In AD 970 it was 'Tudincgatun' and this came from 'Tuda's tun' a settlement of 'Tuda's people'.

Spurious place-name origins abound, not only in popular imagination but sometimes in guidebooks as well. When Queen Elizabeth I inspected her damaged fleet, as it lay at anchor in the Thames estuary after defeating the Armada, she did not say 'Alas, my poor fleet' thus creating Purfleet. And nearby Barking has nothing to do with the Isle of Dogs! Guildford has nothing to do with guilds, nor Wolverhampton with Wolves, nor Bakewell with cooking.

Such examples may sound too obvious, and too silly, but they highlight a basic problem when it comes to place-name study: things are not always as they seem.

It would be reasonable to assume that Walthamstow is derived from 'wald' (forest), 'ham' (homestead) and 'stow' (place or religious site). Each one is a common Saxon element and the place is close to Epping Forest, Essex, which, indeed, once engulfed it. However, in the Domesday Book it was 'Wilcumestou' and this came from 'Wilcume's stow'. In the same way, Grantchester may be supposed to have a Roman foundation, judging from the common suffix, from 'caester' (the Saxon word for a Roman camp).

But here again the supposition would be wrong. In 1086 it was 'Granteseta' meaning 'settlers on the Granta' and it was the Normans who switched the spelling to 'Grancestre' in order to make it easier for them to pronounce.

Even when place-names have the same modern spelling it is not necessarily the case that they derive from the same roots. Aston – a common place-name – can be a corruption either of 'east tun' (eastern farm) or 'ash tun' (ash tree farm). Alston can be 'Halfdan's farm' or 'Alred's farm' and Teddington can be 'Teotta's homestead' as well as 'Tuda's homestead'.

The reverse is also true. The same roots, with the same meanings, can produce very different present-day names. A place-name meaning 'northern dairy farm' can end up as 'Northwich', 'Northwick' or 'Norwich'. The farm belonging to a person called Dudda can become 'Doddington', 'Dodington', 'Diddington' and even 'Dotton'.

The moral of these examples is that exhaustive reference to all earlier spellings is essential, and that researchers should never accept, without question, suggestive derivations. Two good instances which especially bear out these two principles are the recent studies concerning the origins of Lichfield and Leatherhead.

Until a few years ago Lichfield was assumed to be a place-name derived from the Saxon words 'lych' (corpse) and 'feld' (field). Such seemed likely since Lichfield was the site of an ancient battle between invading Angles and resident Celtic Britons. However, it has now been discovered, from more detailed investigation, that the name comes from a Celtic word meaning 'grey' and (before the Saxons introduced the 'feld') the Celtic 'coed'(wood).

Leatherhead is a similar case. Until recently it was thought to derive from the Saxon words 'leode' (people) and 'rida' (a ride, bridleway or riding ford). But today a different, and much earlier, derivation has been discovered. The prefix comes from the same root as that found in Lichfield, a Celtic word meaning 'grey' and the suffix from a Celtic word for a ford – 'ritu' perhaps, being similar to the Welsh word 'rhyd'. As Hoskins said: 'everything is older than we think'.

(d) Misleading Spellings

Even when every conceivable spelling has been found for a place-name, and all possible sources have been studied, the diligent researcher must still be careful. For the very spellings themselves might be suspect.

On the simplest level, there might be mistakes of a purely calligraphic kind. The scribes who wrote down place-names on old documents were not infallible. They might, for example, have copied out names wrongly: misreading some letters, missing out others, even putting some extra letters in where they should not have been. If those scribes were writing down place-names from direct contact with local inhabitants, as opposed to reproducing earlier documents, then the mistakes could be worse. They might have mis-heard the names given, or guessed a spelling if the spoken version had been mumbled.

However, far more significant than all such errors, are those which resulted from a much more fundamental aspect of early documentation.

Until the 18th century there was no such thing as standard spelling. All the spellings found before then were merely attempts by scribes to record the sounds they heard. Letters and groups of letters were used to reproduce pronunciation and, as such, their arrangement was very much determined by the nationality of the scribe and the dialectic nature of the place-name. Imagine, for example, a Norman French scribe writing down a place-name phonetically from a Saxon who spoke in a broad Devonian accent.

From about AD 500 to the Norman Conquest the language of England was Saxon, with a smattering of Danish, and this has been called Old English. But it was not a standard tongue. If accents and dialects can still vary greatly between say, Kent, Yorkshire and Newcastle-upon-Tyne, even with modern mass media and standardisation, consider how wide regional differences must have been in Saxon England. And then consider how much the phonetic spellings might have differed even for two settlements with, ostensibly, the same name.

After the Norman Conquest, a certain amount of French was added to the native tongue which, in consequence, became Middle English. Regional dialects remained strong but now there was a ruling class which, for a while at least, did not speak the principal language of the country. Thus, Norman scribes had to reproduce in writing the sounds they heard from foreign tongues. In many cases they had no letters or symbols to indicate certain Saxon sounds because these sounds did not exist in French. In such circumstances they either wrote down a sequence of letters which they hoped would produce the correct sounds, or else they changed the name to something they could pronounce and then wrote it down in their own way.

With so many variables, and with such an inexact science, it is perhaps surprising that place-name spellings as found in old documents are as consistent as they are. But it is wise to be aware of the dangers.

CHAPTER 2

The Blending of Languages: Migration & Consolidation

▦ INTRODUCTION

Before a detailed study of place-name origins can really be made some background information is necessary. What were the languages that produced our names? Where did they come from? How did they mix? And what sort of society existed to cause our place-name development?

These questions are pertinent since it is only through the answers that we can fully understand the ways in which place-names have evolved. Our place-names have mixed origins because we do, and our society does. Our place-names have a long history because our country does. Our knowledge of Britain in pre-Roman times is a little hazy. All we do know for sure is that the country was Celtic and that the Iron Age had replaced the Bronze Age in about the 6th century BC. Yet, even then, the population was not homogeneous, but was a mixture of peoples.

The Celts themselves had been invaders. Arriving in two waves from about 800 BC they partly displaced and partly intermingled with the tribes already here, such as the Picts and Iberians. The first wave was made up of 'Gaelic' Celts, the second wave of 'Brythonic' or 'Brittonic' Celts. The former group was pushed northwards and westwards by the latter and so formed the origins of the languages and place-names still used in Ireland, North-West Scotland and Isle of Man. The Brittonic Celts settled over the rest of the country and gave their name to 'Britain' (and, incidentally, to Brittany as well). Their language was more akin to Cornish and modern Welsh and it was that language spoken when the Romans arrived.

The Celts had come from Central Europe originally but, by the middle of the first millennium BC, had spread throughout Western Europe. 'Gaul' was a name probably derived from 'Gaelic'. To what extent their language gave a basis to our modern place-names can only be surmised. There are some names which are undoubtedly Celtic in origin – especially those used

Old Sarum, Wiltshire

The Brittonic Celts arrived in the Iron Age, from central Europe, and settled across the best agricultural lands. They favoured scattered farmsteads as a means of colonisation but also built large hill-forts for defence. It is not known what they called Old Sarum and Maiden Castle. The former was Sorviodunum in Roman times, which probably incorporated the old Celtic words soria (meaning unknown) and dunon (fort). The latter is perhaps derived from the Celtic words maia-dun (great hill). Old Sarum was occupied until the 13th century when New Sarum (Salisbury) was built by Bishop Poore. Maiden Castle was destroyed by the Romans who replaced it with their own town nearby, Durnonovaria, now called Dorchester.

Maiden Castle, Dorset

for physical features like rivers and hills – but there are others which still puzzle experts.

Of particular interest to modern place-name researchers are those names which pre-date the Celts. So far only a relatively few have been identified – the Rivers Colne, Humber, Itchen, Severn, Tees, Tweed and Tyne for example – but it is hoped that more will be discovered.

The Roman conquest of Britain lasted about four centuries. In that time the Romans built roads and settlements, cultivated the countryside, and established systems of law and administration. Yet they had surprisingly little impact on place-names. Either they added Latin endings to existing Celtic names – as with 'Londinium' (London) and 'Camulodunum' (Colchester) – or else they added a whole Latin word – so that 'Venta' (Winchester) became 'Venta Belgarum' (Venta of the Belgae). Only very occasionally did they invent an entirely new name, like 'Aquae Sulis' (Bath). But such Latinised names did not last. In almost every case Roman place-names disappeared with the fall of the Empire in the 5th century AD. Perhaps this was because the Romans occupied Britain but did not settle here in great numbers.

The coming of the Saxon tribes was a very different matter. Soon after the departure of the Romans various groups from mainland Europe started to arrive. At first they were raiding parties, plundering the shoreline and coastal valleys, but gradually they turned into colonisers: farming the land, clearing the forest, building villages. By the 8th century they had spread throughout the realm, superseding the Celts both in power and influence. Most of the place-names that exist today can trace their roots back to these three centuries.

The term 'Saxon' in fact includes many different groups. The largest of these were the 'Saxons' themselves who came from what is now northern Germany. Their name derived from 'seax', a sharp, single-edged knife or dagger which they used as a weapon. The second largest group were the 'Angles' from what is now Denmark. Their name derived from the word 'angel' meaning a fish-hook. Whether this group came from a part of Jutland which was shaped like a fish-hook, or whether they were so-called because they traditionally lived on fish is not known. The third group, the 'Jutes', made up the smallest Saxon tribe. They did not come originally from Jutland, as Bede imagined, but from the Rhineland. Generally speaking the Saxons settled in southern England, the Angles in eastern and northern England and the Jutes in the south-east. By the 8th century these three tribes had not only merged into one cultural and linguistic population – the Anglo-Saxons – but the Angles had given their name to what was rapidly becoming known as 'England'.

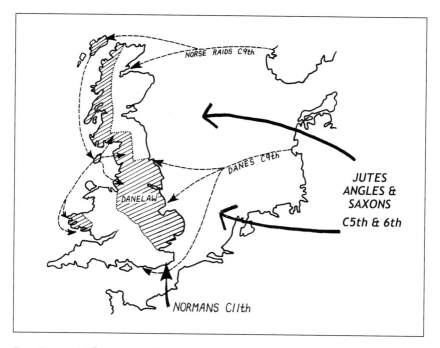

Post-Roman Influences on Place-Names

The Viking invasions began in the late 8th century and continued until the time of the Norman Conquest. As with the Saxons before them, these new invaders first came to Britain just to plunder but later came to settle. By the 10th century they had spread across eastern and northern England and round into Scotland, the Isle of Man and Ireland.

The term 'Viking' was a general term for a warrior, and 'Norsemen' (another term often used for these invaders) merely referred to the men from the north. More accurately they should be labelled Norwegians and Danes. Incidentally, the same people also invaded and settled in Northern France and gave their name to that region whence came Britain's next enemy: Normandy – the land of the northmen.

William I's conquest in 1066 marked the last major influence on our place-names. Although Normandy had been settled by the Vikings a century or so earlier, by the 11th century that part of France was speaking French. And so it was a French influence that now made itself felt in England.

▓ THE MIXING OF TONGUES

It would be a mistake to imagine that, because Britain was subjected to a succession of invasions and foreign colonisations, the language which eventually evolved was an amalgam of diverse and disparate tongues. Nor would it be correct to think that our place-names are the product of disassociated roots.

The Celts, Anglo-Saxons and Vikings all came from the same broad region – Central and Northern Europe. Their languages were superficially different but were based upon the same linguistic origins. They had the same Indo-European roots. There were common sounds, common elements and common structures. Each was an inflective tongue – that is, it had cases and declensions, like Latin – and each used the same alphabet. In the same way, the Northern European languages of today are related: English, Dutch and German, for example are different but similar.

For this reason, it was relatively easy for each successive language introduced into Britain to be absorbed by the existing, native one. This was especially the case with the coming of Danish, which was rapidly merged into Saxon. The mixing of Saxon and Celtic, at an earlier date, was less easy but even here there were enough common elements to make it possible within just a few generations. The truth is that the history of Britain, of the English language and settlement, is the history of adaptation and assimilation, not of dispersal and displacement.

When the Anglo-Saxons arrived they found a country of Celts who had been Romanised. Many spoke Latin, many were Christian and many lived the Roman way of life. So influenced were they, in fact, that books call them Romano-Britons. But they were still essentially Celtic. They spoke a Celtic language (called in some books 'British' or 'Primitive Welsh') and kept a Celtic tradition and culture.

And with the coming of the Anglo-Saxons these Britons did not, for the most part, migrate to the north and west. Some did, of course, but many more stayed where they were. At first they fought the Saxons, then they tolerated them, at last they intermingled with them. In most of what became England the Anglo-Saxons eventually dominated, and the hybrid language which was mainly Saxon and partly Celtic became 'Old English'. Only those regions the Saxons did not reach in any great numbers remained Celtic in character: Cornwall, Wales, Scotland.

The same thing happened when, first, the Scandinavian and, later, the Norman incursions took place. Danish and then French were assimilated into the existing language (which became 'Middle English') with new words and sounds being introduced.

The nature of this language evolution has a significance to place-name study. Because Celtic, Saxon and Danish had common roots and, over a period of 500 years, merged together, it is not always easy for a place-name researcher to identify the linguistic origins of different elements within names. Some elements are found in more than one language; other elements are easily confused with alternatives. Ash tree, for instance was 'aesc' in Saxon and 'askr' in Danish. So what looks like a Saxon place-name might be a Danish one, and vice versa.

Over the last few decades researchers have increasingly begun to realise that names formerly thought to be Saxon may, in fact, be Celtic in origin, and that some Saxon place-name elements may have Celtic roots. Everything is older than we think.

▓ THE CELTIC FRINGE

The areas where the Saxons did not settle in great numbers retained their Celtic way of life. To such an extent, in fact, that Gaelic, Manx and Welsh are still spoken in those parts. Even Cornish, as a spoken language, died out only two centuries ago.

In consequence, the place-names found in western and northern districts of the British Isles remain Celtic. Prefixes such as 'Aber', 'Bryn', 'Glan', 'Llan', 'Pen', 'Pol' and 'Tre' are common and any glance at a map of Wales or Cornwall will furnish more examples of typical Celtic elements.

In the rest of the country – across England – Celtic names are fewer. But they still do exist; many of our river and hill names are Celtic, together with a scatter of settlement names, like Wendover, Lympne, Carlisle and London.

Interestingly enough, however, the names we now use for the separate parts of the so-called Celtic Fringe are derived from the Saxon terms. With the exception of Cumbria and, possibly also, the Isle of Man, the Celtic regions are called by what the Saxons called them.

Scotland: The Saxons called the far north 'Scotia' since it was the land of the 'Scottas' – the Celtic raiders from Ireland. The Celtic version of the name is 'Caledonia' meaning 'the land of tough men'.

Wales: This name derives from the Saxon word for 'foreigner' or 'serf' – 'Walh' and 'Wealh' (plural 'Walas'). The Celtic name for the same area was 'Cymri' from a word meaning 'compatriots' or 'brothers' (now 'Cymru').

Cornwall: This was named 'Cornwealas' by the Saxons, the prefix deriving from the name of the Celtic tribe living there, the 'Cornovii' (the promontory dwellers): hence 'Cornovii foreigners'. The Cornish name for the area is 'Kernow' derived from the same tribal name.

Cumbria: This comes directly from the Celtic original 'Cambras' – the land of the Cymri. In Saxon times this area included all England west of the Pennines and north of the River Ribble plus much of southern Scotland. Today it refers to the land between Morecambe Bay and the Scottish border, west of the Pennines.

Isle of Man: The Romans called this 'Monapia' and it is thought that this was a corruption of the original Celtic god 'Mannan Mac Lir' who was worshipped on the island. The present name is a descendant of this.

▦ THE SAXON KINGDOMS

As the Anglo-Saxons spread across England they superimposed their language and way of life onto the Romano-British landscape. In some places they created new farmlands, new settlements and entirely new place-names. In other places they took over existing farms and villages

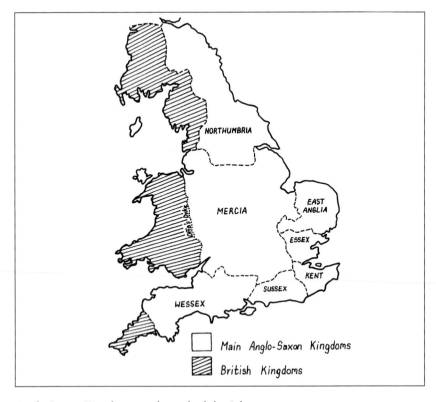

Anglo-Saxon Kingdoms at the end of the 8th century

and re-named them. They did this either by altering the Celtic root to make a name more pronounceable, or by adding their own prefix or suffix to make a Celtic name sound more Saxon. Suffixes like 'ham', '-ton', '-ing', '-wick' and '-ley' are all typical Saxon-derived elements.

As these Anglo-Saxons became established so their tribal differences became more regionally distinctive. At first these tribal districts were vague zones without firm boundaries, but as group loyalties strengthened so they became more cohesive. Eventually separate kingdoms developed.

The Jutes settled in the south-east corner of the country in an area known as 'Cantium' or 'Cent' from the Celtic word 'Canto' meaning 'border land' or 'coastal district'. In due course this name became Kent.

The Angles settled in the east, the midlands and the north. Those in the east (in an area later to be known as East Anglia) were divided into 'north folk' and 'south folk' – whose areas became Norfolk and Suffolk. Those in the midlands settled in districts towards the Welsh border and so were called the 'Mearc' (boundary) people. Their region became 'Mercia'. The Angles settling in the north were at first divided into two tribes, whose districts were 'Bernicia' and 'Deira'. These names derived from Celtic words meaning 'land of the mountain passes', and 'land of the waters' respectively. Later, however, these two groups joined and, since their regions were both north of the Humber Estuary, the new district was known as 'North-Hymbre' – Northumbria.

The Saxons spread throughout southern England, and most of their district names have survived to the present day. The west Saxons settled in Wessex; the south Saxons in Sussex and the east Saxons in Essex. Between the latter two were the middle Saxons – in Middlesex. Within this region was a smaller region, south of the River Thames, called the 'suth ge' (south district). This became Surrey.

By the 7th century three of these Anglo-Saxon kingdoms had become dominant: Northumbria, Mercia and Wessex. They vied with each other for land and power, they fought with each other for supremacy. Some of the smaller kingdoms were swallowed up, or lost their independence, whilst the resident Celts – many of whom continued to live in their own small pockets or zones – were simply brushed aside. The Celtic zone of 'Elmet' for example, in south west Yorkshire, finally disappeared and – as late as the 9th century – the 'Dumnonii' tribe of Devon was finally overcome.

The eventual supremacy of Wessex over the other Saxon kingdoms during the 9th century, under King Egbert and then King Alfred, led directly to the unification of England as a nation state.

Offa's Dyke, Herefordshire

By the 7th century the Saxon kingdoms had been established, with Mercia, Wessex and Northumbria being the largest. Mercia was strong under the pagan King Penda (died AD 655) and later under the Christian King Offa (died AD 796). The latter drove back the Celts and built the famous rampart which still, for much of its length, marks the English-Welsh boundary. Today, Offa's Dyke also provides the route for a long distance footpath, here seen near Kington. In the 9th century Wessex became dominant but increasingly had to fight the Danish invasions. Its most famous king, Alfred the Great (AD 848–900) repelled the invaders at Ethandune (Edington). Alfred's Tower was built in 1772 to mark the spot where the king raised his standard prior to that battle in AD 878.

Alfred's Tower, Wiltshire

▩ DANELAW

In the last decade of the 8th century the first Viking raids took place. The Norwegian invaders landed in the north-east and around Scotland, the Danish invaders landed along the eastern and southern shores. The Saxons did their best to resist these incursions but still the Norsemen came. By the first decade of the 9th century Danish settlements had appeared across parts of Northumbria, Mercia and Essex. By the middle of that same century the Danes had conquered almost the whole of northern and eastern England.

Peace by mutual agreement was the only sensible outcome. And so accordingly, in AD 878 King Alfred of Wessex signed a treaty with the Danish leader Guthrum. By this the Danes agreed to settle only in that part of England east of the line from London to Chester, a line marked by the River Lea and Watling Street. It was that area which became known as the Danelaw.

Within Danelaw, Danish laws and Danish customs were introduced, Danish place-names also appeared. Some settlements were completely renamed but many more were simply made Scandinavian by the addition of Danish elements. Prefixes like 'Beck', 'Booth' and 'Carr' became common, and suffixes like '-by', '-thorpe' and '-toft'. The importance of Danelaw in political terms – as opposed to place-name terms – should not be exaggerated, however. England was not split into two separate entities, two separate countries. The two parts were partners: they shared common economic and social conditions and, very soon also, a common language. By the beginning of the 10th century Wessex had become predominant and Danelaw had been assimilated into Saxon England. Danish autonomy had lasted less than 50 years.

▩ THE DEVELOPMENT OF SHIRES

From the development of separate Anglo-Saxon kingdoms, and of an administratively distinct Danelaw, it was but a short step to the evolution of shires and counties. The Saxon and Danish kings needed to govern and there was no better way to do that than by sub-dividing their realms into smaller districts. These were given their own forms of governance and their own local rulers. They were also given their own further sub-divisions to allow for more efficient control.

The result of this re-organisation was that England developed, at different levels, a patchwork of different kinds of regional or district authorities. At the higher level there appeared 'shires', 'counties', 'duchies',

Watendlath, Cumbria

In the 9th century the Norse invaders sailed around Scotland to settle in Northern England, on a landscape reminiscent of their homelands. They built hamlets and farms in the sheltered valleys and left their word elements in the place-names: dalr (dale), thwaite (meadow), toft (homestead), garth (enclosure) and fell (mountain). Watendlath stands on the edge of a tarn, or mountain lake, and takes its name from the old Norse vatn-endi-lan (lake-end-river). In the Yorkshire Dales this view of Upper Swaledale is taken between Keld (from Norse kelda for 'spring') and Muker (from Norse miur-akr for 'narrow valley'). In the foreground are the ruins of Crackpot Hall, a shooting lodge built in the 17th century. This name probably derives from the local geology – the limestone here being characterised by cracks, potholes, underground streams and the various scars and fissures of a past lead-mining industry.

Swaledale, North Yorkshire

'palatinates', and 'sokes'; at the lower level there appeared 'hundreds', 'ridings', 'wapentakes' and 'rapes'. As early as the 8th century the Wessex kings began to organise their subject peoples into self-regulating districts. These were based upon tribal groups and were set around tribal centres. They were called 'Scirs' and were given their own administrative functions. Within each, a 'reeve' was appointed as the King's representative and – below him – an 'ealdorman' who was to become the most powerful local man, that is, a tribal chief or 'elder'. In due course the 'scirs' became shires and the 'scir reeves' became sheriffs.

The earliest shires were those around the tribal centres of Wilton (Wiltshire), Southampton (Hampshire), Somerton (Somerset) and Dorn or Dorchester (Dorset). The suffix of the latter two derived from the Saxon word 'saete' meaning 'settlers' – the settlers of Somerton, the settlers of Dorn.

So successful were these shires the Wessex kings continued to use them. As their dominance grew, and Wessex swallowed up other Saxon kingdoms, so their shires spread. The tribes that were taken over retained something of their independence and so areas like Sussex, Essex and Kent appeared out of the former kingdoms. By the end of the 9th century most of southern England had been divided up in this way.

Across the area known as Danelaw, a different system of local government was developing. In order to keep a firm hold on their newly-won territories the Danes fortified certain towns and created zones around these to be run by local military leaders. Initially, five towns were fortified – the 'boroughs' of Lincoln, Stamford, Nottingham, Leicester and Derby – but later more were added, including Northampton, Huntingdon, Bedford and Cambridge.

These boroughs seemed to work very well – a fact not ignored by the ambitious King Alfred of Wessex. Accordingly he copied the idea. As Wessex power and influence spread northwards so Alfred built his own Saxon boroughs, or 'burhs'. Sometimes he built new wooden or earth fortresses in existing towns, sometimes he repaired the fortifications of old Roman towns. Thus, in due course, 'Magonsaetan' (the settlers around Maund in Herefordshire) and 'Wreocensaetan' (the settlers around the Wrekin in Shropshire) were created. These were later to be merged into 'Shrewsburyshire' – Shropshire. Also Gloucestershire, Warwickshire and Oxfordshire appeared.

Eventually as the Danelaw itself was consumed by the ever growing power of Wessex so the Saxon shires spread right across the Midlands and into Northern England. In most cases the word 'shire' was simply tacked on to the name of the central fortified town. By the time of the Norman Conquest the Wessex system of local government had reached as far as Yorkshire.

▓ THE CONSOLIDATION OF COUNTIES

When it came to governance and systems of administration, the Normans were not so much innovators as improvers. They inherited the 'shires' and turned them into efficient and strong regional entities. They kept the Saxon-inspired offices of 'sheriff' and 'earl' but created new, more powerful levels of authority. Princes, dukes and bishops, in particular, were given power of jurisdiction over the Saxon and Danish regions, thus helping the Conqueror and his heirs to maintain their hold over England. The boundaries between the shires – now more often called 'counties' from the old French word 'conte' – were more clearly defined; the relationship between the regions and the Crown was more rigorously regulated.

In other words, although Saxon and Danish in origin the modern county map of England dates essentially from Norman times. Across northern England, especially, the counties we now recognise were the product of Norman regional management. During the 12th century, Cumberland and Westmorland appeared (after William Rufus had recovered these territories from Scotland) together with Northumberland and Lancashire. During the 13th century the counties of Durham and Cheshire were consolidated. By the beginning of the 14th century every county in England, and its borders, had been established. And so they remained until Government reorganisation in 1974.

Lancashire: This was created in 1169 by combining three districts: Cartmel in the north, Amounderness in the east and the Mersey lowlands in the south, formerly under the jurisdiction of the Earldom of Chester. Lancaster became county town and Henry II's son John (later King) became Earl of Lancaster, with full regal rights over the county. Much later, in 1352 and after Edward III had introduced into England the new title of 'Duke', Lancashire became both a 'Duchy' and a 'County Palatine' – with the right to appoint a chancellor, judges and Justices of the Peace. To this day, the British Monarch is also titled 'Duke of Lancaster'.

Cheshire: William I built a castle at Chester and established that city as a feudal capital, partly to keep under control the surrounding Saxons and partly to provide a military stronghold close to the border with Wales. Later on, the Earldom of Chester was created and the area of jurisdiction was given palatinate privileges. With the loss of Cartmel to Lancashire, the 'County of the City of Chester' became the Cheshire of today.

County Durham: Back in the 9th century the Danes had given the lands between the rivers Wear and Tyne to St Cuthbert's church. In the mid 10th century the then Bishop moved his headquarters from Chester-le-Street to Durham, where the new Cathedral soon acquired the bones of St Cuthbert himself. Thereafter Durham's importance was assured. Apart from becoming a centre of pilgrimage the city gained military power. A succession of 'prince-bishops' developed a private army and extended their power across much of Northumbria. By the 12th century the Bishop of Durham had become a feudal lord, by the 13th century the area under his jurisdiction had become officially recognised as a 'County Palatine'. This status was to last until 1836.

The 'Sokes': These were areas recognised by the Norman kings as being under the authority of a single landowner, who held rights of 'soch' (jurisdiction). They were areas which did not fall under the authority of any shire or county but, instead, were directly answerable – through their local manorial keeper – to the Crown. The area around Peterborough, for example, was a 'Soke' under the authority of the Bishop of Peterborough. Rutland was a 'Soke' because, in 1204, it was given as a dowry to Queen Isabella by her husband King John and was, subsequently, ruled directly by the Queens of England.

▓ COUNTY SUB-DIVISIONS

Administrative sub-divisions within shires and counties go back as far as the shires and counties themselves. They were created to make easier the jurisdiction of regional districts and to allow for the devolution of power and responsibility. The king delegated authority to sheriffs, earls, dukes and bishops and they, in their turn, delegated downwards their control of local business to stewards and councillors.

England's largest county, Yorkshire, was sub-divided into 'Ridings' during Anglo-Saxon times. There were three of these and each had its own, separate administrative functions. The name derives from the Scandinavian word 'Thrithjungr' (meaning third part) which became, in the Saxon tongue, 'Thrithing' or 'Thridding'. North, East and West Thridding thus appeared (The fictional 'South Riding' was invented by Winifred Holtby whose novel of that name was published in 1936.)

South of the Humber, Lincolnshire – also a large county – was similarly divided into three parts: Lindsey, Kesteven and Holland, the first of which was further sub-divided into 'ridings' or thirds. Lindsey was so named because it was the 'ey' (island) of 'Lindon' (the old name for Lincoln); Kesteven derived from 'ced' or 'coed' (Celtic for wood) and 'stefna'

Regional Image Names

Some areas acquire image names that do not necessarily follow administrative boundaries. Such names draw upon cultural, historic or even literary connections and frequently become terms of affection for particular districts. The term 'Black Country' for the Wolverhampton area was first coined by an American in about 1860 to indicate the belching chimneys but it is now used without any hint of disapproval. 'The Potteries' and Arnold Bennett's term 'The Five Towns' equally have become recognised names for the Stoke-on-Trent district.

Since the beginning of tourism in the 18th century many areas have marketed themselves to attract visitors. Often this has involved the use of famous local inhabitants, either real or fictitious. Thus we have 'Shakespeare Country' (Warwickshire centred on Stratford-upon-Avon), 'Bronte Country' (the Yorkshire Dales centred on Haworth), 'Hardy's Wessex' (Dorset centred on Dorchester), 'Constable Country' (the Essex-Suffolk border centred on East Bergholt) and 'Kilvert Country' (the Welsh-English border district centred on Clyro where lived the Victorian clergyman and diarist Francis Kilvert). Some districts draw on legends: Robin Hood in Sherwood Forest and King Arthur in North Cornwall (Tintagel) and Somerset (Glastonbury). Other image names can be found in travel books and holiday brochures.

The English Riviera This term began in the 18th century but

(Scandinavian for a meeting place); Holland was from 'hoh' and 'land' (Saxon for 'land of the hillspur').

When William the Conqueror divided Sussex up into six 'rapes' he was basing them on administrative districts already created by the Saxons. The name derived from the Saxon word 'rap' meaning 'rope'. It is thought that originally open-air meetings or 'moots' were held within roped-off enclosures. These enclosures themselves became known as 'raps' and the term expanded to include any administrative district controlled by moots. The rapes designated by William I were narrow belts of land extending inland from the coast. Each had its own port and each was defended by its own castle. There were six in all: from west to east, Chichester, Arundel, Bramber, Lewes, Pevensey, Hastings.

Neighbouring Kent was sub-divided in 'lathes', a name derived from the Saxon 'lathe' meaning a division of land. As with the rapes of Sussex these were probably areas based upon ancient tribal districts, with laws and became especially popular in Victorian times – referring to the Torbay region of South Devon. It signifies the area's favourably mild climate and luxuriant vegetation, bringing to mind the true Riviera located on the Mediterranean coasts of France and Northern Italy. The word 'riviera' is taken from the Italian for 'bank' or 'shoreline' and is linked to the old French word 'riviere' which meant 'necklace of precious stones'. In the 1870s the exiled Emperor Napoleon III and his family settled in Torquay, further enhancing the fashionable nature of that district. Thereafter, many Italian-style villas appeared, completing the continental atmosphere.

Poppyland The district of North Norfolk around Mundesley and North Walsham became especially popular following a series of newspaper articles by Clement Scott in 1890. It was in these features that the term 'Poppyland' appeared, referring to the abundance of poppies growing in the meadows thereabouts. The Great Eastern Railway Company then used the name in its advertisements, further adding to the district's fame, and attracting such notables as the poet Algernon Swinburne. Today the name survives in local travel brochures and the North Norfolk Railway is now known as the 'Poppy Line'.

In a similar way, from the 1960s **Metroland** became a popular term for the north-west London suburbs served by the Metropolitan Railway. This name was coined by the poet and writer John Betjeman (1906–1984) on television programmes and in newspaper articles.

court judgements determined by open-air gatherings.

Across northern England – in Northumberland, County Durham and Westmorland for instance – a more common county division was the 'ward'. Each of these had a defensive function, charged with the task of organising local militia against border incursions from Scotland. The name derived from the Saxon word 'weardian' whence we get our modern words warden and warder.

More usual across central and eastern England, however, was the 'wapentake'. Originally a Saxon sub-division, each of these had been set up to help England defend itself against the Danish invasions. Every wapentake had to provide one ship, for service off the east coast. Ironically, perhaps, the Danes themselves – once they had conquered Danelaw – continued using wapentakes as administrative districts within their boroughs. The name has an interesting origin. It is thought that it is a Scandinavian corruption of a Saxon word meaning 'the brandishing of weapons'. At public meetings it had been the custom for tribal members to flourish or wave their weapons to confirm decisions or to cast votes. In due course, the meetings themselves became known as wapentakes and, eventually, the areas for which the meetings were held.

By far the most common sub-divisions, found across southern and western England, were the 'hundreds'. These were designated for taxation purposes and were so-called because they were each made up of one hundred 'hides'. A 'hide' was the amount of land required to support a single family. Naturally, these hundreds varied in size depending on landscape, soil fertility, climate and so on, but they tended to average around 120 acres each. They had certain financial and judicial functions and held regular meetings, or 'moots' to formulate laws and make judgements. These meetings usually took place at special places in the countryside – at particular landmarks or ancient sites. Trees, posts, monoliths, preaching crosses and burial mounds were commonly chosen for such sites. Later on, special 'moot halls' were built.

As time went by some hundreds merged, to become larger than one hundred hides, others disappeared. But their names stuck nevertheless. Huntingdonshire had as few as four hundreds by the 11th century, Buckinghamshire had eighteen, Sussex as many as sixty seven.

Today the only well-known hundreds are the 'Chiltern Hundreds' and this only because of a curious tradition in Britain's political life. If a Westminster MP wishes to resign, the nominal office of 'Stewardship of the Chiltern Hundreds' must be sought. And only by appointment to this can resignation from the House of Commons be accepted. Back in medieval times the post of Steward of the Chiltern Hundreds was set up, in order to bring peace and order to an area notorious for lawlessness. The hills and woodlands of that part of Buckinghamshire sheltered outlaws, cut-throats and highwaymen, who preyed upon local townsfolk and travellers on the London to Oxford road. The Steward was given the authority, not only to organise local law-enforcers, and catch these criminals, but also actually to carry out sentencing.

In 1701, by the Act of Succession, the post of Steward to the Chiltern Hundreds (made up, incidentally, of the Stoke, Desborough and Burnham hundreds) became an 'office of profit' directly answerable to the Crown. As such, it could no longer be held by a person whose allegiance was to Parliament: a person could not serve two masters. Accordingly, to apply for the post of Steward of the Chiltern Hundreds became the method by which an MP could step down from office.

CHAPTER 3

Communication: Tracks, Ways & Roads

······◆◇◇◆······

From earliest times people have been on the move. They have travelled in search of new lands to settle; they have transported goods for the purposes of trade; they have journeyed to find personal or spiritual fulfilment. They have travelled for work and for pleasure. As a result, Britain is covered by a dense network of paths, tracks, lanes and roads. Some of these are national routes, producing countrywide patterns, others are local, just linking village with village, or town with countryside.

Nearly all of these routes have a name – or rather, have two names. There is usually a generic name which describes the type of route – its purpose or its character – and an identity name which distinguishes one route from another – its unique personalised name. Thus we may have 'Roman roads', which are different from, say, 'drove roads', and we may have 'Watling Street' which is a different Roman road from 'Ermine Street'. All these names, of course, have a meaning and origin.

▨ ANCIENT TRACKWAYS

Before the Celts and the Iron Age – back in the Bronze Age or even the New Stone Age – the first trackways developed. The earliest tribes and the earliest invaders sought lands to farm and sites to settle. Britain in those days was densely forested and so these early travellers moved across the hills and mountains, where the soils were less marshy and the forests less impenetrable. They lived, mainly, in the uplands of Northern and Western Britain, and on the escarpments of Southern Britain: in Scotland and Wales, Cumbria and the Pennines, Dartmoor and the Cornish moors; on the chalk and limestone ridges of the Chilterns, Downs and Cotswolds. The Salisbury Plain was especially well-populated and it is no coincidence that here is the site of Stonehenge. Many of the most well-known trackways dating from these pre-Roman centuries radiate out from this part of England.

Icknield Way: This prehistoric trackway follows the line of chalk which runs from Wiltshire to the Wash via the Chilterns and East Anglian Heights. Part of it is now also called the Ridgeway. The name comes from a much later period. In the 10th century AD it was known as 'Iccenhilde Weg' – a Saxon name. It was once imagined that this derived from the Iceni tribe of East Anglia – the same that was led by the British Queen Boudicca in the 1st century AD – but this has now been doubted. The villages of Ickleford and Ickleton, both sited on the Way, are derived from the personal name 'Icel' and so the name of the trackway may be similarly derived. Alternatively 'Icknield' could be a Saxon corruption of an ancient Celtic word whose meaning has been lost.

Pilgrims Way: This route ran from Wiltshire to Dover along the North Downs. It acquired its present name during the Middle Ages when pilgrims travelled this way to visit the shrine of Thomas Becket at Canterbury. There is no record of what this trackway was called in earlier times but its western section in Hampshire, is now called Harrow Way. This derives from the Saxon 'Haerg Weg' meaning 'shrine way'. The 'shrine' here is not, of course, Canterbury but Stonehenge.

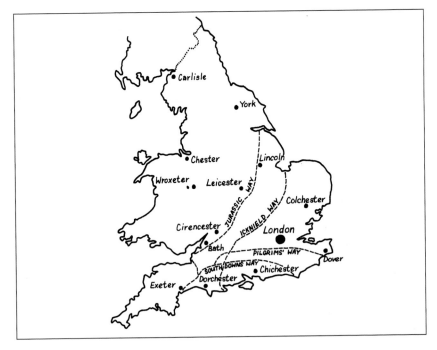

Principal Ancient Trackways

The Ridgeway, Wiltshire

Our ancient routes go back into pre-history and evolved naturally as early peoples found their way across the landscape. These routes tended to follow the hills and ridges which gave access across and above the marshes and forests of the impenetrable lowlands. The Ridgway (a continuation of the Icknield Way) runs from Ivinghoe Beacon in Hertfordshire to Avebury in Wiltshire. Here it crosses the Marlborough Downs close to the famous Hackpen White Horse, cut into the hillside in 1838 to celebrate Queen Victoria's coronation. The Abbots' Way, which crosses Dartmoor from Tavistock to Buckfast, was used by Cistercian monks in the Middle Ages but its route probably goes back to earlier times. Here it runs through Princetown, which grew around the prison (built 1808) and was named after the Prince Regent (later King George IV).

The Abbots Way, Devon

Jurassic Way: This ran from the Mendip Hills to the Humber along the Cotswolds, Northamptonshire Heights and Lincoln Edge. The name is a recent one and derives from the type of limestone of which these hills are made. Geologists call this soft, honey-coloured rock 'jurassic limestone' because it is also found in the Jura Mountains in Switzerland.

▩ ROMAN ROADS

Celtic Britain, when the Romans invaded, was not an uncivilised, subsistence-based country. It was well farmed and industrious. Indeed, it was for this reason that the Romans came: there were minerals and agricultural produce here which the Roman Empire needed. The ancient trackways already in existence were busy trade routes: tin from Cornwall and Devon, iron-ore from the Mendips and Weald, wheat from the fertile lowlands of southern England were all carried across country to ports on the east coast to be exported to Europe.

So the Romans maintained these ancient ridgetop tracks, improving them where necessary and paving those sections where traffic was especially heavy. But the conquerors also built new routeways – long straight ones, mostly radiating out from London. In the four centuries of Roman occupation over 5,000 miles of main road were built, all paved, ditched on either side and cambered.

Roman roads were straight not just because such alignments were easiest to survey and build, or because they represented the shortest distances between points. They were straight because the Romans had a telegraph system. Wooden towers were built at intervals along the roads so that smoke or fire signals could be transmitted. Straight roads, constructed across well-forested country, provided essential sight-lines.

As for the names of these Roman roads, one important point should be remembered. They are not the names that the Romans themselves would have used but the names that the later Saxons gave them. No records survive which indicate what the Romans called their roads. If they did call them anything – and such is by no means certain – then they may have named them after Emperors, Governors or Gods, or else merely after the towns they served. Thus 'Via Caesar' or 'Via Castra Legionum' might have been the name for the London to Chester route.

When the Saxons came to christen Roman roads they distinguished between a 'street' (Saxon word 'straet') and a way (Saxon word 'weg'). The former was used for any road artificially made – normally paved – and the latter for any route which had evolved – normally a wide grassy track. Also, they tended to use general terms for roads and not

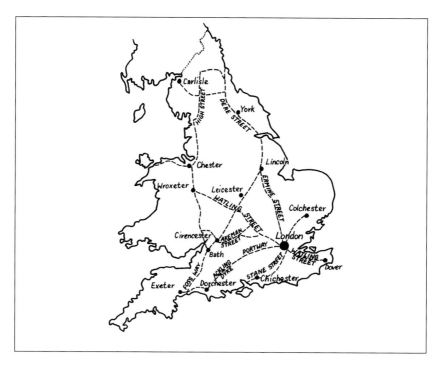

Principal Roman Roads

specific ones: 'hrycgweg' was a common name for any ridgeway, 'portweg' was commonly used for any road or path leading to a town or a market.

Watling Street: This ran from Dover to London and thence to Wroxeter via St Albans. Only the stretch through the latter town was originally called Watling Street, after the Waeclinga tribe which lived thereabouts. In Saxon times St Albans was called 'Waeclingaceaster' and the Roman road here 'Waeclinga Straet'. Only later, in medieval times, did the latter become the name for the entire length.

Ermine Street: Here again, this name originally only referred to a short stretch – that through Cambridgeshire. It was during the Middle Ages that Ermine Street was used for the whole length from London to York via Lincoln. The Earninga tribe lived in the East Midlands.

Stane Street: This road from London to Cirencester was merely called 'stony street' from the Saxon 'stan' and 'straet'.

Akeman Street: Since this road led from Bicester to Bath the Saxons

Peddars Way, Norfolk

The Romans generally built their own new roads and these ran straight, allowing for the fast movement of both troops and telegraph messages. Occasionally, however, they merely straightened existing routes. The Peddars Way, for instance, ran from the river Thames to the Wash and is thought to have been a trade route at least as far back as the Bronze Age. The name could be a corruption of 'peddlars' way'. The Fosse Way (here seen in the Mendip Hills) began not so much as a commercial route between Roman towns but a supply line for a defensive frontier. The foss or ditch (from Lyme Bay to the Humber) acted as an early boundary between lowland England, which had been subjugated, and upland England which had not. Large sections of Ermine Street, from London to York via Lincoln, remain in use today, followed in part by the A10 and A1. Here at Stilton it once formed a section of the Great North Road, the old coaching route of the 17th and 18th centuries. This particular village gave its name to an English cheese, not because this variety was made locally but because it was brought here (from Leicestershire) to be sent on, by stagecoach, to London.

Fosse Way, Somerset

Ermine Street, Cambridgeshire

called it 'Acemannes Straet'. 'Acemannes' was a corruption of 'Aquae Sulis' the Roman name for Bath.

Fosse Way: This is probably derived from 'fossa' meaning 'ditch'. The road, running from Lincoln to Axmouth, had a ditch on either side (as did all Roman roads). Early records just refer to 'Fosse' and later it was 'Fosse Street'. Only since the 15th century has it been Fosse Way.

✹ Trading Routes

From earliest times to the coming of the railways all overland trade took place by hoof and foot. Packhorses and waggons were used, and since most roads and tracks were merely grass-covered ways, transport was extremely slow. For this reason most trade took place over relatively short distances – between towns or from country to town – and most of the routeways to evolve were local in character. Only important goods were carried over great distances along major thoroughfares.

The different kinds of local tracks, to be found radiating out from every village or town, are far too numerous to mention here. For the most part they were simple farm tracks or market ways serving their immediate surroundings. They have survived as country lanes and bridleways, or as footpaths and field edges. Many may have started as 'drift-ways' for cattle or as 'back-lanes' for villagers travelling between cottages without having to use the busier routes.

Nearly all these little tracks have local names. Many of these are self-explanatory – 'Cattlegate', 'Mill Lane', 'Well Lane' – many others derive from Saxon descriptive terms. 'Port weg' (portway) would have been a market lane; 'maer weg' (mereway) would have been a boundary lane; 'bridel weg' (bridleway) would have been a route used by horse traffic. 'Jagger Ways' and 'Galley Lanes' are especially common in northern and southern England respectively, indicating pack-horse routes. The names derive from two Saxon words 'jaeger' (a peddlar) and 'galley', a shortened form of Galloway, a small and strong breed of horse, once used for load-bearing. Other local names for small trackways include 'broad way' (widened by constant use), 'hollow way' (deepened by constant use or sunk into a valley for shelter) and 'ridge way'. In northern England the word 'gate' is often used for a road, derived from the Danish 'gata', and the name 'outrake' is commonly found, indicating a route by which sheep in the hills were brought down to the shearing sheds. In lowland areas 'causeways', 'carseys' and 'carsels' often cross marshy areas on raised embankments or 'caucies'.

The more important trackways which crossed England also have names which are often self-explanatory – drove roads, salt ways and so on – but here it is more difficult to date an origin. Since trade has always been the reason for such routes, their names are apt to change with each period of use. A good example is Peddars Way in East Anglia. This name derives from Saxon 'peddere weg' meaning literally 'traders' way' or 'peddlers' way', but it was certainly used earlier by the Romans who paved and straightened it. But since it links the Wash and Thames without connecting any major Roman settlement the chances are that it is Celtic in origin, or even earlier.

Drove Roads: These evolved to enable cattle and sheep to be taken to market 'on the hoof'. The Saxon word 'drove' meant 'herd' and thus 'drover' meant 'herdsman': animals were driven along wide grassy trackways along which were opportunities for overnight grazing. From about the 10th century onwards two sets of drove roads developed: those from Wales to southern England and those from Scotland to central and southern England. Each route, and even each section of each route, was given a local name: 'Welsh Road', 'Green Lane', 'Hog Way', 'Sheep Street' and so on. Whether these drove roads used existing routeways or created their own new ones is not clear, probably a bit of both.

Salt Ways: These were commonly found everywhere and have origins, probably going way back to Celtic times. Salt was highly regarded then – indeed, it was essential for preserving and cooking purposes. Such was its importance that Roman soldiers were paid a salt allowance – a 'salarium' (from Latin 'sal' for salt) from which we get our modern word salary.

All around Britain's coastline old 'salt ways' led inland, enabling the sea salt produced from evaporation lagoons to be carried to the main towns for subsequent redistribution. There were also numerous salt ways in the Midlands, spreading out from the salt mines in Cheshire and Worcestershire. Droitwich was the main centre for salt extraction (it was once called 'Saltwich') and became the hub of the salt way network.

Lime Ways: All sorts of trackways developed in Saxon and medieval times for specialised traffic: there were peat ways, sand ways, iron ways, lead ways, tin ways and many more. But perhaps the most widespread were the lime ways. Lime was a commonly used fertilizer and was carried from the limestone hills of midland England to the surrounding clay lowlands. The lime carriers travelled in groups or 'gals' – giving rise to such road names as 'Gal Way' and 'Gal Gate'.

Smugglers' Ways: Illegal trade routes developed in the late Middle Ages as taxes began to be imposed on imported goods. Most coastal areas have their smugglers' ways, often indicated by such names as 'Brandy Lane' and

'Kegway' (since alcohol was a common booty). Not a few 'wool lines' and 'cloth ways' can also be traced back to smuggling, since England's wool trade was subject to protective trade registrations. Other goods carried along such routes included tobacco, spices and tea.

▓ NON-TRADING ROUTES

Prehistoric tribes had their processional ways, to places like Stonehenge and Avebury, and the Celts had their trackways to shrines and hill-top forts. The Roman roads, of course, were built partly for military reasons – to enable the legions to move rapidly across country – and the Saxons constructed 'herepaeths' or 'hare straets' as army roads to help in their defence of England against the Danes. So non-trading routeways are not new. However, since the Norman Conquest such routeways have certainly become more common, and all over England names suggest their alignments and former functions.

Abbot Ways: As Christianity spread from late Saxon times onwards so the power of the Church grew. Monasteries sprang up all over the country and monks acquired ever larger estates. By the 15th century the abbeys of England, collectively, were the largest landowners under the Crown. Fountains Abbey, for instance, in the Yorkshire Dales held property throughout the northern Pennines and into the Lake District. There was much contact between the various monasteries and so special routeways developed, linking them together. One such track was the Abbots' Way across Dartmoor, which linked the Cistercian Abbeys of Buckfast, Buckland and Tavistock. Its alternative name is 'Jobbers' Path' – indicating that the monastic yard jobber used it for his wool pack-horse train. Wool was the basis of Church wealth throughout the Middle Ages and many of the abbot ways were used for its transport. Other names which might indicate an abbot way include 'Church Way', 'Holy Way' and 'Nun's Way'.

Pilgrim Ways: Medieval Christian belief relied heavily on 'relics', shrines, holy wells, miracle sites and religious symbols. Accordingly places of pilgrimage appeared all over the country, some of minor or local significance, others of national, or even European importance. Amongst the latter were Glastonbury, which was linked with Joseph of Arimathaea as well as King Arthur, and Canterbury, scene of Becket's murder in 1170. St Albans, Bury St Edmunds, Knaresborough, Chester, Shrewsbury and Evesham were amongst others. The routes taken by pilgrims naturally became 'pilgrims' ways', 'St Thomas ways', 'Shrine ways' and so on. Usually such ways followed existing roads and tracks, but some created

The Modern Road Numbering System

Up to the beginning of the 20th century, roads still fell under the administration of local authorities: county councils, rural district councils, boroughs and parishes. Even major trunk roads came under the control of separate authorities; the Great North Road for instance, was administered by 72 different ones. And while such authorities had the power to repair surfaces they were not allowed to construct new roads across virgin countryside. They could not, in other words, build by-passes to avoid trouble spots.

Road naming also was not standardised. The Great West Road was not so-called throughout its length, but had various local names. So too did the Great North Road. Most county councils accepted responsibility for the maintenance of main roads, but varied as to their definitions. Norfolk and Hertfordshire for example called all important routes 'main roads' and repaired them accordingly. Surrey and Glamorgan, on the other hand, designated hardly any 'main roads' and thus kept down their repair bills.

With pressure from the Roads Improvement Association, the Lloyd George Government at last took responsibility for Britian's main road network, setting up a Road Board. In 1919 this became the Ministry of Transport.

It was in 1920 that the formal classification of roads began, numbering them into A, B and C classes. This produced the system still in use today. It is based on a clockwise rotation centred on London, with numbers increasing from a line due north.

Thus, the A1 runs from London to Newcastle (and beyond), the A2 goes from London to Dover, the A3 London to Portsmouth, the A4 London to Bristol, the A5 London to Shrewsbury (and on to Holyhead), the A6 London to Carlisle. In this way all the roads in a single region should have the same initial number: in East Anglia they begin with 1, in the South-West they begin with 3, in Wales they mostly begin with 4. Where there are apparent anomalies – like the Cornwall to Derbyshire road being the A38 and the Leicestershire to Suffolk road the A14 – numbering is based on where the road nominally starts.

The motorway numbering system tends to follow the same arrangement, each motorway being given the number of the A road it parallels. The possible exception is the M1 London to Birmingham and Leeds motorway. This was so labelled because it was Britain's first major length of motorway.

their own routes across the countryside. One of these was the 'Pilgrims' Way' across Breckland, running from Brandon to Walsingham; another was 'Jugglers' Way', in Wiltshire. The latter commemorates the entertainers who used to accompany pilgrims, lightening both their cares and their pockets.

Military Roads: King Henry I built a new road over the Wenlock Edge, Shropshire, to speed troop movements, and Edward I, during the 13th century, built many new roads in Wales to enable his conquest of that country. But it was General Wade who built our most famous military roads. The one that follows the line of Hadrian's Wall from Carlisle to Newcastle-upon-Tyne (where Wade had his headquarters) is still called 'Military Road', and those which cross the Scottish Highlands are still, collectively, called the 'Wade Roads'. The General was given the task of suppressing the Scots following the 1715 Jacobite Rebellion, and saw the construction of wide, well-surfaced roads as an essential element in the fast mobilisation of his English troops. More recent military roads can be found in regions where army ranges have been allowed, on Dartmoor, the Salisbury Plain and in Dorset for example, and around military camps and airfields.

Burial Ways: Throughout the Middle Ages only parish churches were allowed to have graveyards. This meant that, in areas where parishes were large, the dead might have to be transported over long distances. In places like Dartmoor and Cumbria ten mile trips were common, coffins being strapped on horse-backs. The paths linking outlying hamlets to their parish churches and used for this purpose were called 'lykeways' in southern England and 'corpseways' in the north. 'Lyke' was the Saxon word for a dead body. Local names for such ways include 'Dead Man's Lane', 'Bury Lane' and 'Old Corpse Road'.

✵ TURNPIKES AND TOLL ROADS

Britain's modern road network dates from the 17th and 18th centuries when, for the first time, roads were built and named with a view to a national system. Road maps began to be published and transport services began to be organised. Road surfaces began to be improved and Parliament began to take responsibility for highway repair.

In the early 17th century a network of post roads was established and coach services were started up on a regular basis. Existing roads and tracks were linked up to create countrywide routes and such names as the 'Dover Road', 'Great West Road' and 'Old North Road' were first used. At the same time – in 1625 – John Norden's set of maps was published, *An*

Intended Guide for English Travellers, and these indicated the existence of such routes.

As coach travel increased so the need for better road surfaces grew. The first toll road appeared in Hertfordshire, along a section of the Old North Road, as a result of an Act of Parliament in 1663 which gave companies permission to repair highways and levy tolls to pay for the work. Further Acts of Parliament followed, through the 18th century, and increasingly longer stretches of road were resurfaced.

The first toll roads had turnstile barriers with spikes set into the central pillars. These tapered wooden or iron spikes could be turned round upon payment of the toll. And so the term 'turnpike' roads was born. Subsequently, 'Turnpike Trusts' were set up and it was under their auspices that most of our major trunk roads were created.

Thomas Telford and John Macadam were the two most famous road builders. The former used a surfacing method based on large stones but the latter pioneered a more successful method using small surface stones watered and rolled into smooth layers. These were called 'Macadam surfaces'. Much later – at the beginning of the 20th century in fact – the same method was used with the addition of tar, to bind the stones together. This produced 'Tar-Macadam' surfaces and gave us our modern abbreviation 'tarmac'.

CHAPTER 4

The Natural World: Landscape & Nature

Early settlers lived very close to the land, its shape, elements and vegetation being very important to them. They knew every subtle change of terrain, every nuance of landscape, every river and stream, every type of plant and tree. Such were matters of life and death. A badly chosen site for a settlement or farm could mean starvation; a faulty reading of the natural surroundings could lead to a settlement in decline.

After the Ice Age, which ended around 9000 BC, Britain became an island. Ocean levels rose as the temperatures rose and deep valleys were left behind as the glaciers retreated. The shape and character of the country took on its present form: our mountains, hills and lowlands had been created. As the tundra grassland gave way to forest and scrub so pine and birch woodland took hold, followed by a succession of tree species familiar to us today – broad-leaved deciduous varieties. By the Neolithic Age (4000–2500 BC) most of Britain was covered by a blanket of oak, elm, maple, hazel and elder. Across the lowlands this forest was dense and damp, on the uplands it was sparse and drier.

This was the landscape looked upon by our early ancestors. This was the natural world where they had to settle.

▓ TOPOGRAPHICAL FEATURES

Some of our earliest place-names relate to geographical or structural features. References to hills, slopes, soils, rivers, springs and wells abound, each one helping to describe the site or location of the place in question. And the great variety found in these references not only reflects the subtleties of topographic identification but also the differences between the languages and dialects of the early tribes. There are, for example, a great many place-name elements meaning 'hill'. This is because those early settlers had a rich vocabulary. Several different words for, apparently, the same feature probably distinguished between similar features with subtle differences: a steep hill, gentle hill, conical hill, flat-topped hill and so on. Such differences were important. In addition to this, different tribes had different vocabularies. What the West Saxons, for instance, called a conical hill was probably not what the East Angles called it, let alone what the Celts or Danes called it.

The names of our landscape features themselves are probably the oldest of all. They have survived because each successive wave of settlers tended to re-name only those things which affected them directly – in particular their settlements. Features in the landscape were, to them, merely reference points. When the Saxons arrived they replaced or altered Celtic farm and village names but often kept the names of the surrounding hills and rivers in their original forms. There was no need to change them since those features were not habitative.

Even the place-names that were habitative often had links with the surrounding physical features. When naming a farm or village it was only natural for early settlers to make reference to the site's most obvious characteristic – on a river bank, in a valley, by a steep slope and so on. And when several farms or villages were situated on similar places, adjectives would be used to differentiate: a muddy river bank, a narrow valley, a rocky steep slope.

Celtic Elements: Not only are these found in Celtic place-names but also in many Saxon ones. The Saxons often found it more convenient to alter an existing name to a form they could better pronounce than to change it entirely – especially if Celts continued to live there.

A hill might be indicated by the Celtic elements 'Barr', 'Bre', 'Bron', 'Bryn', 'Menna' and 'Pen'. A river might be 'Aln', 'Dore', 'Esk' and 'Ruan'.

Other Celtic elements include 'cerne', 'carn' and 'charn' (cairn); 'llyn' and 'pol' (pool)' 'ince' and 'enys' (island); 'crug' (crag) and 'nans' (valley).

Saxon Elements: These are, by far, the most common and most varied place-name elements. Different kinds of hills are represented by such words as 'beorg', 'dun', 'hlaw' (how), 'hvall', 'hyll' (hill); different kinds of rivers were called 'broc' (brook), 'burna', 'ea', 'flode', 'lacu', 'rith', 'sic' and 'waeter'. A spring might be 'celde', 'funta' or 'wella'; a pond 'mere' or 'poll'. A valley might commonly have been a 'cumb' (coomb or combe), a 'denu' (dene or dean), a 'dell' or 'slaed' (glade). Other Saxon elements include 'eg' (island), 'mersc' (marsh), 'hamm' (meadow), 'helde' (slope) 'sloh' (muddy hollow) and 'scelf' (ledge).

Scandinavian Elements: These are less common in English place-names. By the time of the Viking invasions, the country was fully settled and the place-names established. Only in the far north and down eastern England

Upland Areas

With few exceptions, the names we now use for our hills and escarpments were already in use by the Norman Conquest. They are to be found in medieval documents, and on early maps, and generally have origins going back to Saxon and Celtic times. It is possible that some of these names go back to pre-Celtic periods but, before such can be proved, more research needs to be done.

Cheviot Hills: This upland area, in Northumberland and across the Scottish borders, took its name from the highest summit called 'The Cheviot'. This is of unknown pre-Saxon origin, the word being Celtic or even earlier. In the 12th century it was 'Chiuiet', becoming 'Chivyet' and 'Chyviot' thereafter.

Chiltern Hills: This name is a corruption of the old Celtic word 'Celtae' meaning high or a high place. This, together with the Celtic suffix 'erno' which made the word an adjective, produced 'celterno' to which the

Saxons added their own word 'hyll'.

The Cotswolds: In documents of the 13th century we find 'Coteswaud' and 'Coddeswold', which suggest an origin of 'Cod's Wald'. 'Cod' was probably a tribal leader and 'wald' or 'weald' was the Saxon word for a woodland (as in modern German). In due course this term became used for high woodland and eventually for any region of upland. The modern words 'weald' and 'wold' are used in this way, as in the Sussex Weald, Lincolnshire Wolds and Yorkshire Wolds. The addition of the modern 'Hills' is therefore superfluous.

Dartmoor: The Saxon word 'mor' is a very common suffix in place-names. It meant not only a moor in the modern sense but any large area of wasteland, be it heathland, marshland or whatever. The Somerset Levels, for instance, are called 'moors'. This particular moorland in Devon is named after the River Dart, a name derived

did Scandinavian topographical names appear. A 'fjall' or 'fell' was a hill, a 'bekkr' or 'loekr' a river, a 'holm' an island. Other elements include 'myrr' (swamp), 'hyrcg' (ridge) and 'kelda' (spring).

▦ DIRECTIONAL NAMES

Early settlers were also conscious of the relative position of the places they settled. Which side of the valley they inhabited mattered to them; on what part of a slope a village was built was important. Such considerations often showed themselves in the names, giving us various directional elements.

from the Celtic word 'derva' meaning oak. Nearby Exmoor has a prefix from the Celtic word 'esca' meaning a fast-running stream.

North and South Downs: These are named from the Saxon 'dun' (pronounced 'doon') meaning a hill. Many hills are called Downs so adjectival affixes are common: Marlborough Downs, Ballard Down and so on. The Black Down Hills are prefixed from the Saxon 'blaec' which was used for any dark place: dark rivers, dense forests, glowering hills.

Mendip Hills: The first element is probably from a Celtic word for mountain similar to the modern Welsh 'mynydd' or 'mynd'. Perhaps the name 'Menedepe' as recorded in the 12th century referred only to the valley which all-but cuts this line of hills in two. Only later did the name indicate the hills themselves.

The Pennines: Strangely no mention of this name exists before the 18th century when Charles Bertram published an account of medieval England by the monk Richard of Westminster. But this account was proved to be a forgery and the monk Richard entirely a product of Bertram's imagination. So was the name 'Pennines' also an invention? If so then Charles Bertram certainly chose the name well. The Celtic prefix 'pen' (headland or hill) makes it sound genuine, and the association with the 'Apennines' in Italy cannot be ignored. Perhaps the Romans saw the similarity of the two lines of hills, both forming national backbones, and named the English version accordingly.

Quantock Hills: The Domesday Book (1086) refers to 'Cantoche' which is thought to be the Saxon version of an earlier Celtic name 'Cantuc', from the word 'canto' meaning circle or rim. The Quantocks form a chain of hills north of Taunton, perhaps being seen originally as a 'rim' along the western side of the Somerset Levels, which were once an extensive marsh and meadow region.

Along valleys running east-west the first inhabitants tended to choose the northern sides, these being south-facing and therefore warmer and sunnier. Along north-south valleys the eastern sides were more popular, these being sheltered from the cold easterly winds. In lowland areas, and especially across marshlands, sites upon small hills or gravel islands were preferred, these giving dry soil conditions; in upland regions sites at the bottom of slopes were settled, where the thin mountain soils mixed with heavy valley soils to give fertile loams. In all these cases the choice of site might have been reflected in the choice of name, giving prefixes or affixes derived from 'north', 'east', 'upper' and 'lower' respectively.

A directional element might also have evolved from a settlement's position in relation to another settlement nearby, perhaps with the same or similar name. If the same tribe settled in more than one place, but in the same location on the same hillside or river, it might have given each settlement the same geographical name but with a distinguishing directional addition. Thus, we might have 'Upper Caldecote' and 'Lower Caldecote', 'East Stow' and 'West Stow'.

Of all directional elements, those deriving from the four compass points are the most common: 'Norton', 'Sutton', 'Easton' and 'Weston' are found together with their variations all over England. Altitudinal references include 'Under', 'Over', 'Up', 'Lower' and 'Nether', these being most common in central and southern England.

▦ Climatic Names

Just as the first settlers were close to the features of the landscape, so they were close to the vagaries of the weather. They grew crops, kept animals and lived in rough wooden or mud cottages which gave only the slightest protection from climatic elements. So they were only too aware of the passing of the seasons and the effects of sun, wind and rain.

This awareness can be seen in some of the place-names used. 'Cold Ashby', 'Cold Eaton' and 'Winscales' are self explanatory; the first inhabitants of these places obviously overcoming the cold or windy disadvantages of the sites in order to enjoy the assets, a good soil perhaps or an important water-supply. 'Somerton' and 'Winterton' are common names, indicating farming settlements only inhabited at certain times of year. Summer-only occupation might have been found in high altitudes or where marshlands dried out, as in Somerset; winter-only occupation might have been common where rivers dried up during the summer months, as in the chalk areas of Wessex.

In the Somerset Levels the reed and willow beds were much wetter than they are today. During the summer months, when they dried out a little, local farmers took their herds down to graze on the rich pastures, living themselves in temporary huts. In winter, the cattle were taken back to the drier uplands of the Mendips and Black Down Hills. In the neighbouring counties of Wiltshire and Dorset almost the reverse situation occurred. The streams flowing over the chalk downs would dry up in the summer leaving the valley floors parched and unsuitable for cattle-grazing. In the winter, however, those same rivers would flow freely, producing damp grasslands. It is no coincidence that one of the main rivers flowing down to the Dorset coast is still called the Winterbourne.

▦ RIVERS AND ESTUARIES

Apart from those river names known to be pre-Celtic in origin like Wey, Wye, Colne, Itchen and Tyne, most of our water courses have names dating from the Iron Age onwards. In many cases they are no more than tautological names, with the present-day words deriving from the old words that simply meant 'river' or 'water'. However, there are a number of river names also, which derive from adjectival words, whereby the original word which described the river led to the river name itself. For example, the River Blyth in Northumberland derives from a Saxon word ('blithe') meaning pleasant or gentle. Similarly the rivers 'Stour' and 'Tove' come from meanings of strong and slow respectively. With older, Celtic river names this was even more common: the Cam, Cray, Frome, Taw and Yeo derived from words meaning 'crooked', 'fresh', 'brisk', 'calm' and 'forked'.

Another group of river names are back-formations and can therefore be misleading to the researcher. A settlement might have been given a name and then, at some later date, part of that name might be transferred to the river upon which the settlement stands. Chelmsford, for instance, was named first from 'Ceolmaer's ford' and then the river became known as the 'Chelmer'. Similarly the Cam was named after Cambridge and the Wandle after Wandsworth.

Avon: This is one of the commonest of all river names. It derives from an ancient Celtic word 'abona', later to be 'afon', meaning 'river'. Related is the modern Irish word 'abhann' and the Scottish Gaelic 'awe'.

Derwent: Another common name, this is derived from the Celtic word 'derva' meaning oak. The rivers Dart and Darent have the same root. Such rivers probably flowed through oak woodlands – oak being predominant in Britain's primeval forests.

Humber: This was called 'Humbrae' in the 8th century and probably derives its name from two Celtic words, 'hu' meaning good and 'ambhas' or 'ambro' meaning estuary. The latter is cognate with the Welsh 'aber'. Whether this estuary was 'good' in a fishing sense, or 'good' in a religious sense is not known. Perhaps it was so-named in irony to placate a destructive river god.

Mersey: This is a relatively recent name: the Domesday Book version 'Merse' shows its obvious link with the Saxon words 'maere' and 'ea', boundary river. The river once formed the boundary between Mercia and Northumbria.

Ouse: Almost as common as avon, this similarly comes from a word meaning river. The linguistic root in this instance is especially interesting. The Indo-Germanic root 'udso' or 'uss' led to a number of related words all across Europe: 'hudor' in Greek, 'voda' in Russian, 'wasser' in German and 'eau' in French. The Celtic 'ud' and Saxon 'use' were similarly connected, the latter producing 'Ouse'. The modern English water has the same root, as does the word otter.

Severn: The origin of this name is vague. In Roman times it was called 'Sabrina', in the 8th century it was 'Saeferne' and the modern Welsh name is 'Hafren'. Though probably Celtic – the River Shannon in Ireland and Savernake Forest in Wiltshire have the same root – its original meaning has been lost. Some people think it derives from the name of a river goddess.

Thames: This is one of our oldest river names. In Celtic times it was 'Tamasa', in Roman times 'Tamesis' and in Saxon times 'Tamisa'. From the Indo-Germanic root – in sanskrit 'tamas' – it appears to have meant 'dark river'. The 'h' was added in Norman times. The rivers Tame, Tamar, Thame, Tay and Tyne probably come from the same pre-Celtic root.

Trent: The Roman name 'Trisantona' suggests a derivation from the Celtic 'tri' (through or across) and 'santon' (road or journey). A combined meaning of 'trespasser' might suggest that the river was prone to flooding for it 'crossed many roads'. The River Tarrant has a similar origin.

Wash: The Saxon word 'gewaese' was originally used to indicate the tidal movements across the sand-banks here, the swash and backwash. Later the word became 'wasshe' and referred to the sand-bank itself, which was reached on foot by a low-tide causeway. Later still, the present name was used for the whole inlet.

▦ COASTAL AREAS

The islands and peninsulas of Britain have always been regions apart. Their physical isolation has resulted in distinct histories and cultures, and in separate social and economic identities. In many cases they were the first areas to be invaded and the last to be subjugated. The names of these coastal regions, in many ways, reflect this uniqueness.

Anglesey: The Saxon name of 'Anglesege' (Angle's island) was probably a corruption of the earlier 'Ongull's ey' (Ongull's island) which was Scandinavian in origin. The Viking invaders who travelled all the way round Scotland settled here in the 9th century. Before then it was a Celtic island which the Romans had called 'Mona' – mountain island.

Penwith: A purely Celtic name for this, a purely Celtic part of Cornwall. It derives from 'pen' (headland) and 'uuid' (aspect) and was so called either because it was a promontory with a wide aspect, or because it was a promontory which could be seen from far out to sea.

Godney, Somerset

Island settlement sites were especially popular amongst early peoples since they offered protection from wild animals, thieves and, indeed, enemy tribes. They could also offer a means of livelihood, the surrounding waters, be they sea, lake or marsh, providing fish and fowl as a food supply. Godney (Goda's eg or island) once stood in a wide marshland that is, today, the Somerset Levels. In the distance is Glastonbury, King Arthur's legendary Avalon – the 'island of apples'. Close by have been found the archaeological remains of lake-villages dating from the Iron Age together with the remnants of wood-pile causeways. Blakeney (black or Blaca's island) was a major port in medieval times but has declined with the silting up of the coastline; today it is a holiday and boating resort. Neighbouring Cley-next-the-Sea suffered a similar fate and is now a mile inland.

Blakeney, Norfolk

Isle of Dogs: This area of East London, within a Thames meander, has a name of debatable origin. It has been said that it was here that King Charles II exercised his spaniels, whilst staying at Greenwich Palace, across the river. However, the name goes back further than the 17th century. Perhaps it was King Edward III (in the 14th century) who trained his dogs here – keeping hounds for hunting in nearby Waltham Forest. Some etymologists say that the name is simply a corruption of 'Isle of Ducks', from the wild fowl once living here in great numbers.

Isle of Portland: This was the island where the estate or territory (Saxon 'lande') was associated with the harbour (Saxon 'port'). Evidently Portland harbour was a natural anchorage long before the Royal Navy took it over. In the Domesday Book it was called 'Porland Insula'. Portland is linked to the mainland by the Chesil Beach, a name from the Saxon word 'ceosol' or 'cisel' meaning gravel or shingle.

Isle of Purbeck: The marshes behind the Dorset town of Wareham once made Purbeck almost an island. It was called Purbicinga in the 10th century and Purebic in the 13th century. This is a Saxon name, deriving from the words for bittern and headland. The suffix is, itself, derived from the old words 'becca' (pick-axe) and 'beck' (bill). It is not known whether bitterns lived here or the island was shaped like a bittern's beak.

Isles of Scilly: These Cornish islands were first recorded in Roman times as Silimnus and Sillina. Later, in medieval times, they were Sulling. It has been suggested that this name derives from the Roman–Celtic Sul or Sulis, the goddess of wisdom. The same deity was found in the name Aquae Sulis (Bath).

Isle of Thanet: Up to the Middle Ages the Stour Valley was a broad expanse of marsh, making Thanet more distinctly an island than it is today. The Celts used to light fires or beacons here to help seamen and so called it 'fire island', the Celtic word for fire being 'tan'. The Romans called the place 'Tanatus.'

Isle of Wight: This name has nothing to do with the white chalk cliffs found here, nor with the Saxon word 'wiht' meaning weight. Instead it is a corruption of an old Celtic word 'gweith' (later to be the Welsh 'gwaith') meaning division. The reference was probably to the tidal currents, the double tides producing flows apparently 'parting' in the Solent. The Roman name 'Vectis' was related to this meaning, deriving from 'veho' indicating levering or turning.

Wirral: The suggestion that this name derives from the Saxon words 'wir' (bog myrtle) and 'halh' (nook, meadow or river head) has been questioned by many place-name researchers. This is because such a derivation does not match the landscape, which is dry and hilly. An alternative suggestion, however, perhaps giving a Celtic origin, has not so far been forthcoming.

▦ FOREST NAMES

Early peoples, of course, had to clear the trees before they could begin to farm and settle. They started where clearance was easier – on the uplands – and so it was in the Scottish and Welsh mountains, the moors of Cornwall and Devon, and on the chalk and limestone hills of England that the first settlements and therefore the first place-names were established.

Throughout the Bronze Age and Iron Age forest clearance continued, so that, by the time the Romans arrived, farmland had spread into the plains and valleys of lowland England. The Saxons, when they came, merely finished the job of deforestation.

With the history of forest clearance it is not surprising that the natural vegetation, and the wild-life, loomed large in the consciousness of those early tribes. Many of the place-names chosen reflected this.

Forests were cleared by cutting and burning and the resulting spaces were usually enclosed with thicket fencing to keep out wild beasts. The ground would then be tilled upon the open space and cottages constructed. When the size of a family or tribe increased, and the clearing could no longer support the extra mouths, new forest spaces would be created. In this way the forests were gradually eaten away.

It follows that many place-names reflect this process of farm and settlement colonisation. There is, for example, a plethora of elements, both prefixes and suffixes, which mean 'clearing', 'enclosure', 'fenced enclosure', 'enclosed field', 'open glade' or 'cleared tract of country', all of which are essentially the same thing. Thus, in Saxon there were the words 'leah', 'feld', 'denn', 'haeg', 'haga', 'camp', 'hamm', 'land' and 'rodu'; in Scandinavian there were the words 'thveit' or 'thwaite', 'garth' and 'toft'. The names of Brandwood, Brentwood and Barnet all derived from 'burnt wood', indicating clearings thus created, and names ending in '-firth' often refer to sites where woodland had given way to brushwood and scrub.

But early settlers were not just interested in their clearings. They also used the woodlands which remained for providing timber and thatch for building and firewood, charcoal for power, and tree products for food. In many areas, and from the earliest of times, woodlands were managed to guarantee regular supplies of poles and staves. 'Coppicing' pruned trees at ground level, to produce long upright shoots, and 'pollarding' pruned trees

Epping Upland, Essex

Most of our great forests are the remnants of the primeval woodland that once covered all England. In some places they have survived because successive medieval monarchs enclosed vast areas as hunting parks, or 'chases'. Epping Forest (named from the Saxon yppe-inga – 'the people on the upland') is the last surviving vestige of the Forest of Waltham which covered half of Essex. What remains today was saved by the Corporation of London, through Act of Parliament (1878) which made that body the official 'conservator'. There is a legend that Queen Boudicca, after her final defeat by the Romans, took poison somewhere along the Roding Valley beyond Ongar and that her ghost still haunts the ancient earthwork at Amesbury Banks near Theydon Bois. The Forest of Dean (named after the Dean villages and from 'denu' for valley) was much depleted in the early 17th century, felling taking place for house and boat building. Under Charles II, however, a Reafforestation Act (1668) led to widespread replanting. The New Forest similarly had to be saved: William III ordered mass tree planting, a Commission was appointed in 1848 to oversee protection, and in 1923 the Forestry Commission was given overall authority. The Rufus Stone is said to mark the spot where William II (Rufus), son of William the Conqueror, was killed by an arrow, not perhaps by accident.

Littledean, Gloucestershire

HERE STOOD
THE OAK TREE,
ON WHICH AN ARROW
SHOT BY
Sir WALTER TYRRELL
AT A STAG,
GLANCED AND STRUCK
KING WILLIAM
THE SECOND,
SURNAMED RUFUS,
ON THE BREAST,
OF WHICH HE
INSTANTLY DIED,
ON THE SECOND
DAY OF AUGUST,
ANNO 1100.

Rufus Stone, Hampshire

just above head height, to allow shoots to spray out above the grazing mouths of cattle.

The importance of woodlands themselves in the local economies was reflected in place-names. As with the vocabularies for clearings, so too early tribes had many words meaning wood, grove, copse, spinney or tree-covered pasture. In Celtic there was 'coed', 'cos' and 'kelli'; in Saxon there was 'wood' or 'wode', 'weald', 'holt', 'sceaga', 'bearu', 'graf', 'hyrst' and 'treow'; in Scandinavian there was 'lundr' and 'skogr'. The names of Staveley and Yardley indicate places where staves and rods were obtained from the woodland; the name of Cowley refers to a former charcoal centre.

As the Saxon period progressed so many of our woodlands gained a further use as 'chases' or hunting grounds. Deer and wild boar were especially prized and many areas of forests were set aside for their pursuit. With the coming of the Normans, forest areas actually expanded, as royal hunting parks were specially designated. For the first time ever, Britain's total area of woodland began to rise and many of the forests we know today can be dated back to this period.

New Forest: On the site of the ancient forest of 'Anderida', this was created by William the Conqueror. Numerous farms and villages were swept away, and people evicted, and strict forest laws were enforced to reserve all game for the Crown. In the Domesday Book it was called 'Nova Foresta'. Incidentally it was under the Normans that the word forest entered the English language.

Epping Forest: Originally this Royal forest stretched as far as Hainault in the south and Ongar in the north. In the Domesday Book it was called 'Eppinges' and later, in the 13th century, 'Eppynggehethe'. It derives from the Saxon words 'yppe' (raised look-out place) and 'inga' (the people of). The present villages of Epping Upland and Upshire correspond to this origin.

Forest of Dean: Bounded by the Severn Estuary and River Wye, this is one of the last remaining stretches of primeval forest in England, containing over 20 million trees. Legend says that when King Alfred defeated the Danes (AD 878) at Ethandun in Wiltshire the remnants of the defeated army escaped across the Severn and took refuge in the wooded hills of Gloucestershire, which thus became known as 'Danes Wood', later corrupted to Dean Wood. In reality, however, this forest probably takes its name from the villages found at its northern edge: East Dean, West Dean and Little Dean. 'Dean' comes from the Saxon word 'denu' meaning valley. In 1016 King Canute designated the area as a hunting ground: the Royal Forest of Dean.

Sherwood Forest: Of late Saxon origin, this was called 'Sciryuda' in

AD 958. Literally, it was the 'shire wood'. The Norman kings greatly enlarged the Forest and imposed harsh penalties on intruders. Such vast areas of Royal hunting forest, all over England, were not created without a good deal of opposition and disruption. There were many bandits fighting the Forest laws, Robin Hood becoming a legendary leader here in Nottinghamshire.

▥ Tree and Plant Names

Different trees had different uses: some produced wood suitable for construction and fencing, others produced foliage for thatching. Resins and fruit were also obtained, and some even had godlike, or mystical, powers to those who had not given up their old pagan beliefs in favour of Christianity. Plants, too, were utilised, some in cooking, others in medicines, yet others in various agricultural techniques.

Most of our tree and plant place-names originate in Saxon times when our woodlands were becoming scarce and people, perhaps, were beginning to recognise their full significance and usefulness.

Thorn was commonly found everywhere and was much used for hedging, either in the form of cut branches entwined or more usually in planted rows. The ash-tree (Saxon 'aesc') and willow (Saxon 'welig') were used for furniture and basket making; the box for containers, hence the name. The lime tree ('linden') was doubly important: its inner bark was used for rope-making, its outer bark for making war shields. Holly was a good substitute for box and also had certain magical qualities, believed to keep away evil spirits (hence its later use in Christmas festivals). It was quite late in the Saxon period when fruit orchards started to appear in the English landscape. The most common were those growing apple ('aeppel'), pear ('pirige') and plum ('plume').

Amongst the shrubs found in Saxon times, heather ('haeddre' or 'lyng') and gorse ('gorst') were used for kindling, fodder and dyes; bramble ('bremel') was used for hedging. Bracken and fern ('braecen', 'fearn') were used for bedding in cattle sheds and, when burned, provided an alkaline ash for fertiliser. Those plants which possessed medicinal properties included broom ('brom'), wild garlic ('hramsan'), mint ('minte') and the water iris ('laefer' or 'flagge'). The latter also gave a yellow dye from the bloom, a black dye from the roots, and on a different plain altogether provided the model for the heraldic symbol of the fleur-de-lys.

For the most part tree and plant place-names are easy to identify because the relevant element has changed in company with the word itself. Thus, names like Oakford, Haselbury, Ashton, Gorsley and Brackley all have prefixes which are closer to the modern words for those plants than they are to the original Saxon roots. This is because the pronunciation of such names has probably stayed the same, so that, when standard spellings were introduced in the 18th century, the modern versions were used.

▣ ANIMAL NAMES

The primeval forests were rich in wild life, in birds, insects and mammals, and early settlers made full use of this natural bounty. They hunted and fished, they gathered eggs and honey, they recycled animal waste – bones, antlers and dung – as fertilizer. From a very early date they also domesticated many of the species around them, to supply food, clothing and muscle power.

With such activities – farming, hunting, gathering – it was natural for many place-names to appear which incorporated animal names. Animals, after all were the mainstay of the agricultural economy. However, not all apparent animal elements are derived directly from the animals in question, so researchers must be a little wary. It was fairly common for tribal leaders to be given names, or nicknames, to reflect their personalities or statures. Warriors, for example, may have been given the names of fearless animals (a wolf, perhaps), athletes the names of fast ones (a hare, for instance).

Throughout Saxon times numerous examples of such human/animal names occur: the famous Jutish leaders 'Hengist' and 'Horsa' were so named from a stallion and a horse; the 7th century Bishop of Rochester was called 'Putta' (meaning a hawk) and one of the Mercian kings was called 'Wigga' (a beetle). 'Eofor' (a boar) and 'Wulf' (wolf) were also common Saxon names.

Domesticated Animals: Cattle provided many a settlement with a place-name – like Oxford and Bulmer – and supported many a local economy by providing meat, milk, hides and bones, as well as being used as beasts of burden. Prefixes derived from 'cu' (cow), 'calf', 'hrither' (another name for an ox) and 'weorf' (a general term for a beast of burden) can also be found.

Sheep had long been reared but with the growth of the wool trade their importance increased. The Saxon word 'sceap' can be seen in such prefixes as 'shep', 'scep', 'scip' and 'scyp', and the Saxon 'ramm' has survived in 'Ram' place-names. Perhaps more common than sheep were goats, which were more tolerant of poor geographical conditions. The Saxon 'gat' or 'gaeten' can still be found in names, so too can 'ticcen' which is thought to have been a word for a nanny-goat. Pig rearing can be assumed for settlements beginning 'Swin' and 'Stig' – the latter coming from 'stigu' for a sty. (A 'stig-weard' was a sty-guardian, hence the modern word steward.) Horses were not commonly used until after the Norman Conquest, although the Danes did enjoy horse-racing – giving rise to a few 'skeith' place-names, from the word for a horse-racing course. Saxon words for a horse ('hors', 'hyrse' and 'fola') are rare in place-names, although 'stod' (stud) is sometimes found. Dogs trained to hunt, herd animals, and protect property appear in place-names usually as 'hunde'.

Wild Animals: Red deer and roe deer were the original native varieties, and the fallow deer was introduced into England by the Romans. The Saxon words 'deor', 'buce', 'hind', 'heorot' (hart) and 'ra' (roebuck) are all found in place-names, often in forms easily distinguishable – Buckden, Hindhead, Hartland and so on. The native hare (Saxon 'hara') features little in place-names but the rabbit introduced by the Normans for food and fur is found in names which included the old French words 'cony' and 'warenne'. The badger (Saxon 'bagga') survives in names like Bagshot but was evidently around much earlier than the Saxons as a place-name element. The Celtic word for a badger was a 'brocc' and this can still be seen in such names as Brockhall and Broxted. (Interestingly, the name 'brock' is still used as a nickname for a badger, a good example of the continuity of the language.) Water creatures like the frog ('frogga' or 'frox'), toad ('tade') and eel ('ael') also can be found, indicating, perhaps, early tribal diets: Frogmore, Tadmorton and Ely for instance. Sadly, a few place-name elements are found derived from animals no longer with us. The beaver ('beofor') was found at Beverley and Beversbrook; the bear ('bera') at Barham and Barford; the wolf ('wulf') at Wolford and Wolvey, and the wild boar ('bar' or 'eofor') at Bosworth and Everton.

Birds and Insects: Game birds, and some others like finches and larks, were eaten and birds of prey were used for hunting and for sport. Bees provided honey and leeches were used, even as early as the Saxon period, for medicines and blood-letting. Place-names from all these creatures can be found. Finchingfield, Swanmore, Cranford, Gosfield and Larkfield are all self-explanatory; place-names including 'earn' and 'hafoc' may indicate eagles and hawks respectively. Game birds, fowl ('fugol') and pigeons were all important in earlier times since they provided fresh meat during the winter months. Names beginning with the element 'Beo' or 'Bee' indicate a place where bee-hives were kept (as in Beoley and Beeby), and Honiton was evidently a place where honey was made. 'Laece' was the Saxon word for a leech and this has given us Latchmere – leech pond.

CHAPTER 5

The Nature of Society: Culture & Belief

⸻⸻••◄◗∞◖►••⸻⸻

As each new group of peoples settled in England it introduced its own social structure: its own culture, hierarchic patterns, beliefs, legends and traditions. Yet these aspects of human society did not necessarily force out those previous social structures that were already established. Instead they merged, mingled or existed side-by-side with the old ways. This happened largely because all the migrant groups were racially linked: they were all Indo-European coming from West and Central Europe. As mentioned earlier, their cultures, traditions, legends and beliefs were broadly related – diverse and different yet inter-connected and holding common elements.

The original Iron Age Celts had not expelled the Picts and Iberians of the Bronze Age or the earlier peoples of the Neolithic Age. They had merged with those resident populations. Likewise the Romans had imposed their authority and culture upon the Celts but had not removed them. The latter simply became Romanised. The same was true of the Saxons (from the 5th century onwards) and the Danes (from the 8th century) when they, in their turn, arrived. They superimposed their own traditions upon the existing social structure. In this way each successive wave of immigrants commingled with those groups already here, not always peacefully it must be said in the initial stages.

The result upon place-names of this sequence of migration, cohabitation and assimilation was to produce hybrids between Celtic, Saxon and Danish elements. Countless place-names, in other words, have become mixtures in terms of linguistic derivations. Celtic roots are found with Saxon suffixes, Saxon names with Danish alterations and so on.

▓ FOLK AND TRIBAL NAMES

A particular outcome of this historic development of place-names has been the preponderance of folk, tribal and personal name elements. In culturally mixed societies people may try to retain their separate identities, often by living amongst their own kind, sometimes by clinging to their own distinct customs and dialects; occasionally by forcibly ejecting those whose lifestyles they do not understand. This aspect of human nature produced, in post-Roman Britain, pockets or districts of different tribal groups. Place-names reflect this characteristic: it was not just 'Cymri' and 'Angle-land' which showed where separate peoples lived. On a much smaller scale places like 'Bretby' and 'Bretton' originated as places where the Britons ('Brettas') lived; places like 'Danby' and 'Denby' originated as Danish settlements. The Saxons called the Celts 'walas' (foreigners) but this did not only give us the present name Wales. It also gave us the names of such settlements as Walbrook, Walcot and Walton.

Another aspect of this desire to retain one's individuality was the evolution of place-names which included the names of tribes, tribal leaders and regional kings.

What is not clear is whether tribal place-names were bestowed or self-invented. Did, for example, other groups from surrounding areas call the place Oundle – home of the 'Undalas' tribe – or did the inhabitants themselves call their own settlement Oundle to show their uniqueness? We may never know. What we do know is that tribal place-names developed from earliest times.

Examples of such place-names include Phepson which was the homestead of the 'Fepsaetan' tribe, Hitchin, the place of the 'Hicce' tribe; Ripon, place of the 'Hrype' tribe; Whichwood, wood of the 'Hwicce' tribe and Uxbridge, the bridge of the 'Wixen'. These probably date from the 5th and 6th centuries since, during later centuries when the Saxon culture became more established, tribes became intermixed and tribal identities diminished.

From where the tribal names themselves derived is another problem for the researcher. Sometimes a tribe was simply named after the place where it lived – the 'Gifle', for instance, were the dwellers on the river Ivel, the 'Gyrwe' were fen or marsh dwellers (at Jarrow) – but often it was named from its original home. Swaffham in Norfolk was the village of the 'Swabians', a tribe originally from Slesvig (West Schleswig) in northern Germany, and Friston in Suffolk was the homestead of the 'Frisians', people from the Frisian Islands off the Netherlands. When a tribe moved more than once, its most recent previous home was often used in its name. Englefield was the open land belonging to the 'Angles', but significantly is located in Wessex. Saxham, the homestead of the Saxons, is in East Anglia.

The most common of all tribal place-names are those derived, not from actual tribes, but from the general Saxon word 'ingas' meaning 'the people of'. Normally these now end in the suffix '-ing' or '-ings' but can also have settlement elements added, that is, those like 'tun', 'ham', 'field' and 'wick' which have meanings such as homestead, farm enclosure, hamlet or farmstead.

Physical elements can also be found at the end of an 'ingas' name – 'den' or 'dean' (valley), 'bourne' (river) and 'ford' for example – when, that is, not found at the beginning. Thus we have simple place-names like Roding, Reading and Hastings, together with more compounded place-names like Hedingham, Haslingfield, Sittingbourne and Wallingford.

Many place-name specialists believe that 'ingas' names are amongst the oldest Saxon names in England – and certainly the fact that they are most commonly found in eastern and south-eastern England seems to support this theory. East Anglia, Sussex and Kent were the first areas to be invaded by the Anglo-Saxons and are especially well-off for place-names including the element 'ing'.

In the old Saxon language 'ing' meant son or descendant and 'ingas' was the plural form. King Alfred was often referred to in documents as 'Aelfred Aethelwulfing' (Alfred, son of Athelwulf) and the 'Wuffingas' were the descendants of Wuffa, one of the first Anglian kings. In 'ing' place-names the plural spelling has generally been lost in evolution but there is little doubt that they referred to 'the people of' as opposed to 'the sons of'. In many cases the 'ing' is preceded by the name of a tribal leader, to whom the people would have sworn an oath of allegiance. Members of a single tribe were not necessarily linked by family or blood ties but did share common backgrounds or social needs, or indeed, common demands for protection.

If 'ing' names really are amongst our oldest place-names, then they probably began as names for districts – for those areas where their tribal groups lived. Only later did they come to refer to specific villages or hamlets – probably to the main settlements in each district.

▣ PERSONAL NAMES

The 'ingas' place-names which begin with a tribal leader's name are not the only place-names which include names of people. A great many others do too – those ending in such elements as 'bridge', 'ford', '-well', '-bury', '-worth', '-ley' and so on. Indeed, it is probably true to say that personal place-names make up the largest single group – more English place-names are derived from personal names than from any other source.

In areas settled by the Saxons, most personal place-names have the personal element used as a prefix – giving us somebody's hamlet, somebody's farm, somebody's bridge and such like. In areas of Danish settlement, however, the personal element often appears as a suffix. Thus,

'Bewaldeth' and 'Brigsteer' are found (meaning 'homestead of Aldgyth' and the 'bridge of Styr' respectively) and not – as they might have been in Saxon districts – something like 'Aldgitham' and 'Stirbridge'.

It has always been assumed that the person referred to in the personal element of a place-name was a tribal leader. And such was probably true for the most part. But it would be wrong to imagine that this was always the case. They could have been local religious leaders, local landowners, local soothsayers or local warriors. Similarly, it would be an error to assume that these personal names always belonged to men. Women had a status in Celtic, Saxon and Danish societies higher than they did in later centuries, in the Middle Ages, for instance. They could own land, employ servants and sign contracts. They could become fortune-tellers (much respected in earlier times) and doctors, and they could set up religious establishments. Indeed, in some cultures they wielded considerable power: widows of kings and earls took on the authority of their husbands and – since brides often received large dowries from their grooms – wives often possessed enormous wealth. Moreover, childbearing was ranked as important and so mothers were respected and honoured. Thus, not a few personal name elements referred to women, not men.

Sometimes the person whose name was used was neither a tribal leader nor a local dignitary or landowner, but a regional king. The Saxon kingdoms survived for several centuries and their separate kings enjoyed considerable power. Some of these sovereigns were great warriors and conquerors, and so gave their names to the places they annexed. Others were popular and so had their names bestowed upon settlements by their grateful subjects. Into the first category probably fell Edwin, King of Northumbria in the early 7th century, who built 'Edwin's Burh' (now Edinburgh), and Penda of Mercia, the last pagan king, who inspired Pendeford in Staffordshire. Into the second category probably came Alfred (hence Alfreton, Derbyshire), Edmund of East Anglia (Bury St Edmunds, formerly Edmundsbury), and Oswald of Northumbria (Oswaldtwistle, Lancashire, and Oswestry, Shropshire).

▦ GROUP NAMES

Apart from incorporating personal names, place-names may also include the names of groups or types. These can be occupational groups, status groups or even sexual groups. Why settlements should have been named after these groups can only be surmised. Maybe such groups lived in those places; maybe they financed their construction; maybe they owned the estates nearby.

Lyme Regis, Dorset

Some settlements have been named directly from Kings: the Saxon monarchs Edwin, Alfred, Edmund and Oswald all being well represented. Other settlements have been given a regal appendage from a monarch's patronage, resulting in names which include 'King' such as Kings Cliffe (Northants) and Kings Lynn (Norfolk). Elsewhere, patronage resulted in 'Regis' names derived from the latin 'regius' meaning king ('regis' for of the king). Lime, as recorded in the Domesday Book, was named after the local river but received its addendum in the 13th century when Edward I made the town a free borough. Today Lyme Regis is a popular tourist resort. 'Hohtun', recorded in the 12th century and meaning hill-spur, received its present name in the 14th century. It had long been under royal ownership, Henry I having cut off the southern part of its manor in order to establish the town of Dunstable. Today Houghton Regis is almost a northern suburb of Luton. 'Graftone', recorded in the 12th century and meaning grove farm, was ennobled in 1541 when the manor passed into the possession of Henry VIII. It is said Henry courted Anne Boleyn here. Grafton Regis, today, is a quiet rural hamlet.

Houghton Regis, Bedfordshire

Grafton Regis, Northamptonshire

Modern Group Names

The tradition of giving regions and groups of people distinctive names goes on. Just as the Saxons called the Celts 'walas' (foreigners) thus producing, in time, the name 'Wales', so people today give certain names to those they recognise as being different from themselves. The Americans nickname the English 'limies' (from the limes English sailors used to eat to avoid scurvy) and the Austrialians call them 'poms' (since the early settlers turned as red as pomegranates in the strong sunshine). The Scots call the English 'Sassenachs', from the Gaelic word for Saxons.

Within England there are nicknames for tourists ('grockles' in Cornwall) and for country dwellers ('yokels'). There are also nicknames for those living in some of our major cities.

Brummies: The people of Birmingham are so-called because the old name for their city was 'Bremingeham', pronounced 'Brummagem'. In the late 17th century counterfeit groats were made here, leading to the word 'Brummagem' or 'Brummie' for short, coming to mean fake of false. This derogatory term was transferred to the inhabitants during the 18th century.

Cockneys: Some people think this derives from the French word 'coquin' meaning rogue, but an older – and probably more accurate – origin is that it is a corruption of the word 'cokeney', a cock's egg. Such eggs, laid by young hens, were usually misshapened and thin-shelled. 'Cokeney' was first used derogatorily by healthy countrymen for weak, soft, effeminate, town-dwellers. In the 18th century it was used specifically for Londoners, but not necessarily only those born within

Amongst occupational groups, warriors were a common source for place-name designation. 'Cempa', 'secg' and 'haegstald' were all Saxon words for a soldier and can be found in such names as Kempshot, Sedgeley and Hexham. The word 'beorn' (hero) can be seen in Barnwell. Huntsmen are commemorated in Huntingdon, bakers in Baxterley, charcoal-burners ('colestres') in Colsterworth and bailiffs ('refas') in Reavely. Smiths, woodmen, merchants, shoemakers and bee-keepers can also be found. Even entertainers are not forgotten. Minstrels ('hearperes') are remembered in the names Harperwell and Harperley, and trumpeters ('bemeres') in Bemerton and Bemersley. Such people, together with tumblers, animal keepers and mummers (folk-play actors), used to travel from fair to fair living off the money or goods given them by their audiences.

the sound of Bow Bells – which was a later, London-based, invention.

Geordies: In the late 19th century this term was used solely for coal pitmen. It derived from the diminutive of the name George. In the early days of coal mining, pitmen used a miner's safety lamp developed by the engineer George Stephenson. These lamps became 'George's' and 'Geordies' and the term spread first to the men who used them and then to all the inhabitants of the area where they lived – Tyneside.

Mancunians: The original Roman name for Manchester was 'Mamucium', this becoming 'Mameceaster' in Saxon times: the 'ceaster' (Roman fort) of the Mamucion – perhaps a Celtic name for a nearby rounded hill. However, the medieval Latin form of the earlier Roman name was 'Mancunium' and it is from this spelling that the modern term for

Manchester folk derives.

Scouse: The use of this word for a native of Liverpool is probably no older than the 20th century, but its origins go further back. It is derived from the scouse stew which has long been part of the diet of Liverpudlians – a meat, potato, onion hotpot. This meal was once called 'lobscouse' and began as a sailors' dish in the days of sailing ships. 'Lob' was a dialectic word meaning bubble or boil and 'scouse' was a term for a course – hence, a 'bubbling course'.

Tykes: Also spelt 'Tikes', this name originated as a term of abuse. 'Tike' derives from an old Norse word for a dog or mongrel and is still sometimes used as a slang reference for a badly-behaved person. However, it has also evolved into a less derogatory term – first meaning a rustic, clownish person from Yorkshire and later meaning any native of that county.

Amongst different levels of society, kings, knights, earls, monks and abbots are well represented in place-names. 'Ceorls' or 'churl-freemen', who owned land and had the right of inheritance, had names like Charlton recorded in their memory; 'holdrs' (Danish yeomen farmers) had Holderness. Even those groups at the bottom of the social ladder can be found in place-names: 'leysingi' (Danish freedmen) in Lazenby and 'cnafa' or 'knapi' (servant) in Knavenhill.

Strangely there are even place-names which include names from the criminal classes: 'Whissonsett' derives from 'wicingas' (pirates – a word originally meaning Vikings) and 'Sattering' from 'saetere' (thief).

Gender group place-names largely consist of those from certain female groups. 'Wives' form the basis for Westow and Winestead; brides give us Bridwell and Britford and 'maidens' produce Maidwell and Maidenhead.

Such names either reflect the status of women in early societies, as mentioned earlier, or derive from analogical references. Thus, a place-name based on the word 'wife' might have been given to a settlement dependent upon another elsewhere; a place-name from 'maiden' might have been used for a new settlement or a settlement known for being peaceful or unsullied.

▓ PAGAN NAMES

Before the Romans became Christians, and converted many of the peoples in their Empire to the new-found religion, the Celts in Britain had a mixture of beliefs. They worshipped various gods, a large number of which were connected with natural elements (like wind and rain) and living things (like woodlands and flowers) and they followed various superstitions and myths. They celebrated seasonal festivals, deified unworldly beings and sanctified special sites – hilltops, wells, springs and so on. They were, in short, pagan.

During the Roman occupation such beliefs were suppressed under a veneer of Christian worship. Adherence to the Church and one God became the established norm and many Celts, or Romano-Britons, really did convert and conform. But many others did not.

Then, upon the departure of the legions, and the coming of the Saxons, paganism re-established itself. the old gods and old ceremonies were restored, now mixed with the gods and beliefs of the newcomers from northern Europe. Christianity did not come again until the 6th century, and even then it was forced to accommodate many of the old established customs before it could be widely accepted.

With this background it follows that many of our place-names have pagan elements or refer to heathen practices. By the time Christianity had become fully integrated into English life most of our settlement names had already been formed. Any Christian elements now found in those place-names were either later alterations or separate additions made to fit subsequent circumstances.

Place-names which incorporate pagan elements seem to fall into four categories: those commemorating former gods and goddesses; those referring to supernatural beings; those which indicate sites of temples or shrines, and those which suggest the one-time practice of sacrifice.

Proof, if proof were needed, that gods and goddesses played an important part in pre-Christian times comes from our days of the week. These names go back 1,500 years and recall seven powerful deities. Sunday and Monday, of course, are so-called from the sun and moon – the gods of day and night, light and dark. Tuesday is from 'Tiw' or 'Tig', the god of war; Wednesday is from 'Woden' (otherwise Odin or Othin), the god of the dead; Thursday from 'Thor' or 'Thunor', the god of thunder; Friday from 'Freya' or 'Frig', consort of Woden and goddess of love and beauty; Saturday from 'Saturn', god of agriculture.

Some of these gods can be found also in our place-names: Tiw occurs in Tewin, Tysoe and Tuesley; Woden in Wednesbury, Wednesfield, Woodnesborough and Othenesburg; Thor in Thunderley and Thundersfield, and Freya in Fretherne and Froyle. Another god who appears in place-names is 'Es' or 'Os' – as in Eisey and Easole.

Whereas the gods were powerful and generally 'good' – that is, the early tribes sought comfort and help from them and offered up prayers and sacrifices – supernatural beings were essentially evil and therefore feared. Place-names which include the names of such things were often those given to sites to be avoided.

Puckeridge, Puxton and Purbrook all contain a prefix derived from 'puca', the name for a goblin (hence the later name 'puck' used by Rudyard Kipling and others in children's stories and legends). This sprite was also known as 'Bug' and 'Hob' – the latter giving us the word hobgoblin – and so we have the place-names Bugley and Hobmoor. Shacklow and Shugborough both contain an element from 'scucca' – a demon or evil spirit; Drakelow and Drakehill contain 'draca' – a dragon. Giants ('thurs') and dwarfs ('dwergs') can be found in the names Thrushgill, Thirlspott and Dwariden.

Features in the landscape like woods, wells, springs and waterfalls were all given special attention, either because they themselves had mystical forces or hidden powers, or because they were the places where supernatural beings lived. In some cases such features became shrines or the sites of temples.

Many place-names with a suffix meaning 'wood' or 'well' have prefixes of pagan origin. 'Wells' especially had religious connotations – being associated with riches and wealth – and became heathen centres. The custom of well-dressing stems from this aspect, as does the surviving tradition of throwing coins into wishing wells. The words 'weoh' and 'wig' meant a shrine or idol and can be found in Weedon, Weoley, Weyhill and Whyly. The numerous words for a temple – including 'alh', 'ealh', 'hergae' – can be found in Alkham, Harrow and Harrowden.

Animal sacrifices to the gods were common, and occasionally human sacrifices were made. These were normally part of autumn festivals, when the harvest had been gathered in and winter was nigh. The gods had to be thanked and implored to return the following year. The Venerable Bede called November the 'month of Blood' such were the offerings made and the creatures killed. It appears that heads were the particular part of an animal which the gods most desired, and many a place-name includes this part of the anatomy. Broxted was derived from badger's head, Evershed from wild boar's head and Shepshed from sheep's head. Pigs' heads seem to have been a common offering, judging from the number of place-names like Swineshead and Swinside. We can only surmise about the derivation of Manshead.

Stonehenge: This is the largest pagan monument in Western Europe and dates from about 2500 BC. Its exact purpose is not known but it is thought that, when first built, it was a focus for the worship of earthly gods. Only later – by the time it was finished in about 1500 BC – did it act as a centre for heavenly observation, sun sacrifices, or for planetary adoration. During the 12th century AD it was called 'Stanenges' and in 1205 'Stanhenge'. This probably derived from the Saxon words 'stan' (stone) and 'hengen' (gallows). The Saxons, no doubt, imagined the shapes of the edifice resembled a series of stone gibbets.

▓ CHRISTIAN NAMES

After the fall of Rome, Christianity was kept alive in the outposts of the Celtic world. Romano-British monks and holy men kept their monasteries, their beliefs and their counsel only in the Irish and Scottish margins. Then, in the late 6th century, St Columba sent out missionaries from Iona into Northern England. At about the same time Pope Gregory sent Augustine and other missionaries to southern England from Rome. King Ethelbert of Kent was the first Saxon monarch to be converted, then others followed. Eventually, only King Penda of Mercia held fast to the old pagan beliefs.

The rivalry between the Celtic church, which had converted northern England, and the Roman church, which had converted southern England, was settled in AD 664 at the Synod of Whitby. By this, England became a Roman Catholic country.

The Vikings, when they came to Britain, were pagan. They sacked the monasteries at Lindisfarne and Jarrow and destroyed Christian relics. But this desecration was not to last. By the terms of their peace treaty with Alfred in AD 878 the Danes accepted mass baptism.

The oldest Christian place-names are mostly found in the Celtic fringe and probably date from the time of the first British missionaries. Depending on region the Celtic words for a church were 'eglos' or 'egles' and 'lan' or 'llan'. These are found in such place-names as Eccles, Lanteglos, Lanivet and Llandovery. Other Celtic place-names are ancient

Ely, Cambridgeshire

The early Christian missionaries, under Pope Gregory I and his emissary St Augustine, operated a policy of religious assimilation, adapting old traditions to the new beliefs. Christian festivals were fixed to pagan dates (such as Christmas to the Winter Solstice) and churches were built on heathen sites, often hilltops. Ely Cathedral was founded as a nunnery in AD 673 by Etheldreda, Queen of Northumbria, on a site consecrated by St Augustine a century earlier. Ely ('eel island') had long been a sacred site holding mystical dominance over the Fens. Later becoming a monastery, the present building dates largely from Norman times. In the Middle Ages Ely was a place of pilgrimage, Etheldreda (canonised as St Audrey) being the town's patron saint. Annual St Audrey Fairs were held, where religious souvenirs were sold. Many of these gifts, however, were made of cheap or inferior material, leading to our present word 'tawdry', a corruption of 'St Audrey'. Burrow Bridge grew up below Burrow Mump upon which St Michael's church (now in ruins) was built on a previously pagan site. The King Alfred Inn here recalls the area's links with the King of Wessex.

Burrow Bridge, Somerset

saints' names – many of which would have been lost to posterity had it not been for the settlements named after them. These included St Austell ('Austol'), St Ives ('Ia'), St Clear, St Eval, St Buryan and St Breock ('Brioc'). Some are not preceded by a 'Saint' but were saints nevertheless – Cornelly, Mawgan, Zennor.

Christian place-names from Saxon times are by far the most common. In most cases the Christian element itself was added to an earlier name, producing various compounds or double-word names.

With a few exceptions, like Godstow, Christchurch and Chrishall, the name of Our Lord does not figure much in English place-names. But 'Church', 'Chapel' and 'Minster' do. When such buildings were constructed either a new village appeared and was given a name to link it with its religious house, or an existing village had the word 'church' or 'chapel' added to its name. Thus, we have Hawkchurch, Whitechapel and Kidderminster on the one hand and Church Stretton, Chapel Brampton, and Iwerne Minster on the other.

Holy places, other than churches, can be indicated by 'stow', as in Stow-on-the-Wold, and 'stok' or 'stoc' as in Stoke by Nayland. Such places were either ancient shrines or sites of old religious houses. 'Cross' similarly, is a common element, found in Crossthwaite, Shallcross, Stump Cross and other such names. The prefix from 'holy' – as in Hallington, Holywell and Holyhead – can certainly be Christian in origin, but not always. The old Saxon word 'halig' also had pagan connotations.

Instead of the words 'church', 'chapel', 'holy' and 'cross' being added to a place-name it was often found to be more convenient simply to add the dedication name. Thus, we have a whole range of place-names incorporating Saints' names: St Albans, St Helens, St Mary Cray, Ayot St Lawrence and so on.

A further group of place-names are those linked to religious orders. After the Norman Conquest numerous abbeys and monasteries sprang up, and in many cases settlements grew next to them. That these settlements were named after the religious communities which, in effect, created them, was only to be expected. 'Acaster Selby' grew up next to Selby Abbey; 'Crowmarsh Battle' next to Battle Abbey; 'Weedon Bec' next to a sister abbey founded here by the monastery at 'Bec Hellouin' in Normandy. The Saxon word 'hiwan' for a religious community is preserved in Hainault and Henwick.

Similar to these place-names are those which refer to the monastic residents themselves: Prestwich, Monken Hadley, Canons Ashby, Abbotsbury, Nunney, Abbess Roding are all self-explanatory. In medieval times bishops were commemorated in names like Bishops

Stortford but in earlier times their Latin title of 'Episcopi' was more often used, as in Huish Episcopi in Somerset.

Finally, there are a few religious place-names stemming from the Knights Templars, who owned much land in medieval England. That organisation was established to seek the recovery of the Holy Land from the Saracens. It was founded in 1119 and grew to be one of the most powerful religious organisations in Western Europe.

It took part in the Crusades and established centres all over England. Later it became corrupt and degenerate, and was disbanded, but not before it had given its name to such places as Templeton, Templecombe and Temple Normanton. In Hertfordshire the Knights Templars established a very large base at a manor they called 'Baldac' – the Norman French name for Baghdad where they had been stationed during the Crusades. This place-name has since been corrupted into Baldock.

▨ DEATH AND BURIAL NAMES

Death was far more of a feature of life in earlier times than it is today. the average age expectancy at birth was below 40 and half of all children died before they reached the age of four. Diseases were rife, malnutrition common and medical practices primitive. In addition, there were almost constant tribal conflicts; murderous villains stalked the highways and punishments for wrongdoers were executed with rigorous efficiency. Lucky the person who lived to a ripe old age!

Cremation of the dead ceased fairly early in Saxon times – probably when England was still pagan – and so place-names with elements indicating such a practice are rare. Amongst the few found are Belgrave and Bylaugh, both of which may include an element from 'bel' meaning funeral pyre. If so, the former would mean 'cremation grove' and the latter 'cremation enclosure'.

As burial became more common so the number of place-names connected with the dead increased. Burial mounds, in particular, are mentioned. The Saxon words 'beorg', 'haugr', 'hlaw', 'haer', 'byrgels' and 'byrgen' all mean barrow or grave-mound and are found in such place-names as Barrowden and Bergholt, Taplow, and Hounslow, Bernwood and Hepburn.

Coffin place-names are not common – although Chessell is derived from 'cest' and 'hyll' (coffin hill) – and those with 'dead' as an element are little more so. A few local names exist, like 'Deadman's Hill' and some village names include 'morth', as in Morpeth and Mortgrove. Both these are associated with places where violent deaths or murders occurred. The same is true of the element 'lic' (corpse) as found in Litchborough.

One group of death place-names which may be of special interest to the local historian is that connected with hanging. Back in Saxon times the death penalty was imposed for even the slightest of crimes. In the 7th century, for example, King Ine of Wessex introduced capital punishment for all thieves, for foreigners who strayed from the King's Highway, and for anyone who walked through woodlands without shouting or blowing a horn (as a warning to huntsmen). In the 10th century King Athelston executed anyone who stole property worth more than one shilling.

The gallows was the usual method of execution, and the Saxon word 'galga' occurs in Galligill and Gowbarrow. Local names like 'Gallows Tree', 'Gallows Gate', 'Gibbet Corner', 'Hanger Lane' and 'Hangman's Folly' are also found, either within towns, or at road junctions in the countryside where gibbets were frequently set up. The place-name Tripsdale means 'rack valley' and derives from 'threpel' – a gruesome wooden contraption upon which the body of a convicted man was fixed, prior to execution.

▓ FOLKLORE AND LEGEND NAMES

In early English society superstition occupied minds as powerfully as any religion. Legends, folk tales, omens and prophecies were thought to be as true as the gospels; witchcraft was feared; magical power revered. Stories about giants, dwarfs and devils were believed, legendary characters were honoured as genuine heroes. In such a culture is it any wonder that many place-names developed which incorporated elements of a mysterious or mythical nature?

Natural landscape features, old burial mounds and, especially, prehistoric earthworks and stone monuments were all given names derived from superstitious beliefs. Devils, witches and giants feature in many of these: 'The Devil's Punchbowl'; 'Devil's Ditch'; 'Gog Magog Hills'; the 'Giant's Cradle'; 'The Witches' Coven' – the list is endless. Other names do not mention supernatural beings themselves but derive from stories connected with such beings. The 'Merry Maidens' in West Cornwall is a case in point. This name refers to a stone circle. Nearby are two standing stones called 'The Pipers'. Legend tells us that a witch saw them all enjoying themselves on a Sunday – the girls dancing in a circle to the music of the pipes – and so turned them all to stone. A similar tale is found at the 'Rollright Stones' in Oxfordshire. Here the stones forming the circle are called the 'Whispering Knights' and a nearby upright is 'The King's Stone'. They were turned to stone before they could conquer all

England. On the Berkshire Downs a Stone Age burial chamber is called 'Wayland's Smithy'. Legend says that a godlike blacksmith still lives there and will shoe any traveller's horse if sixpence is left on the chamber capstone.

One interesting group of place-names is that pertaining to the number seven. Since the most ancient of times this number has been given mystical qualities – bringing luck and producing magic. Days in the week, Wonders of the World, Deadly Sins, all number seven and in Classical Mythology, Atlas and Pleoine had seven daughters. In present-day England we have the settlements of Sevenoaks, Seven Kings and Sevenhampton, and the cliffs of Seven Sisters.

Legendary Heroes: The two most common personages found in place-names are Robin Hood and King Arthur. The former was supposed to have lived during the early 13th century in and around Sherwood Forest, Nottinghamshire, where he helped (illegally) to redistribute wealth and to support Richard the Lionheart against King John. The latter was accredited with medieval exploits revolving around the Holy Grail and the Knights of the Round Table – largely the invention of Geoffrey de Monmouth in the 12th century and Thomas Malory in the 15th century.

Robin Hood is commemorated in various local names in the Midlands, together with the coastal area in Yorkshire called Robin Hood's Bay. This name dates at least from the 16th century and derives from the legend that Robin kept a fleet of ships there, ready for a hurried escape from the Sheriff of Nottingham, if such were needed. It was also thought that Robin used to go fishing there during the summer months.

King Arthur place-names can be found everywhere from Cornwall to Scotland: King Arthur's Cave, Arthur's Stone, Arthur's Seat, King Arthur's Round Table and so on. Most of these names stem from medieval folk tales, but a few may not. Unlike Robin Hood, Arthur does seem to have some basis in fact. It is now thought that a certain King Arthur did exist, probably in the 6th century. He was a Celtic chieftain who proved successful in keeping the invading Saxons back from the further reaches of western and northern Britain.

Hill-top Churches: In pagan times hill-tops were sacred. They were the places where the Celts and early Saxons buried their dead, to be protected by the dragons that lived there. Many became the sites of heathen temples and places of pilgrimage where offerings would be left to placate the dragon hosts.

When England was later converted to Christianity, churches were built on many of these hill-tops. Pope Gregory had said to his missionaries, 'the temples of the idols must not be destroyed, but the temples themselves should be sprinkled with holy water, altars set up and Christian relics enclosed in them'. In this way, he hoped, people would convert more easily. For the same reason, incidentally, the Christian church also adopted many of the pagan festivals – 'Saturnalia' became Christmas, the spring celebrations became Easter – both complete with pagan symbols: mistletoe, holly and ivy; rabbits and eggs respectively.

Since the warrior Archangel Michael was associated with dragon-slaying, the early Christians made him the focus of their hill-top churches, thus to maintain the continuity with paganism. And so we find, to this day, hill-top churches are frequently dedicated to St Michael – St Michael's Mount in Cornwall, St Michael's at Brentor in Devon and many, many more.

CHAPTER 6

The Needs of Society: Co-operation & Protection

W hen the first settlers were searching for potential sites for habitation they had two basic requirements. First, they needed places which gave them a means of livelihood – normally the physical or natural conditions for agriculture. Thus, they would look for shelter from bad weather, close proximity to water supplies, fertile soils and, possibly also, suitable raw materials for building their homes. Their second basic requirement was an environment or position which gave them continuity and safety. They needed security of tenure or ownership and protection from outside dangers, be they natural, animal or human. The former could be provided through co-operation and a strict adherence to laws, taboos and social codes, the latter could be achieved through self-defence and the acceptance of guardianship.

Different societies developed their own particular methods for satisfying these various needs. The Celts, for example, tended to favour a loose social structure in which family or bloodline bonds were strong, settlements were scattered and hill-forts provided defence in troubled times. The Saxons, on the other hand, tended to have a communal social structure and live in nucleated tribal clusters or even fortified settlements. The Normans were even more well-structured socially, introducing strict land ownership rights, castles and walled towns.

The various aspects of social need and cohesion – the co-operation within and between groups and the methods of protection achieved – are reflected in our place-names. And by Norman times most of our settlements in England had appeared and most of their names had evolved into the essence of their present forms. In effect, therefore, the place-names we have today fossilise the character of the society which existed nearly a thousand years ago.

Field Names

The Saxon word 'aecer' (similar to the Scandinavian work 'akr') originally meant a plot of land. In time, however, it came to mean a plot of a particular size – the area of a single 'strip' as cultivated in the 'open-field system'. This became the 'acre'.

With a simple ox-drawn plough the Saxon plough team could till an acre in a day. The width of each plough ridge was measured by a wooden pole or rod 5½ yards long. Four of these poles were laid end-to-end to mark off the total width of a strip (22 yards), this then being regulated by a chain. Ten chain lengths were used to measure the total length of each furrow which thus became 220 yards. This 'furrow long' became a furlong. And so we have the beginnings of our old imperial measures. There were four furrow lengths to each strip which, in turn, was 4,840 square yards in area (that is, an acre).

The unploughed ridges which marked the boundaries between the strips in the open fields were called 'balks' or 'baulks', and the field edges where the ploughs were turned round at the end of each furrow were called 'heads', 'headlands' or 'sidelands'. Areas of ground close to boundaries, or in field corners where ploughs could not reach, were called 'shots', 'shutts' or 'shutes'. All these words are still in use today and can still be found in the names on local farm maps.

Indeed, all kinds of names can be found on local, large scale, maps. It is not only farms and settlements that are given names but fields as well. And many of these go back to Saxon times.

Condition Names: Many field names merely describe the nature of the soil or the character of the land. 'Hungor' (hunger) might suggest a barren field, for example, and 'cloudy' could mean a stony one. Marshy or muddy fields might have such names as 'Gall', 'Quab','Lag' and 'Pudding'. Fields in hollows could be called 'Bottom' or 'Dimble'; those with tall grass 'Fog' or 'Math'.

Dimension Names: These usually refer to some aspect of a field's size or shape. Small plots could be called 'Pleck', 'Pingle', 'Pightle' or 'Stitch'; narrow plots could be 'Screed', 'Slinket',

⬛ THE SPREAD OF AGRICULTURE

From the Bronze Age onwards Britain's primeval woodland was systematically cleared to make way for agriculture. Trees were felled and large tracts of land were turned over to arable and pasture. Fields were opened out and fenced, or hedged, and farmsteads were built. Settlements appeared and, in many cases, were named according to their agricultural character.

'Spong', or 'Croft'. Corner pieces might be called 'Bye' and triangular pieces 'Gore'.

Location Names: The position of a field might lead to such names as 'Inland' (near the farmhouse); 'Butte', 'Hem', 'Skirts' or 'Meer' (near a boundary) and 'Sideling' or 'Hiron' (near a river).

Charity Names: The custom whereby certain fields, were given over to common pasture each year, from August 1st to the following spring, led to the name 'Lammas' being applied to the plots. Elsewhere, the rents or produce of particular fields might be given to some local charity or cause. 'Poors', 'Corpus', 'Church', 'Glebe', 'Parson' and 'Sacred' are all names suggestive of local ecclesiastical charities; 'Chancel', 'Bell' and 'Churchdoor' all tell where the donations are destined. The ceremony of 'Beating the Bounds' took place during the week before Ascension Day. Village officials and inhabitants would follow the vicar around the parish perimeter, in order to ensure that all boundary marks were still in place. At each mark prayers would be said and verses from Scripture read aloud. This caused many fields at parish margins to be called 'Gospel', 'Amen' or 'Paternoster'.

Fanciful Names: Of all field names these are the most curious and the most interesting. They would also be the most rewarding to study in greater detail. Irony and exaggeration are the hallmarks of such names, with not a little dash of humour. Fertile fields might be called 'Fillpockets', 'Land of Promise' or 'Pound of Butter'; infertile fields might be 'Break Back', 'Pickpocket' or 'Quarrelsome'. Oddly shaped plots of land could be 'Leg of Mutton', 'Dogtail' or 'Knitting Needle'. Small plots could be 'Wren Close' or 'Threepenny Piece' – or else, with heavy sarcasm, 'Thousand Acres'. Remote fields are often given names of remote places: 'Bohemia', 'Gibraltar', 'Botany Bay', 'Dunkirk', 'Worlds End'. Another category are those field names taken from famous battles and wars. These probably help the researcher date the time of enclosure: 'Quebec', 'Blenheim', 'Maida Vale', 'Portobello', 'Waterloo' and 'Balaclava' are some of the most common.

Under the Celts forest clearance was piecemeal. Fields were claimed from the woodlands as required, and enclosed irregularly as the natural topography allowed. Farms became scattered, each one representing a self-contained family-based unit. The Celts were not tribal in any close or cohabitative sense. Their homesteads were often isolated and even their villages were loosely knit or dispersed.

Agricultural organisation and settlement development were very different under the Anglo-Saxons. By the time the Romans left in the 5th century extensive areas of forest had already disappeared, England's population had grown and methods of large-scale farming had been introduced. The invading tribes – the new settlers – saw the possibilities and set about turning the landscape into an efficient agricultural entity. And the feudal system helped them do it.

The Saxons were tribal in the co-operative sense of the word. Their society – more than that of the Celts – was based on the village, the manor and the estate. Farmland was run communally and tenants gave tithes (tenths) to their chiefs, measured in either time or money. In return for this 'feudum' (fee, hence the word feudal) each chief or lord of the manor gave back protection, security and education – the latter usually through the auspices of the parish church. Around each settlement were three large fields, each sub-divided into furlongs and strips. Each field specialised – one growing wheat or rye, one barley or oats, and one lying fallow. These were rotated annually, thus giving each field one year in three in which to regain fertility with the help of pasturing animals. Each villager, or tenant, owned a set number of strips distributed about the three fields, thus ensuring equality of crop output and fair apportionment of good and bad soils.

With modifications and natural evolution the feudal system survived for a thousand years, only really being abolished in the 18th century.

▧ ENCLOSURE NAMES

When the Anglo-Saxons first came to England they took over existing Celtic farms as well as creating new farms of their own. Whereas the former were little more than expanded clearings and tended to acquire names which meant 'enclosure', the latter, being more open in character and more distinctive from the surrounding woods, tended to receive names meaning 'field'.

Place-name elements meaning 'enclosure' are numerous. 'Worth' or 'Worthy' can be found in names like Shuttleworth and Selworthy; 'haeg', 'haegen' or 'haga' in names like Haynes and Thornhough. The latter group often referred to fenced or hedged enclosures, as did the elements 'edisc' (as in Cavendish), 'geard' (as in Bromyard), 'hop' (as in Hopton) and 'penn' (as in Owlpen). More specific enclosure names used by the Saxons included 'pund' (pound) as in Putney; 'fald' or 'falod' (animal enclosure) as in Shinfold and 'teag' (grassy enclosure) as in Grafty. The word 'winter' meant a vineyard – the English climate was warmer in those days – and 'ortegeard' meant garden, giving us the modern words yard and orchard.

Midwinter and Orchardleigh are examples of settlements which include these elements.

By far the most common Saxon element meaning field was 'feld' – strictly speaking, a 'tract of open land'. Place-names which included this usually as a suffix are far too numerous to list fully: Hatfield, Marshfield, Enfield, Sheffield and so on. 'Leah' was a word which began by meaning a clearing but later meant 'grassy expanse' this giving us our present words 'lea' and 'ley' for meadowland. The word 'aecer' (plot of land) not only produced our modern acre but can be found in such place-names as Benacre. The word 'hlinc' (hillside terrace) has become 'lynchet' and is found in Linkenholt and Standlynch. 'Mead' or 'meath' (meadow) as in Meadbourne and Runnymede was itself derived from 'mawan' meaning to mow. This survives in the word aftermath which originally meant 'after the grass-cutting'.

▦ ESTATE NAMES

Many of the old words which had originally denoted clearings, enclosures, fields or fenced pastures later became terms for homesteads, manors or even villages. This was because the lands which made up enclosures were so intimately linked with the buildings within them that the same words could be used for either. In effect, enclosures became farmsteads – areas of land within a boundary fence cultivated and inhabited by separate family groups. Then, as populations grew, those same farmsteads often developed into hamlets, as more buildings appeared to accommodate kinsmen, friends, servants and occasional guests. Still keeping the same generic name (the one meaning 'clearing' or 'enclosure') many of these settlements then proceeded to grow into villages and, perhaps, eventually towns.

A good example of this process involves the Saxon word 'ham'. In earliest Saxon times there were two separate words 'hem' and 'hamm'. The former, it is believed, referred to a farm building of some kind, the latter to a meadow enclosure or to a fenced pasture. In time, the two seem to have merged: 'hamm' disappearing from early records and 'hem' changing to 'ham' with the meaning of 'enclosure with a farm building' that is, a homestead. By late Saxon times the same word had taken on the meaning of a manor, an estate, even a village. In other parts of Europe, too, the word can be found in varying forms: in old Gothic it was 'haims', in German 'heim' and in Old Norse 'heimr'. In modern English we retain the word in 'hamlet' (literally 'a little ham').

The Saxon 'tun' had a similar evolution of meaning. At first indicating fence or hedge, it came to mean 'area enclosed by a fence or hedge' and

Saffron Walden, Essex

So important did agriculture become during the Middle Ages that some
settlements were named after the crops which sustained the local economy –
that is, which gave most profit. At Saffron Walden the old village of Waldena
(12th century, from 'denu-walas' – valley of foreigners) had its present adjective
added in the 16th century. The saffron crocus was grown here, a plant used in
medicines and dyes. Much of the saffron produced was exported to Europe.
Wheathampstead derives its name from 'wheat-hamstede' meaning the
homestead where wheat is grown. Cereal farming was important here in
medieval times, but also had a long history. One of the reasons that the
Romans invaded Britain was to gain access to the vast Celtic arable farms.
Wheat had long been exported to Gaul.

Wheathampstead, Hertfordshire

eventually 'enclosure with a dwelling'. From that point its progression to meaning farmstead, hamlet or village was assured. The spelling changed to 'ton' which, in due course, gave us the word town.

Another Saxon word that underwent a change of meaning was 'wic'. This began life referring to a farmstead, deriving as it did from the Latin 'vicus', but later became a word meaning a farm specialising in a particular type of farming. Usually, but not always, this would have been a dairy farm. From this meaning it developed a further significance – that of a place where food was prepared, and not necessarily dairy produce. Perhaps it was from this connection that a separate meaning was created – a place where salt was used or produced. Salt in those days was an important preservative. By late Saxon and medieval times 'wic' had become 'wick', 'wich' or 'wyke' and had become a word with the general meaning of village or town.

Place-names which include the elements 'ham', 'ton' and 'wick' or 'wich' are found absolutely everywhere and need not be listed here. Suffice it to say that they are very common indeed (Nottingham, Hexham, Taunton, Boston, Norwich, Warwick …).

▦ FORTIFIED SETTLEMENT NAMES

Each successive wave of invaders and settlers had to contend with a native population loath to allow them to stay. So they all built for themselves camps and castles for protection. But as these new settlers began to impose their cultures onto the existing inhabitants so the role of their fortified sites changed from defensive to offensive. Military centres grew up to subdue all local opposition. In response, the native tribes themselves established defensive sites, many of which developed as centres for armed resistance against the intruders.

But hostilities did not just exist between invaders and natives; between Celt and Saxon, Saxon and Dane, English and Norman. Within these groups there was also disunity. Each race was not homogeneous but tribal, and territorial or power disputes were commonplace. For long periods the Celtic tribes fought amongst themselves and, later, the Saxons and Danes also. Perhaps only when there was a threat from abroad did these people unite.

In this human climate it is not surprising that not only did many of our towns and villages first develop as defensive or military settlements, but also many of their names now indicate their fortified pasts.

The kinds of settlement which gave early tribes natural protection were headlands, hill tops, islands (offshore, in marshes or in rivers) and lake-

Castle Acre, Norfolk

In medieval times protection continued to be an important requirement in a settlement site. Either villagers found their own method of defence by building enclosed compounds such as found at 'burh' (bury) and 'stocc' (stoke) sites, or else they sought refuge next to castles. Castle Acre grew up within the outer bailey of a Norman castle whose 13th century gateway still survives. The name simply means castle field. At Nunney (the 'eg' or island of the nuns, this being the old site of a nunnery) the cottages gathered around the castle built by Sir John de la Mare in the 14th century. In earlier times the peasant huts would have clustered around the priory for the same protective reason.

Nunney, Somerset

sides. Thus, place-names which include such elements mean these features could be termed defensive in nature. In Celtic place-names the commonest such elements found include 'pen' (headland) as in Penzance; 'bar' or 'bre' (hill) as in Bredon and 'lyn' or 'lin' (island) as in King's Lynn. In Saxon names there are numerous such elements – 'hyll' (hill), 'torr' (rocky peak), 'beorg' (mound), 'eg' (island), 'totaern' or 'tote' (look-out place), 'mere' (lake) to name but a few. Such elements can be found as prefixes or suffixes: Hilton and Foleshill, Tormarton, Bergholt and Smallburgh, Eland and Eastrea, Totham, and so on.

Where no natural phenomena provided defensive possibilities, the early tribes constructed their own artificial features – building earthworks and stone walls, mud or wooden forts, digging ditches and moats; damming rivers and inlets. Thus, many place-name elements refer to such structures: 'eorthburh' (Saxon for earthwork) is found in Arbury and Harborough; 'dic' (Saxon for ditch) is in Dickley and Dowdyke; 'stocc' (Saxon for stick or trunk – sometimes used to mean stockade) is in Stokenchurch and Stocking Pelham.

The most common elements which refer to defensive sites are those meaning army camp, fort or fortified place. The Romans built many a defensive or military base, most of which were taken over by later peoples. The 'colonia' was an army establishment, usually a colony for retired soldiers (hence the present name of Lincoln) and a 'castra' was a fortified camp or walled town. The latter was very common indeed and most were re-established under the later Saxons, who called them 'ceasters' or 'caesters'. Their walls were rebuilt, their gates and towers restrengthened, their streets resurfaced.

The settlements today which began as Roman 'castras' are legion. Normally they can be recognised by their suffixes, which derive from the Saxon version of that word. Thus, we have all those places ending in '-chester', '-cester' '-caster' and '-xeter': Winchester, Worcester, Manchester, Doncaster, Exeter and so on. Some of these have prefixes from older Celtic words (sometimes tribal names or physical features), others have prefixes purely Saxon. Rarely, if ever, are the prefixes from a Roman or Latin root.

Another common defensive element found in place-names was 'burh', a Saxon word meaning fortified place, fort or strengthened manor house. This has given us all number of suffixes ('-burg', '-bury', '-borough', '-brough', '-burgh', '-burrough', '-burrow', '-bere' and '-berry') as well as some prefixes ('Bour-', 'Bur-', 'Bul-' and 'Burra-'). Thus we have such place-names as Peterborough, Shrewsbury, Banbury, Middlesbrough, Bourton, Burton, Burradon and many, many more.

Even fortified places much older than Saxon times were given names by the Saxons from 'burh': the Celtic Iron Age forts of Oldbury Camp, Cissbury Ring, Cadbury Castle, Yarnbury Camp, for example.

The word 'castle' in place-names arrived relatively late – from the 10th century onwards. It derives from the Saxon word 'castel' and the Latin 'castellum'. It was usually introduced to signify a large, purpose-built fortress, of the kind much favoured by the Norman kings. Occasionally, it was used by the Saxons for an ancient earthwork – Maiden Castle, for instance – but this was unusual. Names like Bishop's Castle, Castleton and Castle Bolton are self explanatory.

Hadrian's Wall: Running from Wallsend to Bowness-on-Solway, this was built after a visit to Britain by Emperor Hadrian (or Adrian) in AD 122. It formed the northern boundary of the Roman Empire and a barrier against the unconquered tribes of Caledonia. For much of its length it surmounts the geological feature of the Great Whin Sill. The Saxon word 'weall' is also found in the village names along the wall – Benwell, Wallbottle, Walltown, Thirlwall.

Maiden Castle: No one really knows for sure the origin of this name. Some people think it actually does come from 'maegden' (Saxon for young girl or virgin) either because there was once a temple here to a female pagan god, or because the earthwork was so strong and impregnable that even young girls could defend it. Perhaps a more likely derivation is from 'maia dun' – great hill. In this form it is mentioned in old Roman documents about the attack by Vespasian and his legion on the Durotriges people. The Maiden Castle we see today dates from the Iron Age, probably built around 400-200 BC. It was both the hill-fort, and the permanent civilian settlement, for the Durotriges, a Celtic tribe which lived all across southern England. After the Romans defeated these people and built Dorchester nearby, Maiden Castle became depopulated.

Offa's Dyke: This was dug in the 8th century by the Mercian King Offa, to mark the boundary between his kingdom and Wales. It runs from Chepstow to Prestatyn, a distance of 80 miles, and is still of formidable height. It was called 'Offan Dic' in AD 854 and 'Offedich' in 1184.

Wansdyke: This was built in the 5th century, probably by the Celts against the invading Saxons, who were coming up from the south coast. It ran from Andover to Portishead, on the Severn estuary near Bristol, and was called 'Wodnes Dic' in the 10th century. The name comes from Woden, the pagan god of the dead.

▦ COLONISATION NAMES

The medieval period saw the consolidation of the inhabited landscape. The primeval forest had gone, the wilderness had been tamed. By a process of colonisation and agricultural innovation the late Saxons, Danes and Normans extended the area under cultivation: they drained the marshes, tilled the moors and stabilised the shifting shoreline. As the country's population grew, so the need for more houses and more facilities increased. Everywhere settlements expanded. In a few places some totally new settlements appeared where none had existed.

Mother and Daughter Villages: The Saxon-inspired three-field system of agriculture could not easily adapt to increased numbers. Each village was self-sufficient; the strips were distributed equally amongst the farming inhabitants, and the grazing rights in the encircling woodlands were held communally. So, when the village population grew, the capacity for food production became restrictive. The solution was the creation of colonial settlements. A village experiencing growth would send out a group of farming families into the surrounding forest to set up a new settlement, complete with its own, newly-cleared, three-fields. This new village would then be given a name similar to that of its parent settlement but with a qualifying addition, or adjective. The most common affix was 'Little'. The parent village would then become 'Great' or 'Much', to distinguish itself. Such mother and daughter villages were common; Great Missenden, Little Missenden, Much Hadham, Little Hadham. Sometimes the Latin equivalents were used – Ashby Magna, Ashby Parva, Wigston Magna, Wigston Parva – and sometimes the old Saxon word 'mycel' or 'micel' survived in the name of the parent – Mitcheldean or Mickleover. Occasionally the mother became 'Old' as in Old Sodbury and All Cannings and the daughter became 'Lesser'.

Manorial Villages: After William became King of England he rewarded his Norman kinsmen with lands and estates confiscated from the defeated Saxons. All over England, villages found themselves under new overlordship, with Norman earls and barons becoming their new owners. Sometimes an existing estate would merely be transferred from a Saxon to a Norman – with the latter simply taking over the home and manor of the former. Sometimes an area of land (a group of farms or settlements) would be turned into an owned estate for the first time, with a Norman aristocrat building himself a new manor house, and creating for himself a new domain. The effect of all this upon place-names was the appearance of Norman family names as elements. Most common of all was the addition of the Norman surname to an existing village name as a

Peacehaven, East Sussex

The 20th century saw the appearance of new settlements specifically planned for a post-employed population. These places can be seen as a modern response to the need for co-operation and protection, the elderly and infirm requiring special settlement structures. Improvements in food, sanitation, health and medicine created a larger number of people over the age of 65 and a society in which extra leisure time was expected. Peacehaven was built for retired people and, in consequence, had a preponderance of bungalows and, despite being situated on a cliff-top, a flat and level site. It was named towards the end of the Great War, for self-explanatory reasons. Enham Alamein was simply called Enham until the Second World War (deriving from the Saxon 'ean-ham' for lamb farm). Then it became a convalescence and invalid-care village for war veterans, the addendum then being used. El Alamein, of course, was the scene of Montgomery's decisive victory in 1942 during the North Africa desert campaign.

Enham Alamein, Hampshire

separate suffix. The Trussell family, for instance, took over the village of Marston which thus became Marston Trussell; the Zouch family turned 'Ashby' into Ashby-de-la-Zouch. Other examples are numerous: Newport Pagnell, Melton Mowbray, Shepton Mallet, Beer Hackett, Papworth Everard and so on. Queen Edith, who acquired lands in Rutland, not only produced Stoke Edith but also Edith Weston, thus giving an example of a Norman prefix addition. Where an entirely new manor was created by a Norman family, the name element was often incorporated within a place-name, as found in Williamston, Howton ('Hugh tun') and Marlston ('Martel tun').

When the arrival of a Norman family – or perhaps a Norman monastery or Norman castle – led to a settlement becoming more Norman than Saxon in character, then an entirely French place-name might develop. If, for example, the Saxon inhabitants moved out of a village, or if a new settlement was peopled almost entirely by Norman immigrants, then there was every chance of an alien place-name being invented. Thus, we get Blanchland (white glade), Grosmont (big hill), Richmond (strong hill), Beaumont (beautiful hill), Ridgemont (red hill – from 'rouge mont') and Devizes (boundaries). Where the Norman influence was less, only part of a place-name might be francofied, with prefixes like 'Bel' or 'Beau' (as in Belper and Beamish) and suffixes like 'ville' (village) and 'launde' (forest glade).

New Villages: Sometimes, and for various reasons, new settlements were created and given the word 'new' as part of their names. Newmarket in Suffolk was built in the 13th century – then called 'Novum Forum' – specifically as a market town. It was granted a charter – one of some 2,500 awarded during that century – and was laid out in a formal street pattern. At about the same time New Winchelsea was built in Sussex. This replaced the original settlement of Winchelsea, which had been destroyed by sea storms, and exemplified one of England's first examples of town planning. Newport, in the Isle of Wight, was not a port as such but a commercial centre, built to replace Carisbrooke as the centre of the Island's business. Two settlements which were built as 'ports' were Newquay (Cornwall) and Newhaven (Sussex). The former dates from the 15th century when the Bishop of Exeter authorised the reconstruction of the 'old' quay. The latter dates from the 16th century when a violent storm diverted the mouth of the river Ouse from Seaford, so causing the need for a new estuarine harbour.

Launceston, Cornwall

Castles were usually built on a strong and strategic site commanding wide views across the countryside. The towns which grew around them were actually and figuratively 'at their feet'. Launceston (probably corrupted from Lan Stephen, this being an early religious settlement) developed around a late 11th century castle built to control the main route into Cornwall, between Dartmoor and Bodmin Moor. Totnes (from Totta's 'nes' or headland) had already existed in Saxon times as a major town but was given a boost by the building of the castle in the 12th century. This castle is thought to occupy the site of a Celtic Iron Age earthwork upon which stood a Saxon fort.

Totnes, Devon

▓ BASTIDE TOWNS

After the Norman Conquest, the building of fortified towns became more ambitious, as kings and wealthy land barons strived to protect their newly acquired rural possessions. They constructed not just forts, stockades or strengthened manor-houses, but whole towns built for strategic reasons. Normally in each a large, stone-built castle would dominate, with grid-pattern streets running outwards from a central market square. Around the perimeter would be a town wall, with look-out towers and gateways.

These military strongholds were called 'bastide towns' from the Old French word 'bastir' meaning to build and cognate with the words 'bastille' and 'bastion'. They were most commonly found in border territories – towards Scotland and Wales – where tribal unrest was greater and foreign incursions were more likely. Carlisle and Berwick were bastide towns, so too were Ludlow and Chepstow.

During the 13th century many bastide towns appeared across Wales after Edward I conquered that country and subjected its population to English rule – Pembroke, Harlech and Caernarfon appeared for instance. But these were amongst the last to be built: those across England had been developed much earlier. Launceston, in Cornwall, was constructed soon after the Norman invasion and was already called 'Lanscavetone' in the Domesday Book of 1086. The name either derived from the Celtic words 'lan' (enclosure) and 'scawen' (elder tree) or from the religious settlement nearby of 'Lan Stephen'. Richmond, in Yorkshire, was built a little later. It was called 'Richemund' in 1108, a name derived from the Old French 'richemont' meaning strong hill.

CHAPTER 7

The Wealth of Society: Industry & Trade

A lthough most place-names evolved through the spread of agriculture, natural migration and population growth, many others did not. They, instead, developed from those activities which resulted from the creation of wealth – namely, commerce. Trade, mining, quarrying, and even manufacturing, go back almost as far as farming in the history of human development.

As soon as agriculture could produce a surplus so trade took place, at first using the barter system but, very early on – perhaps as early as the Iron Age – using some form of money. Towns grew and their non-agricultural inhabitants had to be supplied with food, leather, cloth and fuel. They, in turn, provided farms and country dwellers with finished goods – agricultural implements, clothing, household wares. To begin with, most of this exchange of goods was local, but as populations grew and transport improved so trade became more extensive.

Meanwhile, various minerals were being exploited. The bronze of the Bronze Age was an alloy of copper and tin, metals found in the uplands of Cornwall, Wales and the Pennines; and the iron ore which produced the Iron Age came from the Weald, Forest of Dean and the Mendips. By the Roman period, lead, gold and silver were also being mined. Across all upland regions quarries supplied building stone and surfacing shingle. Where local geology allowed, also, lime was being kilned for fertilizer and all-important salt was being excavated. The trade in mineral deposits was immense.

So numerous settlements grew up, some as service centres along the trade routes, others as market centres. Commerce was their *raison d'être* and accessible location their fortune. And their existence can often be suggested by their place-names.

▨ TRANSPORT NAMES

Roads and rivers provided the major transport arteries. Pack-horse caravans and cart trains bumped their way along the ancient trackways,

Roman roads and mud-lined trade ways; sailing barges and freight-carrying rowing boats plied the navigable streams. Places where roadways crossed, or rivers met, were especially good locations for settlements. Places where roads crossed rivers – at fording or bridging points – were better still. And places where river-crossing points coincided with upstream limits to sea navigation were the best of all. Much coastal traffic took place, and ships were an important means of transport from the Iron Age onwards. The most inland places they could reach – heads of estuaries for example – naturally became trans-shipment points, where goods would be transferred to and from river barges and road carts.

Place-name elements indicating settlement location upon an overland trade route include 'straet' and 'weg'. These Saxon words, meaning street and way were used where routes were well established, the former often being found on Roman roads, the latter on old established trackways. Thus, we have examples like Stretton, Stratford, Wayford and Wayhill. The Saxon words for path ('anstig', 'stig' and 'paeth') are found in place-names of less important transport-orientated settlements, such as Anstey, Wolsty and Alspath. The same is true of the words 'faer' (passage) as in Denver and 'lanu' (lane) as in Laneham.

Of far greater importance – and therefore more common – were those settlements sited on river crossing points. In these cases, the most often found elements derive from 'ford' and 'brycg', the former being the older of the two since bridges frequently replaced earlier fords. Indeed, there are considerably more 'ford' place-names in England because, even when a bridge was subsequently constructed, a settlement would normally keep its original name.

Whilst the 'ford' element usually provided the suffix – as in Wallingford (on the Icknield Way) and Buntingford (on Ermine Street) – it can be found as a prefix: Fordham, Fordington, Fordley for instance. Frequently the place-name element accompanying 'ford' is descriptive or adjectival: broad, muddy, wide and so on. The names Bretford and Stapleford both suggest that the ford in question was made out of planks or boards.

The 'bridge' element, similarly tends to be a suffix, as in Tonbridge, Cambridge and Stalybridge. The relatively few examples where it forms a prefix include Bridgwater and Brighouse. One interesting aspect of 'bridge' place-names is the incidence of river names within them. In other words, a meaning of 'bridge over the River ...' is their most common derivation. 'Ford' place-names, conversely, have a greater variety of first-element meanings, as found in Barford (barley ford), Heyford (hay ford), Gateford and Shefford (sheep ford). It is, perhaps, significant that the village of

Swinford (pig's ford) was changed to Stourbridge after the construction of a stone bridge over the River Stour.

Other crossing-point elements found in place-names include 'ferye' (as in Ferrybridge), 'waed' (as in Biggleswade) and 'lad' (as in Cricklade and Linslade). The latter meant 'difficult crossing place'.

Where settlements were located at trans-shipment points, at places where boats or ships were loaded, elements meaning 'landing place' or 'wharf' may be found. These include 'hyo' and 'hyth' (as in Erith, Rotherhithe), 'staeth' (as in Statham and Brimstage), and 'hwearf' (as in Wharton and Wherstead). At coastal locations other elements may be identified: 'fleot' (estuary) in Benfleet and Northfleet; 'port' (harbour) in Portland and Southport, 'mutha' (estuarine mouth) in Exmouth, Tynemouth and Portsmouth.

▓ MARKET NAMES

Most towns – even perhaps large villages – had a market at which local farmers could sell or barter their produce. Normally held once a week, these markets acted as district or regional focal points where all kinds of trade took place, all kinds of business were transacted. Some towns grew up especially because of the market facility and its associated potential for wealth creation. Charters and royal warrants allowing for markets to be held were much sought after, since these were almost a guarantee of commercial success. Settlements which grew specifically as market centres became the hub of route networks. They also, frequently, acquired a reference to market in their names.

In the Middle Ages – after the Norman Conquest – a place-name often had the word 'market' simply added. It was a Norman French word and cognate with the modern French *marché*. Thus we had 'Stow' becoming Stowmarket and 'Bosworth' becoming Market Bosworth. But before then – in Saxon times – a different element was used. The Saxon word for a market was 'ceap' and the word for a market place was 'ceping'. From the latter evolved the place-name element 'chipping' (as in Chipping Sodbury, Chipping Norton, Chipping Barnet); from the former evolved our modern word 'cheap'. The place-name Chapmanslade derives from 'ceapmann' meaning a merchant or market trader.

▓ MINERAL NAMES

Every village of any size had its own mill and, where possible, its own quarry. The mill would have been powered either by water or wind (but

Budleigh Salterton, Devon

Perhaps the two most important raw materials in pre-industrial England were salt and charcoal. Salt was used to preserve food and was found in sea-water and in underground rock deposits. Charcoal was used as a fuel for heating and power, the first energy supply for smelting and foundry work. At Budleigh Salterton there was a 'salt-aern', variously described as a salt-house or salt-works. Either this was a salt lagoon where salt was evaporated or else a place where salt was stored. In 1210 the town was just called Saltre, the addendum coming later (from Budda's leah or 'clearing' and linking it to nearby East Budleigh). At Coleford there was a ford over which charcoal was carried or, alternatively, a ford near which charcoal was made. The name was Colford in the 16th century. The settlement stands in the Forest of Dean which was a major centre for charcoal burning in Saxon times.

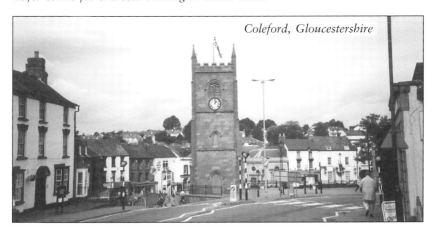

Coleford, Gloucestershire

normally water) and would have produced all the settlement's needs in flour and bread. The quarry – a particular feature in upland areas – would have provided millstones as well as building materials for the settlement's construction. Since such features were so common, it is perhaps surprising that place-names which include 'mylen' and 'cweor' elements are few and far between. There are some examples, however, including Millbrook, Mells and Millbourne; Quarndon, Quarrendon and Quorndon.

Salt was an important substance from earliest days, used as a preserving agent. Apart from the salt deposits found naturally in Cheshire, there were 'salterns' (salt lagoons) dotted all around the coastline where sea-water was evaporated. Accordingly, salt place-names are relatively common, especially around England's shores. The village of 'Ash' (ash tree) in the Cornish-Devon border became Saltash after saltworks were set up on the Tamar in the early 14th century. Salter, Salterford, Salthouse and Salthrop are other examples, the last named deriving from the Saxon 'sealt hearpe', an apparatus for sifting salt. Budleigh Salterton in Devon derives its affix from 'sealt-aern' – one of the salterns mentioned above.

Charcoal was another important substance, burned for fuel supplies from the Bronze Age onwards. Indeed, it was by using charcoal power that the Bronze Age could create bronze out of copper and tin smelted together. 'Col' was the Saxon word for charcoal and is found in the place-name Coleford in Gloucestershire. This stands on the edge of the Forest of Dean, an area where charcoal-burning has been practised since early Celtic times. The place-name Colsterworth is from the Saxon 'colestre' meaning a charcoal burner, and Cowden is from 'col dun' – charcoal hill.

▓ INDUSTRIAL REVOLUTION NAMES

The Industrial Revolution, which began during the 18th century as a result of agricultural improvements, increased populations and labour mobility, technological inventions and the development of coal as a fuel supply, led to a fundamental shift in the human character of Britain. An essentially rural society was replaced by an urban one – the countryside depopulated as the towns grew, industrial production formed the basis of Britain's economy instead of agriculture. Not surprisingly, in this upheaval, many new industrial settlements appeared with names to match their functions.

Mineral Towns: Two of the most important commodities were iron and coal, and places where these were produced often incorporated these

Iron Bridge, Telford, Shropshire

With the Industrial Revolution came an explosion of England's urban population: towns, cities, ports and factory villages expanded rapidly. Abraham Derby's famous bridge across the river Severn in 1774 gave its name to the town that grew around it. In due course an urban zone engulfed this whole area, becoming Telford New Town in 1963. This was named after Thomas Telford, the engineering pioneer and road builder. Maryport was called Elnefoot until 1750 when a new port was built for the coal industry. It was given its present name by its founder Humphrey Senhouse, whose wife was called Mary. Other ports also acquired names from their founders: Fleetwood (Lancashire) from Sir Peter Fleetwood-Hesketh and Porthmadog (Porthmadoc) in North Wales from William Maddocks.

Maryport, Cumbria

minerals in their names. There was Ironville, for instance, in Derbyshire, and Ironbridge in Shropshire. The latter was named after the famous iron bridge over the river Severn. This was designed by T.F. Pritchard and opened in 1781. It had been cast at Abraham Derby's foundry in 1774, at nearby Coalbrookdale (not, incidentally, named from coal but from 'cold-brook-dale'), and was the first cast-iron bridge to be built in the world.

Downstream from Ironbridge is Coalport – from 1790 the home of the Coalport China Company – and in Leicestershire is Coalville, named from the home of the colliery owner William Stenson. Other towns named from 'coal' indirectly are those which grew up around coal-mines, such as Trimdon Colliery and Shotton Colliery, both near Sunderland. These are located near the villages of Trimdon and Shotton respectively.

Transport Names: Canals, and later railways, formed the main commercial arteries of the Industrial Revolution and so had their own impact on the place-names of Britain. Stourport was built specifically as a canal town – the 'port' being on the river Stour where a new canal was dug to link the Severn with the Trent-and-Mersey Canal. Most of the canals themselves were named after the places they served, but there were exceptions. The Bridgewater canal for instance is not in Somerset but in Lancashire where its construction was financed by the Duke of Bridgewater. The Grand Union Canal is so-named from its pre-eminence as the major waterway linking northern and southern England, its extension through London – the Regents Canal – being named from the Prince Regent, later King George IV. The Royal Military Canal, running from Hythe to Hastings, was not built for commercial reasons but – as the name suggests – for strategic purposes. It was constructed as part of the country's defences against a possible Napoleonic invasion and named in honour of George III. The nearby Martello Towers, incidentally – built for the same purpose – were so-called from the round tower at Cape Mortella in Corsica which the English fleet had great difficulty in capturing in 1794.

The great railway towns of Swindon, Crewe and Eastleigh had names from the older settlements to which they became attached but railway station names were not always taken from the settlements they served. The Victoria stations in London and Manchester were named after the Queen; Waterloo Station was named after the battle in 1815 at which Wellington defeated Napoleon; Euston Station (also in London) was named after the Marquis of Euston who owned the land on which it was built. Verney Junction, on the Oxford to Bletchley line, was named after the local Verney family and Earlestown (Lancashire) was named after Hardman Earle, a director of the North-West Railway Company.

Model Villages: The living and working conditions common during the Industrial Revolution were notoriously bad, with poor-quality terraced housing, insufficient sanitation, long working hours and inadequate safety precautions in the factories and mills. Here and there, however, attempts were made to improve the lot of the working classes: factory and education acts were passed by Parliament, public health facilities were provided, extra leisure time given. In particular, certain humanitarian industrialists – philanthropic factory owners – built their own 'model villages' where pleasant, well-built artisan housing was the norm. One of the first of these villages was New Lanark, near Glasgow, built by Robert Owen, and another, in Wales, was New Tredegar built by Lord Tredegar. But not all these 'model villages' were called 'New'. Saltaire and Akroyden, both in Yorkshire, were named after Titus Salt and Edward Akroyd respectively. The former – built in 1853 – covered 25 acres and included 820 dwellings, 45 almshouses, numerous churches, schools and public baths, but not a single public house. Salt was a Quaker and believed in temperance. The latter – built in 1861 – sought to promote house ownership amongst workers through a building society which later became the Halifax. Bournville was laid out in 1879 next to George Cadbury's chocolate factory near Birmingham. It was built next to the river Bourne and was originally to have been called 'Bournbrook' after the local mansion. The prefix 'ville' was later adopted, however, to suggest a stylish mixture of the English 'villa' and the French 'ville' (town). Bournville subsequently gave its name to a type of dark chocolate. Port Sunlight, on Merseyside, was laid out in 1888 by William Hesketh Lever, the soap manufacturer, and was named from one of his product brands. Sunlight soap continued to be made there until well into the 20th century.

Pub Town Names: Occasionally during Victorian times a new urban development would take place not around a mill or factory but around a public house. In such instances the name of the tavern might actually be transferred to the town. Two examples are Waterlooville, in Hampshire, and Craven Arms, in Shropshire. The former grew up around an inn called the 'Heroes of Waterloo', named to commemorate the sailors (rather than the soldiers) who had fought at the Battle of Waterloo in 1815 and who had disembarked, upon their return to England, at nearby Portsmouth. The subsequent settlement was given the suffix 'ville' in accordance with the Victorian fashion for that

Shopping Centre Names

Place-names continue to be invented, offering further scope to those interested in our sense of place – the etymological researcher, local historian and regional geographer. The names of some of our modern shopping centres, for example, provide ample opportunity for investigation. Brent Cross is situated in the North London suburbs. Is it so called because it is in the borough of Brent, or because it stands over the course of the river Brent, or because it was built by the company Brent Walker? And surely The Galleria in Hatfield, Hertfordshire, is so named because it stands above the A1 road tunnel, 'galleria' being Italian for tunnel. The famous Metro Centre in Gateshead, is a name that recalls both the Metro underground system of Paris and the Metro train service of Tyneside – 'metro' being a fashionable shortening of 'metropolitan'.

Bluewater: This stands in Greenhithe, on the south side of the Thames estuary. Opened in the late 1990s, it does not take its name from the five apparently blue-coloured lakes nearby which occupy former gravel pits. Instead it was christened from the two firms which originally planned the complex: Blue Circle (a construction and cement company) and Sheerwater (a development company).

Cribbs Causeway: This is situated near Bristol close to the M5 motorway. Before its construction in the 1990s a section of the A4018 was called Cribbs Causeway, a name possibly going back to the Middle Ages. In those times, revised causeways (or 'causeys') were built where packhorse or drove ways crossed marshes and floodplains, thus allowing for their year-round use. Here the old causeway ran across the meadows of a tributary of the river Avon. A map dated 1777 shows 'Cribbs Causeway and Farm'. Cribb was a personal name: perhaps the original builder of the road or else the original owner of the farm.

Lakeside: This is in West Thurrock, on the north side of the Thames estuary. It opened in 1990 and was sited close to a large man-made lake (flooded quarry workings). The name was chosen to suggest pleasant surroundings where shoppers would enjoy spending a long day.

word and as used at Bournville. Craven Arms developed around the pub of the same name, built at the beginning of the 19th century to rival the older 'New Inn' nearby, and named after the Earls of Craven who had held the local manor of Stokesay. This pub was close to an important road junction which, itself, became known as the Craven Arms. When the railway station was built close by, the same name was adopted and, accordingly, with the growth of the settlement, the name stuck. The suburb of Cliftonville, at Margate, has a similarly interesting derivation to its name. It grew up around the Cliftonville Hotel, itself situated in Clifton Street. The hotel had adopted the 'ville' suffix, partly because it was a fashionable place-name addition and partly because it echoed the already famous suburb of Cliftonville at Brighton.

▓ RESORT NAMES

Together with industrialisation and urbanisation, the 18th and 19th centuries also saw the development of travel and tourism. Factory production may have brought with it housing squalor and workplace hardship, but it also made profits. Initially, only the upper reaches of society benefited, but as wealth percolated downwards so more and more people reaped the rewards. The middle classes, as we know them, were born and even the working classes began to see their lot improve by the second half of the 19th century. Leisure time increased and people started to take holidays. Bank holidays were officially established and annual leave became a common feature of working life. In response, resorts developed, both at inland 'spas' and at the coast, where the newly discovered joys of the seaside could be indulged. Of course, many of these resorts merely grew up at existing settlements, but some were entirely new and took on place-names entirely their own.

Spa Towns: Although the use of geological waters for health and healing goes back a long time – the Romans developed Bath as 'Aquae Sulis' and the Saxons renamed it 'Bathu' after the hot springs found there – the development of spa towns did not really begin in earnest until the 17th century. Most such resorts – Epsom, Buxton, Cheltenham, Harrogate – kept their original names unaltered but some did not. Tunbridge Wells was so christened after the medicinal springs there were popularised by King James I (Tonbridge later adopting a different spelling to distinguish itself) and Leamington was given its 'Spa' appendage at the beginning of the 19th century. In fact, the latter became known as Royal Leamington Spa in 1838 to commemorate a Royal visit, eight years earlier, by the Duchess of Kent and Princess (future Queen) Victoria.

Royal Towns: Leamington was not the only town to acquire a regal appendage. As early as the 13th century Lyme Regis in Dorset had been granted royal prerogatives, and in modern times Bognor Regis was designated. Bognor acquired its royal suffix in 1929 after George V had gone there for convalescence, following a serious illness. That king's liking for this particular seaside resort is paradoxically remembered in the story of his deathbed pronouncement 'Bugger Bognor' – his last convalescence trip evidently not having worked.

Seaside Resorts: Coastal holidays became especially popular when the railways came: when the middle – and even the working – classes could afford to travel out from the urban centres. Most of our modern seaside towns date from this period – the second half of the 19th century – as do many of their facilities, like piers, esplanades, amusement arcades, souvenir shops, boarding houses, cliff-railways and so on. Most of these resorts were the expanded versions of existing towns, like Southend-on-Sea, Torquay, Hastings and Scarborough; some were specially built but named from nearby villages, like Clevedon, Frinton-on-Sea and Swanage; a few were built and named from scratch, like New Brighton (Wirral), Westward Ho! and Peacehaven. Westward Ho! near Bideford, was developed shortly after the publication of Charles Kingsley's novel of that name (in 1855). The story in that book was largely set in North Devon and the name of the resort was chosen partly as a memorial to the author and partly to lure tourists.

Peacehaven, in Sussex, has an even more unusual history as a place-name. The town was developed during the Great War as a plotland speculation – areas of land being sold off to buyers wishing to build their own retirement or holiday homes. In 1916 the instigator of the scheme, Charles Neville, announced through the newspaper a competition to find a name for his new resort. In due course a winner was chosen: 'New Anzac-on-Sea' – a name meant to commemorate the Australian and New Zealand Army Corps, which was stationed nearby and which had fought bravely in the hostilities. However, arguments subsequently arose over the legality of the competition, and over the suitability of the winning name. So, in 1917, Neville decided to use his own invention: Peacehaven. Not only did this indicate a 'peaceful haven', he said, but also expressed a wish for a peaceful end to the war.

▨ URBAN NAMES

Since the end of the 19th century, population growth, increased human mobility, the greater use of road transport, and the growing desire to live at lower housing densities have all led to rapid urban growth. Towns and

Letchworth Garden City, Hertfordshire

At the beginning of the 20th century, town planners saw the advantages of combining urban and rural features – a concept leading to the Garden City project. Letchworth was the first to be built, begun in 1903 (around a much older settlement whose name derived from the Saxon 'loc-worth' meaning lock or bar and enclosure). It combined large industrial premises, well-appointed terraced and semi-detached houses and wide tree-lined streets. It happened, also, to be sited along the prehistoric Icknield Way that ran from Norfolk to Wiltshire. Welwyn Garden City was begun in 1919 and is now a popular, low-density town where fountains and greenery surround a central, modernised, shopping centre complete with railway station. The original village of Welwyn derived its name from the Saxon word 'welig' for willow tree.

Welwyn Garden City, Hertfordshire

cities have mushroomed, ribbon developments have spread ever outwards, urban planning has become a major force. New kinds of place-names have appeared to suit the modern age.

Garden Cities: Towards the end of the 19th century, a new concept in urban construction began. Inspired by such people as Ebenezer Howard, the housing reformer, this concept perceived towns as rural enclaves, with tree-lined avenues, open gardens and low housing densities giving urban areas the advantages of the countryside. At first 'Garden Suburbs' were built based on this notion – Bedford Park in West London built in 1875, Hampstead Garden Suburb in 1907 – but later, entire 'Garden Cities' were planned. Welwyn Garden City was built in 1919 just south of the old village of Welwyn. In this way the 'Garden City' appendage appeared.

New Towns: Since 1946 various 'New Towns' have been designated by Act of Parliament, to house the overspill populations from the big cities. Generally these were located on 'green field sites' – on land not previously developed – but were sufficiently close to existing villages to borrow their names, with the words 'New Town' tacked on. Hence, Harlow New Town was built near the old village of Harlow, Stevenage New Town near old Stevenage. In time the 'New Town' suffix was dropped as the old village became engulfed. However, occasionally new names were invented for these New Towns. One such was Peterlee (County Durham) which was named after a popular local miner, trade union leader and reformed drunkard called Peter Lee. Another was Telford in Shropshire. This New Town is an amalgam of the old towns of Dawley, Wellington and Oakengates. It was designated in 1963 and named after the Scottish civil engineer Thomas Telford. The choice was an apt one: Telford started his career as surveyor of public works in Shropshire and later planned the construction of the main London to Holyhead road (now the A5) which runs through the town now bearing his name.

Conurbations: As towns and cities merge into each other, to form urban zones, so new place-names must be invented. In 1965 London and the old county of Middlesex were combined for administrative reasons and 'Greater London' was created. Ten years later – as a result of the Radcliffe-Maud Report of 1969 – other conurbations became officially recognised – Greater Manchester, Merseyside, West Midlands and so on.

In other parts of the world even conurbations have begun to merge, forming vast urban regions, and these have been given names. 'Boswash' is the name given to the urban belt from Boston to Washington via New

Old Harlow, Essex

Garden Cities were not built after the Second World War, partly due to expense and the shortage of land. They were costly to design, build and cultivate and their relatively low population density was seen as wasteful. Instead, New Towns were constructed. These, generally, appeared next to existing villages whose names they simply acquired. Today, the old remnants of the original settlements can still be found within wider urban sprawls. Old Harlow (named from the Saxon 'here-hlaw', meaning meeting place mound) stands adjacent to its modern counterpart which was established in 1947. Milton Keynes village was originally named from the Saxon 'middel-tun' (middle farm) and the Norman manorial owner Lucas de Kaynes. Now it stands as a quiet, green oasis within a vast urban zone dating back only to 1967.

Milton Keynes, Buckinghamshire

York; 'Tokama' is the region of Tokyo and Yokohama; 'Randstad' is the Rotterdam-Amsterdam-The Hague-Utrecht corridor in the Netherlands, so-called from its 'ring' or 'horseshoe' shape. If such 'megapoli' develop in Britain, we can only guess at their future names. The London to Birmingham urban corridor along the M1 motorway; the 'U' shaped urban belt from Sheffield to Manchester via Nottingham and Derby: what will these be called?

CHAPTER 8

Names Within Towns and Villages

———••◦⧫◦••———

J ust as place-names have evolved – or have been invented – to distinguish between settlements, so they have developed to distinguish between areas and places within settlements. Where the population was relatively small, in Celtic and Saxon villages for instances, street or building names were probably not needed. A thoroughfare might be the only one of its kind and thus would not require a name; a house or business premises would probably be known by the person living there or by its function. Thus, along something simply called 'the lane', might be located 'the herdsman's cottage' and 'the forge'. No other identification would be deemed necessary.

When names were used, they were probably either descriptive in origin or else honorary, commemorating some personage. As far as we know the Romans had streets and buildings named after points of the compass (such as 'east gate') and the names of gods or political leaders ('Via Apollo', perhaps); the Saxons had names that used descriptive or functional adjectives (such as 'the pink cottage', 'the Judge's house' or perhaps 'town end farm').

It was not until medieval times that the naming of streets, houses and public buildings really became widespread.

▓ STREET NAMES

Most thoroughfares have a double name, with a noun preceded by an adjective. The noun is the term used in each case for the alignment itself – 'street', 'lane', 'road' or whatever – and the adjective describes or distinguishes its character – its shape, function or merely its mark of identification. Before the Industrial Revolution of the 18th century, most thoroughfare names evolved and became established by use; after the Industrial Revolution (and especially with the development of suburbs and planned housing estates) they were generally the product of invention or deliberation. Those which evolved tended to have meanings, with the names actually telling us something about their thoroughfares; those which were created artificially were more often arbitrary tags for identifying otherwise similar settlement features.

The word 'street' derives from the Saxon 'straet' meaning paved road. It was normally used for principal routes, from Roman roads to main shopping, transport or trade routes, and survives as one of our most common thoroughfare nouns. Lane (from Saxon 'lanu') was used for less important trackways, as was the noun, way (from Saxon 'weg' and cognate with the Latin 'via'). The word 'gate' meaning a thoroughfare (as opposed to a gate) derives from the Danish 'gata', for street, and is common in the towns of northern and eastern England. The word 'alley' arrived in England after the Norman Conquest and comes from the old French 'alee' – linked to the modern French verb 'aller' meaning 'to go'. Interestingly the modern word 'road' – now so common – did not appear until the 15th or 16th century. It comes from the old Saxon word 'rad' meaning the act of riding, from which root we also get the word 'raid', originally referring to an attack by horsemen. The first roads were probably so-called because they were used by horse traffic.

Medieval Descriptive Names: Some of the earliest street names were merely descriptive, referring to a thoroughfare's character, destination or habitation. Chief routes were often called High Street or Fore Street; minor routes might have been Back Lane (running behind the houses) or Nether Street. Names such as Broad Street, Crooked Lane, Bow Street, Clay Street, Stonegate and Stinking Lane described the shapes or surfaces or routeways originally; names with such adjectives as 'upper', 'lower', 'ridge', 'hollow', 'north', 'south', 'east' or 'west' are all self-explanatory. Cul-de-sacs were often called Blind Lane or Pudding-bag Lane, secluded roads could have been Love Lane or Grope Alley. Destination street names might either have been locally applied – Moor Lane, Park Street, Church Road – or else the product of a thoroughfare's ultimate objective – London Road, Oxford Street, Salisbury Street and so on. Where distinct groups of people settled in certain thoroughfares, habitative street names resulted: Danesgate, Petty France or French Row, Fleming Road, all appeared in medieval towns as a result of immigration from North-west Europe, as Catholic persecution of Protestants spread. Continental persecution of Jews also led to Jewish ghettos appearing in many English towns during the 15th and 16th centuries, resulting in such street names as Jew Lane, Jury Street and Old Jewry. Lombard Street or Lombardy Road arose from the arrival of North Italian bankers into England during the early 16th century.

Often it was not so much the inhabitants of a road that gave it a name but the owners of the land over which the road ran. A general reference might have resulted in such names as Lordship Lane, Manor Road, Queen's Street or Kings Road: more specific references might have led to actual surnames being used, like Russell Street, Monkton Lane, Williams Road, Bennett Street, and More Way. Occasionally, it was not a landowner but a particular resident who was responsible for a street name.

Another type of descriptive name is that found when a thoroughfare is named after some townscape feature – a geographical site or an important building. Well Lane, Bridge Street, Marsh Road, Brook Street, Windmill Lane and Spital Street are all self explanatory – the last being from 'hospital street'. The fortified nature of medieval towns can be recalled from such names as Castle Street, Ludgate, Barbican, Bailey Lane and Bargate; the importance of religion in earlier times can be guessed from the preponderance of such names as Priory Lane, Almshouse Road, Paternoster Row, Abbey Road, Meeting Lane (referring to a chapel or meeting house) and any number of church dedication names – St Michael's Street, St Andrew's Road and so on. Punishments were once meted out in Gallows Street or Hanger Lane and criminals were interned along Gaol Street or Cage Row. The existence of public houses often gave rise to such street names as Angel Street, Greyhound Road and Bell Lane, whilst sporting venues gave us Bullring Alley, Bear Lane and The Butts – the last name being from the earth mounds constructed behind the targets used for archery practice. Sometimes even nicknames became official street names: Thieves Lane, Rotten Row (from 'raton row' – a smelly rat-infested alley) and, sarcastically, Paradise Street.

Medieval Trading Names: One particularly large group of descriptive street names which developed during the Middle Ages was that based on traders and merchants. From earliest times, towns were market centres and many thoroughfares evolved as focal points for specialised crafts or sellers. Similar traders tended to group together, to share site advantage and attract increased custom. Costermongers tended to set up single-commodity markets to enable product regulation and price control. In those days of limited literacy, recognised trading signs went up above shop-fronts: three sugar loaves indicating a grocer's shop; a highlander indicating a tobacconist; a large coloured glass bottle, or carboy, for an apothecary or dentist. The red-and-white pole indicating a barber's shop derived from the fact that barbers also acted as surgeons (blood-and-bandage being the emblem); the pawnbroker's triple ball sign derived from the coat of arms of the Italian Medici family who were money-lenders and bankers.

General market areas in medieval times frequently took on such names

Keswick, Cumbria

Keswick's Moot Hall was built in 1813 and continues to function as the town's main focal point where locals and visitors alike gather. The ground floor now holds a Tourist Information Centre and the first floor room is used for lectures and meetings. It stands in the Market Square, where regular markets still operate. 'Moot' comes from the Saxon word 'gemot' (or 'mot') meaning meeting or place of assembly. In early times each town or village might have an assembly of freemen which would sit as a court or council. Whether or not these freemen had much real power is a moot point! Pannier markets, found in many towns, are named from a 'pannier' – a basket for carrying bread. Panarium was Latin for breadbasket, deriving from 'panis' for bread (and cognate with the modern French word 'pain' and Italian 'pane'). A pannier, in due course, became a word meaning any large basket, usually carried by pack-animals. In medieval times farmers and traders would carry their goods to market in panniers and often, too, would sell their wares straight from the open tops. Incidentally, the same etymological root gives us the word 'pantry' – originally a bread store.

Bideford, Devon

Bideford Pannier Market
Market Hall Open Tues. & Sat.
Butchers Row Shops Open Mon. to Sat.

as Cheapside, Cheap and Eastcheap (from the Saxon 'ceap' for a market); Portgate or Port Street (from the Saxon 'port' for trading centre); or, more simply, Market Street or Broad Street (wide roads often being used for stall-selling). More specialised markets had more specialised names accordingly – Milkmarket, Leathermarket, Cornmarket and so on. Once common names like 'Wincheap' (waggon market), 'Ritherscaepe' (cattle market) and 'Strawecheping' (straw market) are now sadly defunct. Some of these specialised markets were extensive indeed: in 14th century Norwich there were 40 butchers' stalls gathered together, 45 fishmongers and 28 poulterers. The word 'fair' is also found in market town, derived from the old French word 'feire' meaning a gathering of merchants. Hence, we have 'Horse Fair', 'Cloth Fair', 'Butter Fair' and the like.

Street names originating from traders' workshops, grouped along specialised thoroughfares, are common but are not always recognisable. Fish Street, Salters Lane, Wood Lane, Spicer Street, Mercers Row, Drapers Road, Shoe Lane, Butterwalk and Butchers Row are all self-explanatory, but the Shambles, Barker Street and Baxter Lane are less obviously connected with traders. 'Shambles' derives from the Saxon 'scamel' meaning a stool or bench – later referring to butcher's table. Hence, 'Shambles' were places where meat was cut and sold. 'Barker' is a corruption of the Saxon 'barkere' (a tanner) and 'Baxter' of the Saxon 'baecestere' (a baker). 'Finkle Street' was a road where fennel ('finkel') was sold and 'Pilcher Gate' was the place where makers of fur coats set up shop. 'Sherrers Row' was 'shearers row' for cutters of woollen cloth – and 'Tenters Close' was a place where cloth-makers worked. A 'tenter' was an artisan who stretched cloth on a frame of hooks or spikes – hence the expression about being 'on tenter-hooks'. Some streets actually sold cooked food – as is still common in towns around the Mediterranean. These had such names as 'Cook Street', 'Coke Row' and 'Petty Cury' (from the old French word 'curie' meaning kitchen).

Numbered Streets: In Britain the naming of streets and numbering of houses within streets was enforced by a regulation of 1805. The spread of towns and the growth of suburbs necessitated such an order. But the idea of actually naming streets with numbers – 'First Avenue', 'Second Avenue' and so on – goes back further. It all started in the late 17th century, not in Britain but in the former British colonies across the Atlantic. In 1682 William Penn, the philosopher and classical scholar, founded the city of Philadelphia. But, being a Quaker and stern critic of any system which set one man above another, he strongly disapproved of the custom already beginning there of naming streets after their most important occupants –

the local mayor, judge or whatever. Accordingly he instigated the numbering system, naming the streets from east to west 'First', 'Second', 'Third' ... In due course other cities in New England followed Penn's example – notably New York – and the fashion crossed the Atlantic, to be taken up in British towns during the second half of the 19th century.

Suburban Street Names: With the Industrial Revolution and the spread of industrial suburbs, street names became unsentimentally descriptive – Commercial Road, Factory Lane, Canal Street, Railway Cuttings, Station Road. Such names did not have today's grimy connotations since they were newly designated and satisfied the contemporary image that industrialisation, urbanisation and modern technology were desirably linked with progress. The names of speculative builders – or the places in Britain where these builders were born – were also used in street names since the instigators of town growth were proud of their work and wished to be remembered. Landowner names were similarly transferred to the streets which now covered their formerly verdant acres: the Dukes of Devonshire, Northumberland, Bedford and Norfolk – together with lesser nobles like Ashburnham, Beaufort and Hartington – were not averse to having their names or titles preserved on the name boards in the roads which were laid out over their manorial estates.

As the 19th century wore on, and confidence in technological progress, artistic advancement and political stability grew in the public psyche so street names took on a distinctly robust character. The Queen was commemorated in such names as Victoria Street, Jubilee Road and Coronation Street; famous military victories were recalled in Trafalgar Road, Waterloo Street, Wellington Terrace and Nelson Street. Group names started to appear – sets of streets names, with themes, applied to estate roads. From the Crimean War came roads named after Inkerman, Alma and Balaclava; from the Boer War came roads named after Kimberley, Pretoria, Ladysmith and Mafeking. The Empire gave us groups of names from foreign capitals – Canberra, Salisbury, Khartoum – and the Houses of Parliament gave us groups based on statesmen – Gladstone, Diraeli, Palmerston, Russell. The literary world produced poet or writer groups – Byron, Shelley, Wordsworth, Scott, Kipling, Dickens; the artistic world painter groups – Millais, Turner, Constable.

Group names continued into the 20th century but with the decline of Britain's world role and disillusionment with military power – notwithstanding the victories in the two World Wars – these became less patriotic. By the 1920s and 1930s sets of streets were being named after trees – Acacia Avenue, Birch Road, Lime Street – or geographical features –

Derwent, Windermere, Coniston (being lakes in the Lake District), Snowden, Skiddaw, Plinlimon (being mountains).

Another characteristic of street names designated in the 20th century is their use of alternative nouns. Street, Road and Lane began to give way to Avenue, Close, Drive, View, Crescent and Way. In due course – by the 1960s and 1970s – even these were superseded, this time by non-thoroughfare words, such as Stables, Mead and Court. It even became fashionable for streets to be given single country-based names: Treecroft, The Arbours, The Paddocks, Lingswood, The Links, and so on.

Suburban street names not only indicate the age of the thoroughfares to which they refer but also reflect the social aspirations of the people who created them, and the people for whom they were intended. They are the products of the conceits, the ambitions and the hypocrisies of past generations.

▩ House Names

In country districts, in hamlets and villages, house names evolved as essential elements, providing the only means of identification for homes and other buildings. In towns, however, where house numbering systems are normal, they are generally superfluous. However, they do provide character, individualism and interest, and can have informative or amusing derivations.

Originally, house names would have been simple and descriptive. Still to be found in rural areas, they may be ownership-based like Jenkin's Farm, Morgan's Cottage or Glebe House, or architecture-based like Three Chimneys, The Pantiles, White Cottage or The Gables. Sometimes they refer to the surrounding features – Copper Beeches, The Larches – sometimes to the climatic character of the location – Windy Corner, Southside, Sunnybank. Occasionally they suggest a building's earlier use – The Old Barn, The Old Post Office, Chapel Cottage. But all such names are similar in that they are unpretentious and informative. They all satisfy the main requirement of a house name: to aid identification.

With suburban growth, however, house names proliferated and became more self-conscious. They were devised instead of evolved; they became less descriptive and more discursive. They developed in such a way that they began to tell us less about the house and more about the residents.

Victorian householders tended to choose solid, reliable-sounding names, with just a hint of rural aspiration and class consciousness. They continued with the tradition of descriptive names – The Laurels, The Red House, Hilltop or Sea View – but frequently added a note of grandeur: Balmoral appeared as a house name (even for the humblest abode), together with such names as Oakwood House, Lakeside, Larchthorp Towers and Springdene Manor.

When the first tenement blocks were built in the first half of the 19th century, the word 'Tenement' often appeared in their names. But as the century progressed, and that word became debased, linked as it was with squalor and overcrowding, so different names were employed – notably 'Buildings' and 'Mansions'. During the following century the tenements descendants were built – tower blocks of flats – and yet new names were used, including 'House', 'Rise', 'Point' and 'Heights'. The adoption of euphemistic terms to describe multi-layer living was not the sole preserve of the Victorians.

The 20th century saw the widespread appearance of humorous, idiosyncratic house names and it is, perhaps, on these that the researcher or local historian may concentrate with greatest reward. There are names which jokingly refer to house numbering – Numbawun, Nyneteign, Century House – or to house attributes – The Shack, The Igloo, Bleak House. Some names recall literary connections, like House at Pooh Corner, Wind in the Willows and Shangri La (from James Hilton's novel *Lost Horizon*), whilst others imply the economic state of the owners, like On the Rocks, Stony Broke and Skynt. Another interesting group of house names is that which reflects the owners' names: 'Petrita' would have been invented by a couple called Peter and Rita; 'Marian' by Marion and Ian, 'Barwen' by Barry and Wendy. With the coming of cheap travel, package holidays, and greater tourism generally came an influx of foreign house names. Happy holidays or even honeymoons may be indicated by such names as Capri, Innsbruck and Ibiza while the foreign language Chez Nous and Casa Nostra might have been the choice of those householders who so enjoyed their 'villa' holidays on the Mediterranean. Dunroamin, however, could be the house of someone whose travelling days are over.

▨ PUB NAMES

The first inns appeared, probably, in Saxon times as lodging houses situated along the old trading routes, and in market towns, giving rest and refreshment to travellers and merchants. The word 'inn' originally meant a bedroom or chamber but later developed the meaning of a 'suite of rooms'. (In such a sense the word survives in the 'Inns of Court' where lawyers have 'chambers'.) In due course, inns provided ale and other beverages to non-residents, and so became focal points for town and village life. Many were run by monasteries or churches, others were set up by individuals either too old or infirm to work on the land, or else too foreign to belong to any tribal or village group. Innkeepers were frequently outsiders – Britons in Saxon areas, Saxons in Danish areas, ex-seamen in country areas.

By early medieval times taverns had also appeared where accommodation was not provided. These were normally found only in settlements and specialised in selling alcohol – locally-made cider, mead, and beer, imported wine and spirits. The beer was often brewed by the tavern owner himself, or by the local church authorities in order to supplement ecclesiastical funds (hence, the frequent location of public houses next-door to churches).

The first trade sign hung up outside inns and taverns showed a bush. This derived from the evergreen-topped stick held by Bacchus, the Roman God of Wine, and symbolised a vine or bunch of grapes. The old saying 'good wine needs no bush' derives from this tradition. To distinguish themselves from each other, later public houses put up additional signs to indicate their names to a largely illiterate public. Such pictorial signs have continued to be used to the present day, giving us the most visible of all medieval traditions to have survived in our modern settlements.

The general term 'public house' (or pub), incidentally, to refer to all inns and taverns – be they descended from pilgrim hostels, drovers inns, coaching inn or transport taverns – came into use during the 19th century. It developed as licensing laws were introduced and official definitions became necessary.

Public house names can be grouped into categories. They can tell us not only the age of a pub but also, perhaps, something of its history and importance. They can also tell us a great deal about the economy, politics and superstitions of earlier societies.

Heraldic Names: These were popular throughout the Middle Ages, when most people owed allegiance to some noble lord or other, and most villages came under the authority of a manorial estate. In times of strife they were further employed to demonstrate patriotism, to indicate the sympathies of the landlords, or to placate the feelings of the politically conscious customers. Names taken from Royal Coats of Arms, throughout medieval times, include the White Lion and Blue Lion and the Dragon. The White Hart was the badge of Richard II and the Swan was part of the emblem of Henry V. The Red Lion was John of Gaunt's heraldic symbol – he was the son of Edward III and instigator of the first parliament. The Wars of the Roses threw up a plethora of pub names and signs: the Blue Boar and

Football Club Names

Another group of names found within settlements, and which would repay further investigation by the dedicated historian, is that connected with sporting clubs and their venues. Football clubs, for example, have some interesting names.

Soccer, in its present form, dates back to the second half of the 19th century when various amateur clubs were formed, linked with churches, public schools, factories and sporting societies. Most of the club names still in use go back to that time and reflect the character of the early game. The common suffixes 'City', 'Town' and 'County' are, of course, purely descriptive, whilst 'Rovers', 'Wanderers' and 'Rangers' all suggest that the original teams travelled a great deal to play their matches. Perhaps with no regular venues of their own, they had to use various other grounds The suffix 'United' either suggests that a team was formerly composed of players brought together from disparate societies or clubs or else that a team was held together by an agreed set of aims or principles – a 'unified team'. Some football teams have unique names peculiar to their own circumstances

Arsenal: This club was originally founded in 1886 at Woolwich, East London where workers in the Brass Gun Foundry formed a team to represent the Royal Arsenal. Later the club moved to Highbury, North London, and severed its links with the Woolwich Arsenal works, but its name – and its nickname, the 'Gunners' – stuck.

Crewe Alexandra: This name is thought to derive from a visit made to the club, at about the time of its foundation (1877), by Princess Alexandra, wife of Edward, Prince of Wales. Crewe was a railway town and the Princess also visited the rail junction where she christened a steam engine.

Crystal Palace: This club is based in Sydenham, South London, where the famous Crystal Palace was re-erected in 1854, having served as the prime exhibit at the 1851 Great Exhibition in Hyde Park. This vast iron and

White Boar were badges of the House of York – as was the White Rose – whilst the Red Rose indicated support for the House of Lancaster. The Rose and Crown symbolised the marriage of Henry VII to Elizabeth of York, which brought the civil war to a close. The Greyhound was also a badge of the Tudor dynasty. The Unicorn appeared with the coming of the Stuarts to the English throne, and the White Horse with the arrival of Hanoverians.

glass structure had been designed by Joseph Paxton as the largest glass building in the world. Sadly it was burnt down in 1936, but its name has lived on as a park, a railway station and, of course, as a football club.

Plymouth Argyle: Here, 'Argyle' is an alternative spelling for 'Argyll'. The two founders of the club, F. Howard Grose and W. Pethybridge, shared rooms in Argyll Terrace, Sutherland Road, in the Mutley district of Plymouth. This estate was built in the 1880s when the Argyll and Sutherland Highlanders were stationed nearby. Grose suggested that their new club should be inspired by that regiment's team which had recently won the Army Cup. Accordingly, Plymouth Argyle's first strip was green and black quarters, reflecting the Highlanders' tartan.

Port Vale: There is no town called Port Vale but there is a district within The Potteries called the 'valley of ports'. Near to Burslem, the Fowlea Brook (a tributary of the river Trent) is used by the Trent-Mersey Canal as a site for various wharfs – called 'Middle Port, West Port, New Port and Port Vale Wharf'. The latter further created a Port Vale Street and a Port Vale House close by. So when the football club was founded in 1876 (and re-founded at the beginning of the 20th century) it chose a local name.

Sheffield Wednesday: This club was founded in 1867 by a group of cutlers who ran little workshops located close together in the 'stainless steel' district of Sheffield. These craftsmen, however, could only play football on Wednesday afternoons – when there was half-day closing.

Tottenham Hotspur: White Hart Lane football ground, in the High Road, Tottenham, stands on a site formerly owned by the estate of the Percy Family, the Dukes of Northumberland. When the football club was founded recognition of this ownership was made in the name, for the son of the first Earl of Northumberland – who died in 1403 and was immortalised by Shakespeare as a bold courageous warrior – was called 'Henry Hotspur'.

Royal Names: Most of our kings and queens are represented in pub names, sometimes by name but more often by inference – the name being something like The King's Head but the sign showing pictorially which king is meant. Charles II was especially popular and led to many names other than King Charles, such as The Royal Oak (alluding to the story of Charles' use of an oak tree when hiding from the Roundheads) and The Rose Revived (alluding to the Restoration). The George and the Royal

Naseby, Northamptonshire

In the Middle Ages most shops displayed signs to show their functions, since the general literacy rate was very low. Today, pub signs are, perhaps, the last remnants of this tradition and, as such, repay further investigation. Apart from telling us something about the social and economic background of these establishments, they can also help us date their first appearance (although not always the age of their buildings, which could have been reconstructed). Thus, the Royal Oak might originate from the time of Charles II's Restoration (1660) and the Kings Head (showing George III) might originate from the late 18th or early 19th century. The Marquis of Granby might also date from the 18th century despite the nobleman's appearance here: he was a philanthropist, and also a hero of the Seven Years War (1756–63).

Coleford, Somerset

Harlow, Essex

George are commonly found but probably refer to Georges II or III rather than I or IV, who were not as popular. The Prince of Wales and the Feathers (normally the Prince of Wales' feathers) also tend to refer to the Georges, whilst their royal sons were represented by such names as Duke of York, Duke of Cambridge and Duke of Kent. The 18th century saw a mass pub-building programme as the towns grew and the Industrial Revolution produced a burgeoning working class. The Queen Victoria is a fairly common pub name but few 20th century monarchs are represented.

Animal Names: Some of these are corrupted or shortened forms of earlier heraldic names, others are connected with those times when agriculture was all-important. Into the former category might come the Lion, Boar, Hart and Swan, into the latter might be the Bull, Cow, Goat, Horse and Pig. Hunting was represented by such names as the Fox, Hare, and Stag and sport by such names as Cock, Falcon and Bear. Often these animals names are preceded by colour adjectives the Black Bull, the White Horse for instance – for possible superstitious reasons.

Black Lion: Heraldic sign of Queen Philippa, wife of Edward III. Black is a very common colour in pub names, possibly because the Gin Act of 1736 made landlords drape their signs in black velvet, or add 'Black' to their pub names, in order to distinguish them from other trader signs, none of which used black because of its associations with evil and back luck.

Cat and Fiddle: There are various suggestions as to the origin of this name, more than one of which could be true. It might refer to Catherine la Fidèle, French wife of Peter the Great of Russia; to Catherine of Aragon, or to Caton le Fidèle, a brave and faithful knight who became Governor of Calais in the late 16th century. It could be connected with the 18th century nursery rhyme 'Hey diddle diddle, the cat and the fiddle ...', or else with the tradition that all inns and taverns used to keep a faithful cat (which controlled rats and mice) known in French as 'la chatte fidèle'.

Elephant and Castle: This is probably not a corruption of 'Infante (Infanta) de Castile', the title of the King of Spain's son (or daughter) – but a description of the Cutlers' Company crest which shows an elephant surmounted by a 'howdah' – the covered seating platform used by important travellers.

Pig and Whistle: Some people say that this is derived from two Saxon words – 'piggen' (a pail or drinking vessel) and 'wassail' (health or 'be in health'). In former times beer was served in piggens and customers would drink to their health. However, in the 17th century the phrases 'to whet one's whistle' and 'to go to pig and whistles' (meaning to become financially ruined by over-drinking) were in common parlance. Thus, there was possibly a back connection – pubs becoming nick-named 'pig and whilstles' (ruin houses) and landlords subsequently taking up the title officially.

Cock and Bull: This is not a pub name, but the subject of a nice story connected with two separate pubs. 'The Cock' and 'The Bull' were both in Stony Stratford, Buckinghamshire, and a fierce rivalry once existed between the two landlords. Each tried to outdo the other in the amount and nature of the gossip brought in by travellers. So exaggerated became the tales related, that they were called 'Cock and Bull stories' – a phrase which has survived to this day.

Trade Names: These often arose for pubs which especially catered for workers in a particular craft, or else acted as meeting places for such workers. Occasionally they recalled the landlord's own employment prior to his adoption of a publican's way of life. And in imitation of the heraldic pub names elsewhere, the word 'Arms' was frequently added: Bricklayers Arms, Fishmongers Arms, Miners Arms and so on. Sometimes the landlord's own trade was commemorated – Bunch of Grapes, Malt Shovel, Jolly Brewer, etc.

Chequers: This name probably does not derive from the fact that games of draughts were often played in public houses where chequered boards were provided. Such pubs certainly existed – and still do – but the name goes back earlier than this tradition. One possibility is that the chequered pattern formed part of the Fitzwarren coat of arms, and it was a noble from that family who was given the task by Edward IV of licensing ale-houses. Another possible origin stems from the fact that many landlords used to act as unofficial money lenders and currency exchangers (especially at pubs located near ports). In medieval times a chequered board was used by money dealers for counting, adding and subtracting – leading to the word 'exchequer' for a finance department.

Crooked Billet: In very early times an oddly shaped piece of wood or stick was often used as a cheap, easy and effective way of acquiring an inn sign. In later times, a shepherd's crook, a bishop's crosier, a farmer's yoke or a soldier's sword might have been used.

Five Alls: This is popularly linked to an old jingle which referred to the way the country was run: 'the King rules for all, the parson prays for all, the lawyer pleads for all, the soldier fights for all, and the taxpayer pays for all'. However, it is possible that the name goes back further than this, and is a corruption of 'awls' – the pointed tools used by leather, cloth and metal workers for making holes.

Famous People Names: It has always been common for pubs to be named after certain individuals who have, in some way, endeared themselves to the public. Such people might have been aristocrats (Earl of Derby, Duke of Devonshire and so on); warriors (Lord Nelson, General Gordon, Duke of Wellington, etc.); politicians (Disraeli, Palmerston, Lord Salisbury, Gladstone, etc.) or writers and artists (Dr. Johnson, Samuel Pepys, Joshua Reynolds, etc.). John Peel – the Cumberland huntsman immortalised in the song 'D'ye ken John Peel' – is well represented in North West England, and Dick Whittington – four times Lord Mayor of London – graces many a pub name in the South-East. The fictitious Robin Hood can be found on pub signs throughout the Midlands, as can the only-too-real highwayman Dick Turpin. One of the most popular characters to be remembered in pub names was the Marquis of Granby. He lived in the 18th century and served in the army during the Seven Years War. He was much loved and respected by his men, not least because he used his own money to set up those senior non-commissioned officers who became wounded and discharged, in their own public houses so they would not starve. Not surprisingly, perhaps, the good marquis died penniless and owing £37,000.

Miscellaneous Names: Of all other pub names not easily categorised, some of the more interesting are the following:

The Bell: This name is often found where pubs are situated next to churches, and possibly suggest a former link between the two institutions. Such pubs possibly sold church beer. Similar names include Blue Bell, Ten Bells and Ring O'Bells.

Cross Keys: These are the arms of the Pope, of the Bishops of Exeter, Ripon and Peterborough, and of any church dedicated to St Peter, since they represent Jesus' 'keys of the kingdom'. This was, in consequence, a popular pub name before the Reformation. When Henry VIII broke with Rome many pubs holding this name became the 'Kings Head'.

Green Man: Some think this refers to the 'green' man – that is, the man employed in each village years ago to look after the village green. However, more likely derivations are that it refers either to Robin

Hood, dressed in his 'lincoln green' cloth; or to a forester or woodman; or else to Jack-in-the-Green. The latter was a mythical, pagan pan-like figure – the father/son demi-god complementing 'Mother Nature' – who was imitated by medieval youths, dressed in greenery, at May Day celebrations.

Punch Bowl: At the end of the 17th century political passions ran high, as the House of Orange replaced the Stuarts. Whigs, who supported the former, took to drinking punch; the Tories, who supported the latter, preferred sherry (sack) and claret. Taverns patronised by the Whigs often took up the name 'Punch Bowl' to show their sympathies.

Three Compasses: This was the sign used by carpenters, masons and joiners and was transferred to those pubs where such artisans met. However, the interesting feature of this pub name – as with other pub names like Three Bridges, Three Fishes and Three Arrows – is the use of the number three. This has long been a number with certain mystical or magical connotations. In pagan times it was thought to bring luck, and so was used, in various forms, at religious services, in shrines and for burials. Groups of monoliths and ancient settlement sites were often set up in multiples of three and three-sided shapes were used in ornaments. The Christian church incorporated this use of the number in the Trinity, the Three Wise Men or Three Kings, and still to this day some people think it is unlucky to walk under a ladder – thus splitting the triangle formed by the ladder, wall and ground.

Saracens Head: Like the 'Turks Head' this name goes back to the time of the Crusades, when knights travelled to the Holy Land in order to expel the Moslem infidels. Noble families who took part in the Crusades often incorporated a Saracen's Head into their own coats of arms, from where it was transferred to inn signs.

▓ THEATRE AND CINEMA NAMES

The names of theatres, cinemas and other centres of entertainment provide a rich source of study for the local historian. Like pub names many can be traced back to medieval times, or earlier, and can be related to historical events. Indeed, in some cases they derive actually from pub names, since taverns were often the birthplaces of playhouses – and here Shakespeare's Globe and Rose theatres might be examples. Others have originated from personal names, street or mansion names, antiquarian names and, sometimes, mythological names.

Alhambra: During the late 19th and early 20th centuries, theatres and cinemas were built in grand and opulent styles, often with ambitious architectural features – marble columns, mural paintings, curved balconies and the like. Such places were frequently given names to match: exotic and impressive. The original 'Alhambra' is a 13th century Moorish palace in Granada, Spain where marbled terraces and mosaics intersperse with water gardens and intricately-carved cloisters. Other, similarly inspiring names used for playhouses include 'Granada' itself, 'Plaza' (Spanish paved square) and 'Rialto' (from the famous bridge in Venice).

Coliseum: When the impresario Sir Oswald Stoll opened his brand new theatre in London's St Martins Lane (in 1904) he wanted to call it after the famous amphitheatre in ancient Rome. Unfortunately, he could not spell and so christened his new playhouse 'Coliseum' instead of 'Colosseum'. The name stuck, and now theatres and cinemas elsewhere, which are called the same, use both spellings.

Dominion: This name derives from the Latin 'dominus', originally meaning 'master of the house' but later (from medieval times) meaning an area that fell under a supreme authority, state or prince. During the heyday of the British Empire the term was used for a self-governing colony or territory (such as Canada). It was during this latter period that 'Dominion' became a sufficiently grand name to use for a theatre. The name 'Empire' was similarly used.

Hippodrome: In ancient Greece and Rome a 'hippodrome' was an open-air course for horse and chariot-racing – from 'hippos' (horse) and 'dromos' (course). In Western Europe, from the 17th century onwards, the word was used for a circus arena. The first theatre to bear the name, however, was Batty's Hippodrome, built in London for the Great Exhibition in 1851. The place was a success and so the name caught on – later being used for theatres and cinemas all over Britain.

Lyceum: The original Lyceum stood outside ancient Athens and was the gymnasium and garden where Aristotle taught. It was named after the nearby temple of Apollo Lyceus. Apollo was the god of the muses, inspiring music and poetry. The famous Lyceum theatre in London opened in 1809 (rebuilt in 1834) and later achieved fame under Sir Henry Irving. It became a dance hall after the Second World War.

Odeon: During the 1930s the impresario Oscar Deutsch set up a company to build a chain of cinemas, each to be an architectural gem with lavish fittings and grand ornamental details. The name he chose for his company, and for his cinemas, was to be symbolic of the great age of the picture palace: 'Odeon'. It was taken from the ancient Greek 'odeion' (and the Roman 'odeum') which was an amphitheatre used for musical rehearsals and contests. So successful were Deutsch's cinemas that others were built, and the name Odeon became synonymous with 'moving pictures'.

Palladium: In classical legend this name was given to a large wooden statue of Pallas which stood in Troy. It was supposed to have fallen from Heaven and its preservation was vital to the safety of the city. When the statue was later moved, Troy was destroyed. The god Pallas was linked to Athena, the goddess of wisdom, and a 'palladium' became a word symbolising safety and sound judgement.

Phoenix: This became a common name for a theatre or cinema which had been rebuilt. It comes from the mythical bird, worshipped in ancient Egypt, which burned itself every 500 years or so to be rejuvenated and then to rise again from its own ashes.

Ritz: The first Ritz Hotel (in Piccadilly, London) was opened in 1906 and named after its owner, the Swiss hotelier Cesar Ritz. Soon the establishment became a by-word for luxury and high fashion. Other Ritz hotels later opened in Paris and New York and the name Ritz remained synonymous with quality.

Savoy: The original theatre, whose name other entertainment centres have since copied, was built in 1881 along the Strand in London. It was financed out of the profits of the Gilbert and Sullivan operas (since called the 'Savoy Operas') and managed by the owner and impresario Richard D'Oyly Carte (founder of the D'Oyly Carte Opera Company). It was built on the site once occupied by Savoy Palace, a mansion granted by Henry III to Peter, Count of Savoy.

Vaudeville: This name is taken directly from the word for a form of entertainment, originally a play interspersed with dances, songs and comic tunes. Such shows were popular in the 19th century and have survived, in modified form, to the present day as 'revue' and 'variety'. Vaudeville is a corruption of 'Vau de Vire' (Val de Vire) – a valley in Normandy, France, where theatrical entertainments were composed during the 15th century. These became popular in the French Court and so crossed the channel to the English Court.

SECTION
B

COUNTY GAZETTEER

Bedfordshire

☒ AMPTHILL
The early versions of this name – Ammetelle in the Domesday Book and Amethull in 1202 – tell us that it derives from the Saxon words 'aemett' (ant) and 'hyll' (hill). Ant-hills, or ant infested hills, must have been common in the neighbourhood. The word aemett, incidentally, not only gave us the modern word ant but also the dialect word 'emmet'.

☒ BEDFORD
This was once Bieda's or Beda's ford, an important Saxon crossing point over the river Ouse. It is not known who Bieda or Beda was but he is likely to have been a local tribal leader. In AD 880 the place was called Bedanford, in the Domesday Book (1086) Bedeford. A little way upstream was once the 'tun' (farmstead) by the 'cambo' (a Welsh or Celtic word meaning a bend in a river) called Camestone. This is now called KEMPSTON.

☒ BIGGLESWADE
This was originally Biccel's Gewaed, which grew into Pichelesuuade (Domesday Book 1086), Bikeleswada (1181) and Bygelswade (1486). Biccel or Bicca was probably a tribal leader and 'gewaed', or just 'waed', was a ford – literally where people and animals could wade across the river Ivel.

☒ CARDINGTON
The Domesday Book version of this name, Chernetone, was a corruption of the Saxon 'Cenred-inga-tun', the farmstead of Cenred's people. The initial letter of the personal name was probably pronounced softly (senred) until the Scandinavian settlers arrived, which led to a harder sound – as found in the 13th century spelling (Kardinton) and the present pronunciation.

☒ DUNSTABLE
This has long been an important junction settlement, situated where the ancient Icknield Way was crossed by the Roman Watling Street. The Roman posting station or fort of Durocobrivis was replaced by a Saxon village. Called Dunestaple, or Dunestapla, in the 12th century, this was earlier known as something like 'Dunna's Stapol' – the latter word meaning a post or landmark, probably a route marker or mile-post. It is not known who Dunna was.

☒ FLITWICK
This place-name, together with nearby FLITTON, derives from the Saxon word 'fliet' or 'fleot' meaning fleet or stream. Thus we had the 'wic' (dairy farm) by the stream' and the 'tun (farmstead) by the stream'. In the Domesday Book (1086) the former was Flicteuuiche and the latter Flictham. The river Flitt was named after these settlements and not the other way round.

HOUGHTON REGIS

Known simply as Houstone in 1086 this name derives from two Saxon words: 'hoh' meaning a hill-spur and 'tun' meaning a farmstead or village. In the 14th century the estate passed to Royal ownership and the Regis was added. The present spelling was first used as early as 1323.

LEIGHTON BUZZARD

This name goes back to the Saxon words 'leac' and 'tun', the former meaning, originally, leek, but later vegetables generally, and the latter meaning farmstead. Hence, this settlement began life as a vegetable farm or market garden. In the Domesday Book it was Lestone and in 1140 Lectona. The appendage has nothing to do with birds of prey, but derives from the name of the village's first resident clergyman or prebendary Theobald De Busar. In 1254 the name was recorded as Letton Busard.

LUTON

This name has the same origin as Leyton in East London, for it was the 'tun' (homestead) on the river Lea. That river, in fact, rises in the hills just outside Luton and flows southwards to the Thames just below Leyton. Luton has had various spellings: Lygetun (792), Loiton (1086), Leuton (1293). It is thought that the river Lea derives its name, not from the Saxon word for meadow, but from a Celtic root meaning 'bright river'.

SANDY

As might be expected, this derives from the Saxon words 'sand' and 'eg', meaning sandy island. In the Domesday Book (1086) it was Saneia. This village stands at the north-eastern end of an infertile greensand ridge that rises above the clay lowlands which would once have been marshy and well forested. Nearby POTTON was Pottun in the 11th century, probably meaning 'farmstead where pots were made' – this place being sited on the clay.

STOTFOLD

Recorded as Stodfald and Statfalt in the 11th century, this village was probably the site of a stud fold or horse enclosure. The Saxon words 'stod' (stud or herd of horses) and 'falod' (animal enclosure) are common place-name elements since rearing horses was an important part of medieval farming.

TODDINGTON

The Saxon suffix here probably derives from 'dun' (hill) rather than 'tun' (farmstead) since the early spellings were Totingedone (1086) and Tudingedon (1166). Thus it was 'the upland of Tuda's people', the inga element signifying a tribe. The early use of 'tot' in the same name might lead to confusion since such a prefix might come from 'totaern' meaning look-out post, as it does further south at TOTTERNHOE (look-out house).

▦ WOBURN

The Domesday Book lists this name as Woburne, suggesting a direct link with its origins – from Saxon 'woh' (crooked) and 'burna' (steam). So it was a place built next to a winding river; called Wauburn in 1200. However, in pre-Norman times the name probably referred less to a village and more to a district. In AD 969 we find Woburninga Gemaeru meaning 'the boundary of the people of the crooked stream', which suggests a valley-based group of inhabitants.

Berkshire

▦ ALDERMASTON

Aeldremanestone in the Domesday Book (1086) and Aldermannestun in 1167 clearly indicate that this name derives from 'Ealdorman's tun' – the homestead of the alderman – the chief shire officer.

▦ ASCOT

This began as 'east-cot', the eastern cottage, sheep shelter or woodman's hut. It was Estcota in 1177 and Astcote in 1348. The term 'Royal Ascot' appeared in more recent times, when the racecourse here began to acquire royal patronage.

▦ BRACKNELL

The 10th century versions of this name, Braccan Heal and Brachan Heale, were very close to the original form – Bracc'a Healh (or Halh) meaning 'the corner of land belonging to Bracca'. Whether this was the same tribal leader who gave his name to BRACKLEY in Northamptonshire is not known.

▦ COOKHAM

The Domesday Book version Cocheham, together with the earlier Cocham, derived from the Saxon words 'coc' or 'cocc' (hillock or heap) and 'ham' (homestead) or 'hamm' (meadow). The village stands on a bend in the river Thames, below a hill once known as Cocdun. The word 'coc', incidentally, has survived into modern English, in the word haycock.

▦ CROWTHORNE

This town almost entirely dates from the second half of the 19th century, developing after the building of Wellington College and Broadmoor psychiatric hospital. The name was first mentioned in documents of the early 17th century, referring to a road junction where stood 'a thorn tree where crows gathered'.

▦ HUNGERFORD

It is not known why, exactly, this place was called 'hunger ford' (Huntreford in 1101, its present spelling in 1148). Perhaps the soils here were poor and provided the inhabitants with scarce food supplies; perhaps the name was a description of the ford itself – being narrow, shallow or frequently dry.

✳ LAMBOURN

This village name is taken from the name of the stream here, this being derived from the Saxon 'lamb-burna' – lamb's river. The area has long been a sheep grazing district and the river itself was probably used for washing the animals. In AD 880 the settlement was called Lambburnan, in 1086 Lamborne.

✳ MAIDENHEAD

During the 13th century this was variously spelled Maydehuth, Maydenhith and Maidenhee – all derived from 'maegden hyth' meaning maiden's landing place. The village evidently grew as a Thames-side wharf but why it was named 'maiden's' is not known. Perhaps it was where young girls assembled for some religious ritual.

✳ NEWBURY

The Domesday Book name Ulvritun (Wulf's tun or homestead) became Neuberie shortly after the Normans built a new settlement here. This was, literally, a 'niwe burh' (new fortified place). It was founded partly to help establish Norman rule and partly to act as an important market centre. The old Roman fort of 'Spinis' is recalled by the present name of SPEEN, in the suburbs.

✳ PANGBOURNE

This was originally the name of the river itself, now called the Pang but formerly known as the Pangeborne (as noted in the Domesday Book). Earliest records give us Peginga Burnan – the burn or stream belonging to Paega's people.

✳ READING

This was the centre for the 'ingas' (people) of Reada, a tribal leader whose name or nickname derived from 'read' – Saxon for red (possibly owing to his red hair). The settlement was Readingum in AD 871 and Reddinges in 1086.

✳ SLOUGH

The area here was once known as Slo from the Saxon word 'sloh' meaning mire or marsh. It was an unpopulated, low-lying district next to the Thames. Widespread development did not start until the 20th century, when an industrial estate replaced an old army depot.

✳ THATCHAM

This simply means thatched homestead, deriving from 'thaec' and 'ham'. The village was Taceham in the Domesday Book. The Kennet valley was once marshy and thus provided thatching reeds for all the surrounding settlements. The area must also have been insect-ridden, since nearby MIDGHAM derives from the Saxon 'mycg healh' meaning midge-infested nook.

✳ THEALE

Being recorded as Thele in the 13th century, this name probably comes from the plural form 'thelu' of the Saxon word for a plank ('thel'). Thus, it was probably the site of a bridge or path made of planks – possibly over the surrounding wetlands. The area was certainly damp in those days, as indicated by the nearby TIDMARSH ('Tydda's marsh').

▨ TWYFORD

In the Domesday Book this was Tuiford, being the site of two fords (or a double ford) – in Saxon this would have been 'twi-fyrde'. The Thames valley was then a flat, watery grassland, as suggested by other local names like WHISTLEY (meadow glade) and RUSCOMBE (from the 11th century Rothescamp meaning 'Rot's pasture field').

▨ WINDSOR

Windesores, as recorded in the Domesday Book, either came from a personal name Windel or from the Saxon word 'windels' meaning a windlass. Probably the latter since Windsor is situated on the Thames and the word 'ora' (producing the suffix above) meant river-bank or landing-stage. Old documents referring to 'New Windsor' – Niwan Windlesoran, for instance, mentioned in the 12th century – probably indicate that part of the town which grew up around the recently-built Norman castle.

▨ WOKINGHAM

The personal name found in this place-name, Wocca, probably also gave us the names WOKEFIELD and WOKING. It is a pity we do not know who he was. Woking was the 'inga (people of) Wocca' and 'Wokingham the 'ham (homestead) of 'Wocca's people'. In 1227 we had Wokingeham.

Buckinghamshire

▨ AMERSHAM

In the 11th century this name was spelled Agmodesham and Elmodesham; in the 13th century it was Aumodeshame – all of which indicate a derivation from Ealgmund's ham. 'Ham' was a Saxon word often used for a village somewhat larger than a 'tun', which was more likely to be used for a farmstead. Tribal leader-based place-names like Amersham are common – and are especially common here in Buckinghamshire for some reason: for example, AYLESBURY comes from Aegel's 'burh' (fortified place), HAMBLEDON comes from Hamela's 'denu' (valley), OLNEY comes from Olla's 'eg' (island), WINSLOW comes from Wine's 'hlaw' (burial mound).

▨ BEACONSFIELD

The origin of this name is exactly what it sound like – a 'beacon in a feld' (open country or clearing – giving us the word field). But the questions arise: where was this beacon and why was it there? Three miles away, near the village of Penn, is Beacon Hill – which may answer the first question. As to the second – beacons were often used by the Saxons either to transmit fire-signals and messages (as the Romans had done) or to warn of approaching enemy attack. In 1185 this village was recorded as Bekenesfeld.

BUCKINGHAM

It would be tempting to think that the prefix here comes from either 'boc' (Saxon for beech tree) or 'bucc' (Saxon for buck or a male deer). In fact it derives from the personal name Bucca. The rest of the name comes from 'inga' (the people of) and 'hamm' (meadow): 'the river lands of Bucca's tribe'. In AD 918 it was Buccingahamm, in the Domesday Book (1086) it was Bochingheham.

CHALFONT ST GILES & CHALFONT ST PETER

Two villages named from the 'funta' (Saxon for spring or well) belonging to Ceadel (possibly a tribal leader) but distinguished by their church dedications. As early as the 13th century there is a Chaufunte Sancti Egidii and a Chaufunte Sancti Petri.

CHESHAM

In the 10th century this was Caestaelhamm – derived from 'ceastel' (Saxon for a heap of stones and cognate with the words 'caester', a Roman fort, and 'castel', a castle) and 'hamm' (meadow). The former was probably the circle of stones on which the church was built, the latter was the land close to the river Chess. This river name, incidentally, is a back formation, named from the town.

HIGH WYCOMBE

The early forms of this name, Wichama (8th century), Wicumun (10th century), indicate a derivation either from two Saxon words 'wic' (homestead, specialised farm or secondary settlement) and 'ham' (village), or else from a single Saxon word – the dative plural of 'wic' which was 'wicum' (meaning at the farmsteads). The distinguishing adjectives of 'High', 'West', 'Marsh' and 'Chipping' appeared as populations spread outwards: Westwicum (AD 944), Wycombe Marchaunt (1340), Chepingwycomb (1478). The 'High' in High Wycombe means important rather than raised up – just as High Street is used for a main road.

IVINGHOE

This was the 'hoh' (spur of land or ridge) of Ifa's people – a name relating to its position on the Chiltern Hills. Known in the 11th century as Evingehov this village was once an important trading centre, situated on the ancient Ridgeway track that ran from the Wash to Wiltshire and beyond (here called the Icknield Way).

LINSLADE

The earliest recorded spelling, Hlincgelad (10th century), tells us that this name derives from the Saxon words 'hlinc' (slope, bank or ridge) and 'gelad' (passage or water course). Thus, the place was situated on a route through the hills, possibly referring to the river Ouzel, which divides this place from Leighton Buzzard. Incidentally, the Ouzel, which flows into the Ouse, was once called the Whizzle Brook (weasel stream) and, before that, had been known as the Lovat, a Celtic name for a fast, seasonal river.

▓ MARLOW

It is possible that this was a settlement originally built on or next to a dried-up lake, because the early spellings suggest that the name comes from 'mere' (pool) and 'laf' or 'lafe' (remnants or remains). In 1015 it was Merelafan and in the Domesday Book it was Merlave. Perhaps the river Thames changed course at this point, leaving an abandoned meander to silt up.

▓ MILTON KEYNES

Although this new town dates only from 1967 its name – taken from one of the villages engulfed by the modern development – goes back to Saxon times. In the Domesday Book it was Middeltone – from 'middel' (middle) 'tun' (farmstead). Many other 'Milton' names in England derive from 'mylen tun' (mill farm), but not this one. In the 13th century the estate here was taken over by Lucas de Kaynes, thus giving us the present affix.

▓ NEWPORT PAGNELL

From Neuport in the Domesday Book (new town) this became Neuport Paynell in the 13th century after the manor had come into the ownership of the Paynell family. This was one of the new market towns built by the Normans after their victory in 1066.

▓ PRINCES RISBOROUGH

Originally this was just called Hrisanbyrge (in 903) and Riseberge (in the Domesday Book 1086): the 'beorg' (hill) covered with 'hris' (brushwood). Only later did the distinguishing addition appear: 15th century records mention Pryns Rysburgh, so named because the estate had been held by King Edward III's eldest son, the Black Prince. Two centuries earlier documents mention nearby Monks Ryseberge, so named because that estate was held by Christchurch, Canterbury.

▓ STOKE POGES

Well-known for its links with Thomas Gray and his *Elegy written in a Country Churchyard*, this village was known simply as Stoches in the 11th century. This was a corruption of the Saxon word 'stoc' (religious or secondary settlement) or 'stocc' (stump or tree trunk). In 1255 the manor was acquired by Hubert le Pugeis.

▓ WENDOVER

The settlement takes its name from that of the river here, which is of Celtic origin.

Cognate with the Welsh words 'gwyn' (white) and 'dwfr' (river), it probably arose from the fact that the stream flowed over the chalk of the Chilterns, rather than because it foamed. The village was Waendofron in AD 970, Wendovre (1086) and Wandoure (1195).

Cambridgeshire

▦ CAMBRIDGE

The derivation of this name is most interesting, since it demonstrates how completely – and yet logically – a place-name can change. In AD 730 it was Grantacaestir, for it was a 'caester' (Roman fort) on the river Granta. But by AD 875 a bridge element had replaced the fort element, the name becoming Grantebrycg. By the time of the Domesday Book of 1086 this had been shortened to Grentebrige. Then, under the Normans, it was further changed to allow for French-speaking tongues – becoming Cantebruge whence the modern name evolved. Meanwhile the nearby village now called GRANTCHESTER had altered from an original Granteseta – the 'saete' (dwellers) on the Granta. The river Cam is a back-formation from Cambridge. The river Granta derives from a Celtic root meaning 'marshy river'.

▦ CHATTERIS

The early spellings of this name, Caeteric in AD 974, Chateriz in 1080, Chatric in 1200, suggest a derivation either from a Saxon personal name – Ceatta perhaps – or from an older Celtic word – 'ceto' meaning a forest. The suffix, it has been imagined, comes not from the more usual meaning (ditch) for the word 'ric' but from the less usual 'strip of land'. There is a low, narrow ridge running across the Fens just north of Chatteris which might once have been called a ric in that sense.

▦ CHERRY HINTON

This has a fairly clear derivation, coming from the Saxon words 'higna' (monks or nuns) and 'tun' (farmstead). In the 11th century it was Hintona and Hintone; in the 13th century Hyneton. The fruity affix appeared sometime in the Middle Ages, after the local religious order had started to grow cherries. The possibility that Hinton comes from 'hea' (high or upland) and tun is less likely, considering the ecclesiastical connections.

▦ ELY

The Venerable Bede wrote that this place – known as Elge in his day – was named from the fact that eels were caught thereabouts. He was right, for etymology bears him out: 'ael-ge' meant eel district. A century after Bede, in AD 890, the place was called Elig – 'eel island' – with a corruption of the 'ge' to 'eg' suffix; in the Domesday Book it had achieved its present spelling. Ely is an ancient and attractive town, standing high up above the Fens. It was probably the centre of a Saxon administrative district long before the English shires were born.

❋ GODMANCHESTER

There is a legend that this town was founded by the great Danish King Guthrum but early spellings (Godelmingum in the 9th century and Godmundcestre in the 11th century) suggest otherwise. The actual founder was more likely to have been a local tribal leader called Godhelm or Guthmund. The suffix, of course, comes from the Saxon 'caester' since this was the site of the old Roman town of Dovigutum, or Durolipons. Ermine Street crosses the river Ouse here.

❋ GUYHIRN

This began as the name of a district rather than a village – La Gyerne in 1275 – and derives from the Saxon 'hyrne' meaning a corner or angle of land. The prefix, from an old dialective word 'gye' for saltwater ditch probably refers to the fact that the tide could reach as far inland as this along the water-channels.

❋ HUNTINGDON

The suffix here seems to derive from the Saxon 'dun' for a hill, although there is no apparent landscape feature to support this. The town stands on the river Ouse meadows. Perhaps the word referred to a raised levée or river bank. The prefix comes either from Hunta, a personal name, or 'hunta', a huntsman. In AD 921 the settlement was called Huntandun and in 1086 Huntedun – so no clues there. The area was, however, once part of a royal hunting ground.

❋ KIMBOLTON

This name derives not from Cym's 'bothltun' (farm building) but from Cynebald's 'tun' (farmstead). In the Domesday Book it was Chenebaltone and in 1130 Cheneboltona. Cynebald was possibly a tribal leader.

❋ LEIGHTON BROMSWOLD

Originally this was simply called Lestona (1070) or Lectone (1086) being a name derived from 'leac-tun' – technically a leek farm but in fact a more general vegetable farm or market garden. The present affix appeared in the 13th century (in Letton-super-Bruneswald) but it did not, apparently, originate as a distinguishing part of the parent name. It is thought that Brun's wold (weald, wood or upland pasture) began life as a totally separate settlement adjoining Leighton. It has since disappeared leaving only its name behind.

❋ MARCH

In the 10th century this was called Mercc and Merche, probably derived from the Saxon word 'mearc' meaning a boundary (from which we get our modern words march and mark). Either this town marked the edge of the original Wash (now much silted up by the Fens) or else it was the northern limit of the district belonging to Ely Cathedral.

▦ MOLESWORTH

This name is derived, neither from the Saxon 'meolc' meaning outlying nor from the Danish 'muli' meaning headland or craft, but from the more mundane personal name Mul. The suffix comes from 'worth' meaning an enclosure or clearing. The Domesday Book lists the place as Molesworde.

▦ OUTWELL

This, together with nearby UPWELL, comes from 'wella', the Saxon for spring or stream. The prefixes were introduced to distinguish between the two places; 'Up' suggesting a higher location and 'Out' perhaps indicating that it was built outside, or beyond, the parish boundary of the other, older settlement. In AD 970 Outwell was called Uuyllam, in the Domesday Book Utuuella, in 1202 the more recognisable Utwell.

▦ PETERBOROUGH

In the 8th century the Venerable Bede called this town Medeshamstedi – Mede's 'hamstede' (homestead). Mede was probably a personal name, although some etymologists link it to an old Saxon word meaning a whirlpool (presumably one in the river Nene hereabouts). By AD 972, however, the place had become simply Burh, this being written Burg in the Domesday Book of 1086, meaning town or borough. This change arose from the fact that, during the 10th century, the town grew as an important market centre around a newly-built Benedictine abbey (which replaced an earlier monastery destroyed by the Danes). Subsequently the name of the abbey's dedication was transferred to the town's name, which became Burgus Sancti Petri in 1225 and Petreburgh in 1333. The present cathedral stands on the site of the old St Peter's Abbey.

▦ ST IVES

This town is named after St Ivo whose bones were allegedly discovered here at the end of the 10th century. Before then it had been called Slaepe (in AD 672), possibly because of the 'slepe' or slippery slope on the muddy banks of the river Ouse. After the great discovery, the place became known as St Ivo de Selepe (during the 12th century). It grew as a manorial settlement attached to nearby Ramsey Abbey and as a pilgrimage centre. Eventually its old name was dropped altogether.

▦ ST NEOTS

St Neot, the story goes, was a Cornish hermit who founded a monastery near Liskeard during the 9th century, and was subsequently buried at a place in Cornwall now called after him. As a martyr he was much revered, and his grave became a centre of pilgrimage. Then, during the 10th century, his bones were dug up and brought to Huntingdonshire, to be re-interred at Eynesbury, then called Eanulfesbyrig. This village thus became a centre for pilgrimage and took on the name of the saint – S. Neod in 1132, S. Neoti in 1203. The name EYNESBURY survives as a suburb of St Neots.

Sawtry

This was recorded as Saltrede in the Domesday Book and undoubtedly derives from the Saxon 'seal-tera' meaning salt-maker or salt-seller. This could have been either a landing place from where salt was sold or even a settlement where sea-salt was produced, the Fens being more coastal in those days. Salt, of course, was essential for preserving food and 'salt ways' crossed the country as trade routes.

Soham

From Seagham (10th century) to Seham (13th century), it is evident that this name derives from the Saxon 'sae-ham' meaning lake homestead. There is no lake here today but the Domesday Book mentions one and the flat lands to the west are still known as Soham Mere. Nearby is the National Trust-owned Wicken Fen, preserved as one of the last stretches of the original fenland landscape.

Stukeley

This has the same derivation as Stewkley in Buckinghamshire – from 'styfic' (stump) and 'leah' (grove, woodland clearing). From being a single village – Stivecleia in 974 and Stivecle in 1086 – it became a double village as the population grew producing the 'mother' with the adjective 'Great' and the 'daughter' or colony village with the adjective 'Little'.

Waterbeach

This was once simply called Bechia (11th century) or Beche (13th century) from the Saxon word 'baece' meaning stream or valley. It stood on the river Cam. But another village nearby had the same name! So, by 1242 this had become Waterbech and the other one had become Londbech (now LANDBEACH), the latter being on drier land away from the river.

Whittlesey

The 10th century version of this name, Witlesig, tells us that this comes from Witel's island, the suffix being the Saxon 'eg'. In the Domesday Book it was Witesie. Other modern 'ey' endings in this region also derive from the same root: RAMSEY (wild garlic island) and THORNEY (thorny island).

Wisbech

The prefix in this name could be from the river Wissey or from 'wisc', Saxon for a damp or marshy meadow. The suffix could derive from the Saxon word 'baece' or 'bache' (stream or valley) but is more likely to come from 'baec' (ridge or raised ground). Wisbech is built on a slight rise in the Fen meadows. The early spellings include Wisebece (AD 656), Wisbece (1086) and Wissebeche (1291). It is neither the Wissey nor the Ouse that now flows through here but the river Nene.

Cheshire & Wirral

⊞ ALSAGER

The 13th century spelling Alisacher gives us the origin of Aelle's field, the suffix coming from the Saxon 'aecer' meaning a plot of land (hence our modern word acre). The field's owner is named in this instance.

⊞ BIRKENHEAD

This derives from the Saxon 'bircen heafod' or else from the old Norse 'birki hofuth'. Either way the meaning was the same – birch tree head. The 'head' probably referred to Bidston Hill rather than to the Wirral peninsula. In 1150 the name was Birkened, in 1278 Birkenhead.

⊞ CHESTER

In the 2nd century AD this town was named after its river, now called the Dee but then called the Deoua or Deva. To the Romans it was Civitas Legionum and to the Welsh it was Carlegion, in both cases meaning 'the city of the legion'. But to the later Saxons it was Legacaester (in AD 890), the suffix 'caester' (Roman fort) being tacked on to a root derived from the Roman name. Why the prefix should later be dropped (to produce Cestre and Ceaster in the 11th century) is not known.

⊞ CONGLETON

The derivation of this name – spelled Cogeltone in the Domesday Book and Congilton in 1282 – is still a matter of debate amongst place-name experts. Clearly the suffix comes from the Saxon 'tun' meaning farmstead. But the prefix may either come from 'kangr', the Scandinavian word for a river bend, or else from 'canc-hyll', the Saxon for a steep-sided or rounded hill. The town stands on a bend in the river Dane and below a conical hill, so either derivation could be correct.

⊞ CREWE

The early spellings here – Crev (1086), Cruue (1288) and Crue (1346) – suggest an interesting derivation from an old Celtic word 'cryw', meaning a ford or stepping stones. It is thought that this word was, itself, derived from 'creel' – a fish basket. It was once the custom to set a wicker fence across a river, next to a crossing point, in order to trap fish. In due course the name for the wicker net was transferred to the ford. Here at Crewe it was not so much a river as an area of marsh which had to be crossed.

⊞ ELLESMERE PORT

This industrial town was built in the 18th century at the point where the Ellesmere Canal, an arm of the Shropshire Union Canal, joins the river Mersey. At first it was called Whitby Wharf or Whitby Locks (Whitby being a town here, now a suburb). The present name relates to the town of Ellesmere in Shropshire.

❖ HELSBY
This is a Viking name, the prefix coming from 'hellir' (cave) or 'hiallr' (hillside ledge) and the suffix from 'byr' (village or homestead). In the Domesday Book it was recorded as Helesbe, this becoming Hellesby by the 13th century.

❖ HESWALL
Eswelle in the Domesday Book and, more significantly, Haselewelle in 1252, can be traced back to the Saxon 'haesel-wella': hazel, spring or stream. There were once hazel woodlands here, in the Middle Ages much used for making fencing, hurdles and basketry.

❖ HOYLAKE
This settlement was developed in the 18th century around the Royal Hotel at Little Meols. In 1766 it was called Highlake, but this was a misspelling of 'Hile Lake'. The Hile, or Hyle, was the roadstead offshore – the area of deep water used for fishing and mooring. Whether this name comes from the Saxon 'holh' for hollow or from 'hygel' for hillock (in this case, a sandbank) is not known. Further corruptions of the name have resulted in 'Hoyle Lake' and the present spelling.

❖ KNUTSFORD
There has long been a theory that this name comes from Cnut's ford, and that, in consequence, Knutsford has links with Royalty – Cnut being the famous King Canute. But no evidence has been found that this monarch was associated with the town, and no site has been discovered for the supposed ford. In reality the person who gave his name to Knutsford was probably not the king, and the ford was probably a causeway across Tatton Mere and marshland. In the Domesday Book the town was Cunetesford, in 1282 Knottisford.

❖ LYMM
This name has changed little over the years: it was Lime in 1086 and Limme in 1260. Either it comes from an ancient Celtic river name, similar to Lymn, Lympnee and Lemon, meaning elm river, or else it comes from the Saxon word 'hlimme' meaning roaring brook.

❖ MACCLESFIELD
The whole district around here was once densely wooded, called Mackley Forest, and so it is not surprising that this name derives from Maccel's or Macca's feld. A 'feld' was an area of open land or clearing, giving us the field of today. In the Domesday Book it was called Maclesfeld, in 1183 Makelesfeld. Who Maccel was is not known but he also gave his name to nearby Macclesfield Forest.

❖ NANTWICH
This was originally just Wich (in the Domesday Book) which meant dwelling, village or dairy farm. In the 12th century, however, it became Nametwihc –

the 'named' (renowned) village – since the salt deposits had been discovered. In due course the wich, wick or wic took on the extra meaning of salt-works – thus producing MIDDLEWICH, NORTHWICH and DROITWICH in the same area.

⌗ RUNCORN

Though designated a New Town in 1964 the name goes back to the Saxon words 'rum' (roomy, wide) and 'cofa' or 'core' (cove, bay) – referring to Mersey Estuary. In AD 915 it was actually called Rumcofa, this changing to Runcore by the 13th century.

⌗ SANDBACH

Called Sanbec and Sandbec in the 11th century, and Sandbache in 1260, this name comes from 'sand-baece' – a sandy-floored stream or valley. There is a tributary here of the river Wheelock and the region became well-known not for sand but for salt-extraction.

⌗ WALLASEY

Coming from 'walh' and 'eg', this name was Walea in 1086. It meant welsh island (plural of 'walh' was 'walas' – hence Wales). Later another 'eg' was added, unaccountably, producing Waylayesegh – Waley Island. This northern end of the Wirral was once an occasional island, being cut off at high tides.

⌗ WEAVERHAM

This, of course, comes from the name of the river, which has been variously spelt Weever, Wevere and Wiure. This name is derived from an ancient Celtic word meaning winding river. Here the village name (Wivreham in the Domesday Book) simply meant 'homestead on the Weaver'. Interestingly, the village of WERVIN, near Ellesmere Port, also derives from the river Weaver, leading some historians to suggest that the Mersey estuary was formerly called the Weaver estuary.

⌗ WILMSLOW

This was once a sacred place: Wilhelm's 'hlaw' (burial mound). In the 13th century it was Wilmislowe. A later holy place can be found nearby: PRESTBURY, which comes from 'the priest's manor'. This was Presteberie in the Domesday Book.

Cornwall

⌗ BODMIN

Bodmine in the Domesday Book, followed by Botmenei in the 12th century, suggest an entirely Cornish-Celtic derivation – from 'bod' or 'bot' (house, dwelling) and 'meneich' (monk or, possibly, sanctuary). King Aethelstan founded a monastery here in AD 926. Nearby Bodmin Moor was once called Fowey Moor from the river that helps drain it.

✖ BUDE

This spelling goes back to the 15th century, when it was also called Bedebay. The settlement was named after the river here which indicated an ancient Celtic root of 'boutto', 'boyd' or 'byd', all of which meant muddy or turbulent river.

✖ CAMBORNE

This name is not derived, as it might seem, from Saxon ('camb' meaning a ridge and 'bourne' or 'burna' meaning a stream) but from two Celtic words – 'cam' or 'cambo' meaning crooked and 'bron' meaning a rounded protrusion or breast-shaped hill. The hill in question is probably Camborne Beacon, just south of the town. In 1291 the place was called Cambron, in 1309 Camberoun.

✖ FOWEY

Both the town and the river were called Fawe and Fawy in the 13th century, names originally applied just to the latter. The origin is straight from old Celtic: 'fau', 'fou' or 'fawi' (beech tree) and 'cy' or 'y' (water, stream). The same suffix can be found in other West Country river names – the Tavy, Wylye, Bovey, Carey and so on.

✖ HELSTON

This is a hybrid place-name, partly Celtic, partly Saxon. To the Cornish 'hen-lis' (old – court or hall) the English added 'tun' (homestead). In the Domesday Book (1086) it was Henlistone, in 1186 Helleston. The river Hel is a back-formation, named after the town. The Hel's original name was the river Hayle (found elsewhere in Cornwall) which derived from the Cornish 'heyl' meaning estuary.

✖ LAUNCESTON

The Domesday Book spelling, Lanscavetone, suggests this is a hybrid name, the Saxon 'tun' (farmstead) being added to the Celtic 'lan Stefan' (the church site of St Stephen). The 14th century version (Lanceton), interestingly, is close to the present pronunciation of the name.

✖ LISKEARD

Here the prefix is easy to understand – from the Celtic 'lis', 'lys' or 'les' for a court, hall or palace – but the suffix is more problematical. It is certainly Celtic but could derive from 'caer' or 'ker' (castle or fortified settlement), 'ruid' (free – that is, not owned by a Saxon), 'carow' (stag), or from a personal name like Carrad. In the Domesday Book the place was Liscarret, before which it had been Lyscerruyt.

✖ LOSTWITHIEL

It is thought that this whole part of Cornwall was once called Withial, a name probably meaning high woodland from the Celtic words 'gwydh' (trees) and 'ial' (upland). If true then the name of this town means 'end of withial' – 'lost' being Cornish for tail. In early medieval times the place was Lostwetell or Lostwhidiel.

▓ MARAZION
Taken from the Cornish words 'marghas' (market) and 'byghan' or 'bechan' (small), this town was called Marghasbigan in around 1200. 'Little Market', possibly in relation to that at PENZANCE (holy headland). The old and alternative name for Marazion – Market Jew – is in fact a corruption of a neighbouring place called Marchadyou in 1200. This meant either South Market ('dyow' = south) or Thursday Market (from 'yow').

▓ MEVAGISSEY
In the 15th century this was Mavagisi, this being a corruption of the Cornish saints' names Meva and Isy (or Ida), to whom the local church was dedicated. The adjoining PORTMELLON comes from the Celtic word 'melin' (mill) and nearby GORRAN HAVEN is named after the Celtic saint, St Guron.

▓ MULLION
The old Cornish name Eglosmeylyon translated into Sancti Melani (13th century), the church here being dedicated to St Melan. The town stands on the western edge of the heathy downs of GOONHILLY, from the Celtic 'goon-helhy' (moorland-hunting), an area once covered by oak woods and renowned for a particular breed of pony.

▓ NEWLYN
There are few early sources for this name, other than a 13th century record of Luelyn, probably from the Celtic words 'lu' and 'lyn' meaning fleet and pool respectively. The derivation possibly refers to the deep water bay offshore now called Gwavas Lake, Newlyn long being a major fishing centre. Neighbouring MOUSEHOLE does not have a Celtic origin. This was Musehole in the 13th century and takes its name from a large cave nearby.

▓ PADSTOW
The legend tells us that St Petroc landed here in the 6th century in his coracle from Ireland and founded a monastery. He might well have done, for the name is a corruption of 'St Petroc's stow' (holy place). Sancte Petroces Stow in 981 became Padestou by 1361. Padstow was the ecclesiastical capital of Cornwall until the 9th century, when the Saxons arrived.

▓ POLPERRO
The prefix here probably does not come from the Celtic word 'pol' (meaning pool, pot or cove) but instead is a corruption of 'porth' (port). In the 14th century this village was called Portpira. The suffix is from Pera, a personal name. The holiday resort of LOOE, to the east, takes its name from the Celtic word 'lo' or 'logh' meaning inlet.

✳ REDRUTH
Being Ridruthe in 1259 and Riddruth in 1291 it is thought the most likely derivation of this name is from old Celtic: 'rid' (Welsh 'rhyd') for a ford; and 'ruth' or 'rudh' (Welsh 'rhudd') for red. Literally, therefore, it was 'ford red' – such a reversal of words being common in the Celtic language. The colour might have referred to the soil here. Some etymologists, however, maintain that the suffix comes instead from an ancient word for a Druid – an interesting idea.

✳ ST AUSTELL
A great many Cornish settlements are named after church dedications and ancient Celtic saints. This town, called Austol in 1138, commemorates the 6th century monk St Austol. ST ERTH was named after St Ercus, Bishop of Slane in Ireland; ST IVES after the Irish virgin St Ia who landed there in the 6th century; ST JUST probably after St Justus of Beauvais, the 3rd century martyr.

✳ TINTAGEL
If this derives from Saxon it means Togol's 'dun' (hill); if it derives from Celtic then it comes from 'tagell' (throat, gorge, constriction) and 'dyn' (fort). The early spellings – Tintaieol (1205) and Tinthagel (1229) are inconclusive but the old local name Dyndajel seems to support the latter possibility.

✳ TRURO
The 12th century versions – Triuereu and Triueru – might indicate an origin here from Cornish 'tri' (three) and 'erow' (an old land measure like the yardland). The Saxon equivalent can be found in a village in Wiltshire – TINHEAD, which means 'ten hides'.

Cumbria

✳ AMBLESIDE
This name is purely Old Norse in origin, from 'amelr' (a sandbank next to a river) and 'saetr' (a shieling or temporary shelter). 'Transhumance' has long been a common practice in Lakeland, whereby cattle are taken up to the high grazing pastures in summer, and down to the sheltered valleys in winter. Here at Ambleside (Amelsate in 1275) there would have been water for the animals and huts for the herdsmen.

✳ ASPATRIA
The spellings used in the 13th century, Ascpatric and Askpatrik, clearly show an origin from 'askr' (Norse for ash tree) and Patric (possibly referring to the Celtic saint). Interestingly, this is a Viking-British place-name, implying that this area was not heavily settled by the Saxons.

▦ BARROW-IN-FURNESS

The early versions of this name (Barrai in 1190, Barray in 1292) come from the same root as Barra in Scotland – namely the Celtic word 'barro' meaning the tip of a promontory. To this the Scandinavian settlers added 'ey' for island, possibly referring to the Isle of Walney. The peninsula as a whole takes its name from old Norse 'futh' or 'futhar' and 'nes' – rump headland. Perhaps it was so called from its long central depression. In 1150 it was called Futh Thernessa.

▦ BEWCASTLE

This place could well have been called Bewchester since the suffix derives not from 'castel', as might have been supposed but from the Saxon 'ceaster' for a Roman fort. In 1178 it was Buchecastre and in 1272 Bothecaster. The prefix comes from the old Norse word 'buth' meaning a booth or shelter. Perhaps the old fort – or the stone from it – was used for a sheep or shepherd's hut.

▦ BORROWDALE

The river Derwent here was once called the Borghra or Borgara, a name derived from the Old Norse words 'borg' or 'borgar' (fort) and 'a' (stream). To this the Scandinavian settlers merely added 'dalr' (valley) to apply both to the area and to the settlement. In the 13th century it was Borgordale and Borcheredale.

▦ BOWNESS

On this site once stood the Romano-British settlement of Maia, a name from the Celtic root 'maros' meaning great. It was built on a commanding headland and known as the 'higher place'. The site has survived but not the name. Bounes in 1225 was taken from the Saxon 'bos-nes' (or, Norse 'bogi-ness') with the descriptive meaning of bow headland.

▦ BUTTERMERE

The spelling of this name has changed little – Butermere and Bottermere in the 13th century – and the meaning has remained descriptively clear. It was so called because the 'mere' (lake) was surrounded by rich pastures which allowed grazing cattle to produce good butter-making milk.

▦ CARLISLE

The 5th century name, Luguvallium, is thought to have derived either from the Latin, meaning the wall of Lugus, or else from an old personal name, Luguvalos – 'as strong as Lugus'. Lugus was a Celtic god. In the 8th century the Venerable Bede called the place Lugubalia, this being shortened to Luel by the 11th century. To this form the Welsh added the word 'caer' or 'cair' (city, fortified place), giving us Caerleoil in 1130. The present spelling is due to Norman influence, giving the name a French-sounding suffix.

▦ CARTMEL

The origin of this name could be either old Norse or Saxon. If the former it would have been 'kartr-melr'; if the latter 'ceart-meal'. In both, however, the meaning would be the same: rough sandbank. Here the 'rough' might mean rocky, sterile or gorse-covered. In the 12th century the place was known both as Kertmel and Ceartmel.

▦ COCKERMOUTH

As one might suppose this was the mouth of the river Cocker – called the river Coker in the 13th century. An ancient river name this, going back to a Celtic root like 'cucra' or 'crwce', and cognate with the Irish 'cuar', meaning crooked or perverse. Thus, it was a crooked or winding river. The settlement here was called Kokermue in 1195 and Cokermuth in 1253.

▦ GRASMERE

It is thought that the original name for this place was Grisse, from the Old Norse words 'gres' (grass) and 'saer' (lake). If this is true then the later addition of the word mere was superfluous. In the 13th century it was Ceresmere and Gresemere – the two versions possibly indicating differences in Saxon and Norse pronunciations. It was 'grassy lake' either because the shores provided good pasture or because the water was clogged with reeds.

▦ KENDAL

This town was called Cherchebi in the Domesday Book and Cherkaby Kendale in the late 11th century. In more recent times it was Kirkby Kendal. Elsewhere other Kirkby villages grew up, each adopting its own distinguishing addendum. KIRKBY LONSDALE was Kircabilaeunesdale in 1090; KIRKBY STEPHEN was Cherkaby Stephan in the same year. In common was the root meaning church village (in Old Norse 'kirkiubyr') Kendal was named from the dale (valley) of the river Kent; Lonsdale from the dale of the river Lune, and Stephen from an early landowner (although the Abbot of St Mary's Abbey, York, to whom the estate was bequeathed, was also called Stephen, or more accurately Stephanus). Of these three settlements Kendal was the only one to drop its original name and become known only by its addendum.

▦ KESWICK

This has exactly the same derivation as CHISWICK in London, except that here the initial spelling and sound has been hardened by Norse influence. It comes from the Saxon 'cese-wic' meaning a cheese farm. With BUTTERMERE across the fells, Cumbria was evidently a major dairying district in former times. In 1276 it was called Kesewik.

▦ LOWTHER

This castle name – Lauder in the 12th century and Louther in the 13th century – comes from the local river and is derived either from Celtic or from Old Norse. If the former then its origin is the root word 'lautro' or 'lavatres' (meaning bath, waterway, canal); if the latter then it is based on 'lauthr' (meaning froth or lather – hence foaming river).

▒ MARYPORT

The old settlement here was called Elnefoot (or Ellnesfoote), being the mouth (end) of the river Ellen. But in 1750 a new harbour, or port, was built for the coal industry, and a new village appeared. It was named after the wife of the founder Humphrey Senhouse.

▒ PENRITH

This name – unchanged since the 12th century – derives from the Celtic words 'pen' (head, hill or chief) and 'rhyd' or 'rit' (ford). The crossing point was probably that over the river Eamont near BROUGHAM CASTLE, itself derived from Saxon 'burg' (fort) and 'ham' (homestead). Here stood the Roman fort of Brocavum (heathery place).

▒ RAVENGLASS

The prefix in this name comes from Old Celtic 'rann' or 'rhan' meaning a share or plot of land and not from 'hrafn', the Norse word for raven – although such birds were common here. The suffix comes from a personal name – Glas perhaps. Rengles in 1170 became Reynglas in 1250, the present spelling appearing soon afterwards. The name of the old Roman fort here, Glannoventa was from Celtic 'glan-venta' – place by the river bank.

▒ RYDAL

This goes back directly to 'ryge-dael', Saxon for rye valley, or dale where rye was grown. The name has not changed much since 1240 when it was Ridale. The lake of Rydal Water was formerly known as Routhmere, from the river Rothay. Some people think this derives from Old Norse 'rauthi' for trout.

▒ SHAP

From Hepe in 1228 and Yhep in 1241, this became Sheppe in 1300. Derived from the Saxon word 'heap' (meaning a pile of stones and probably referring to the old stone circle to the south of the town), the initial letter 'S' was possibly added due to confusion with the word 'sceap' (meaning sheep). The area around here has long been a sheep-grazing district.

▒ TORVER

This is a purely Viking name, from 'torf' (turf or peat) and 'erg' (shieling or hut). In the 13th century the village name was spelt Torvergh, evidently the pronunciation then being similar to that used today. It was obviously a humble settlement of mud cottages. Further north was the grander village of CONISTON whose name is a Scandinavian version of the Saxon name Cyninges-tun, meaning 'the king's manor'.

⊞ ULVERSTON

The Domesday Book entry, Uluvestun, suggests that this is a hybrid name, combining a Viking personal name (Ulfar) with a Saxon suffix 'tun' (meaning farmstead). Interestingly, on the other side of the Lake District, ULLSWATER has a name from Ulf's lake. This may or may not be the same tribal leader, since Ulfa was a common Scandinavian name.

⊞ WHITEHAVEN

In the Middle Ages this was spelt Withofhavene and Wytofthavene. The town hence took its name from the nearby headland, which in old Norse was called 'hvita hofuth' (white headland). The haven or harbour was evidently built below the headland. Long before its 18th century expansion, Whitehaven served as the trading port for neighbouring MORESBY (whose name derives from 'Morice's by' – the settlement belonging to Maurice).

Derbyshire

⊞ ASHBOURNE

This is clearly named after the river: the stream where ash trees grow, from the Saxon word 'aesc'. In medieval spellings it was Esseburne and Ascheburn. There are many tree-based names hereabouts (for example, Mapleton, Birchover, Thorncliff, Ashford) indicating a forested area in which timber was an important resource. Further north, CHAPEL EN LE FRITH comes from chapel in the woodland (from the Saxon 'fyrh' or 'fyrth').

⊞ BAKEWELL

The spelling in the Domesday Book, Badeqvella, was preceded in the previous century by spellings much closer to the original form: Badecan Wiellon and Badecanwelle. Badeca must either have been a very successful tribal leader, or else must have possessed a common name – for the villages of BAGINTON in Warwickshire and BARKFOLD in Sussex are also named after him. Here the 'wella' – stream or spring – could have been prized since the medicinal qualities of the waters hereabout have long been known.

⊞ BELPER

This is of purely Norman origin, coming from the French words 'beau' or 'belle' (beautiful) and 'repaire' (retreat). It was probably so named by a Norman baron, proud of his new acquisition. In the 13th century it was recorded as Beaurepeir and Beurepeyr.

⊞ BOLSOVER

It has been suggested that this name comes from three Saxon words – 'bulan' (bullock), 'laes' (pasture) and 'ofer' (slope or edge). Certainly some of the early spellings seem to support this, Bolesoura in 1167 and Bolesor in 1230, and the grassy promontory east of the town appears to give credence. But the Domesday Book version – Belesovre – reduces the possibility. Instead the name might derive more mundanely from a personal name: Bele's ofer.

▦ BUXTON

Sadly, perhaps, the old Roman name for this town has not survived – Aquae Arnemetiae (the water of Arnemetia the Roman goddess). Instead we have a name which goes back to 'bug-stan' – Buchestanes in 1100, Bucstanes in 1230. A 'bugan-stan' was a rocking or logan stone, that is, a large boulder that rocked when pushed. The site of such a stone has not so far been found, nor have historians decided upon the significance of a buckstone. Incidentally, the Saxon word 'bugan' – to bend or rock – has given us the word buxom (formerly spelt 'bucksome') which originally meant generous or yielding.

▦ CHESTERFIELD

This was Cesterfelda in the 10th century and Cestrefeld in the 11th century, clearly from the Saxon words 'ceaster' (Roman camp, from the Latin 'castra') and 'feld' (clearing or field). The settlement was sited on the Roman road Ryknild Street which linked Doncaster with Worcester. Chesterfield itself was the centre of an important lead-mining industry in Roman times.

▦ DERBY

Here the Scandinavian settlers of Danelaw changed the old Saxon name of Northworthige (north worthy or enclosure) to their own name Deoraby. This derived from 'djur' (deer) and 'byr' (homestead). The village was probably close to a deer-park – perhaps the same one which gave us DARLEY nearby (from Saxon 'deor-leah', deer grove or clearing).

▦ EYAM

This is a corruption of the dative plural of the Saxon word 'eg' meaning island: 'egum' – at the islands. In the 1086 Domesday Book it was Aiune, in 1236 Eyum. The settlement was sited between Jumber Brook and Hollow Brook.

▦ GLOSSOP

This name has not changed much over the years: Glosop in the 11th century, Glossope in the 13th century. It comes from Glott's hop (valley or island in a fen). The personal name here is possibly related to the Saxon word 'glotsen' (to stare) and might refer to that person's facial appearance. Hop is found in many other place-names around the Peak District, such as HOPE, HASSOP, ALSOP EN LE DALE, and DRADNOP, all of which are situated in valleys.

▦ HATHERSAGE

The 13th century spellings of this name – Haueresheg and Hathersegge – show a clear link with the origin: the Saxon word 'haefer' (billy-goat) and 'ecg' (edge, steep ridge). The animals were probably grazed on the Millstone Edge pastures.

▨ MATLOCK

Judging from the name this has long been an important centre. The Saxon word 'maethl' or 'maethel' (assembly or gathering) was combined with 'ac' (oak) to produce a place-name that was Meslach in the Domesday Book and Mathlac in 1233. An oak tree probably acted as a focal point for a 'moot' where local administration was established by public will. Interestingly, Matlock stands on the river Derwent whose name is of Celtic origin meaning 'oak river'.

▨ SWADLINCOTE

From Sivardingscotes in the 1086 Domesday Book it became Swardlincote in 1309. To the personal name Sweartling was added the Saxon word 'cot' or 'cote' meaning a cottage or shelter. 'Cots' were more humble than 'tuns' and 'hams' (which meant homesteads) and so Sweartling was less likely to have been a tribal leader and more likely to have been a hermit, 'churl' (freeman) or farmer.

▨ WIRKSWORTH

It is thought that the prefix here comes not from 'weorc', the Saxon word meaning work or fortification but from Weorce, a personal name. If so then the same man probably also gave his name to WORKSOP in Nottinghamshire. The suffix 'worth' meant enclosure. In AD 835 the place was Wyrcesuuyrthe, in the Domesday Book Werchesuuorde.

Devon

▨ BARNSTAPLE

There is not much doubt about the origin of the suffix here – it comes from the Saxon word 'stapol' meaning pile, post or staple. It is the derivation of the prefix which is debatable. Either it comes from a personal name – Bearda, or it comes from 'barda' meaning a beaked ship (warship) – whose genetive plural was 'bardna' (of the warships); or else it derives from 'beard' meaning hirsute. Thus, the 'post' indicated either an assembly point or 'moot' – known by its owner or by its twig or stick embellishments – or a mooring place. The early spellings include Beardastapol (AD 979) and Barnestaple (1086).

▨ BUCKFASTLEIGH

This originally was the 'leah' (grove or clearing) belonging to Buckfast – a nearby village whose own name derived from 'bucc' (male deer) and 'faesten' (stronghold or thicket). From just being known as Legh in 1286 it became Leghe Bufestr and Bucfastenlegh in the 14th century.

▨ CLOVELLY

This was Clovelie in the Domesday Book and Cloveli in the 13th century. Interestingly, there is a tiny hamlet a short distance inland now called Velly and known as Felye in medieval times. It is thought that the latter derives from the

Saxon word 'felg' (meaning wheel) and refers to a circular ridge or small hill. The prefix 'cloh' means cleft or ravine. Thus, Clovelly was the ravine near Velly. Today the narrow, steep main street is a draw for tourists.

▦ COMBE MARTIN

The Saxon word 'combe' or 'cumb' (narrow valley) is a very common place-name element and hence it is generally found linked to another element, so that places can be distinguished from each other. Here the manor was held by 'Nicholas, son of Martin' according to 13th century Charter Rolls. It was Cumbe Martini in the 13th century. Neighbouring ILFRACOMBE belonged to Alfred's people (being Alferdingcoma in 1168, from Alfred-inga-combe) and PARRACOMBE was the pedlar's valley (being Pedrecumbe in the Domesday Book).

▦ CREDITON

This town takes its name from the river Creedy which was known as the Crydian in AD 739 and Cridia in 1244 – an old Celtic name probably based on the word 'critio' for winding one. To the name of this river the Saxons added the word 'tun' (farmstead) – thus producing Cridiantune (in AD 930) and Chritetona (in the Domesday Book).

▦ CULLOMPTON

This settlement is named after its river: the 'tun' (homestead) on the Culm. In the 9th century it was Columtun. Upstream there is also CULMSTOCK (the 'stocc' or trunk by the Culm) and UFFCULME (the stretch of river belonging to Uffa). The river name itself is from an ancient Celtic word meaning winding river.

▦ DAWLISH

The Dawlish Water here was once called the river Dalch or Doflisc – a Celtic name meaning dark stream (from 'dubo', black, and 'glais,' stream). Then the settlement which began as Doflisc Ford became Douelisford (in about 1200) and Dawlysshe (in 1483).

▦ EXETER

The Greek geographer Ptolemy in the 2nd century AD called both the town and the river here Iska – derived from an ancient Celtic word for water (cognate with such other river names as Axe, Esk and Usk). From this the Romans called the place Isca Dumnuniorum, after the local tribe which gave its name to the county. By the 9th century it had the Saxon name Exanceaster – the Roman fort of the Exe – and by the time of the Domesday Book (1086) it was Essecestra. The present spelling is due to the Normans.

▦ KINGSKERSWELL

In the Domesday Book this was simply Carsewelle, deriving from the Saxon meaning cress spring – watercress being a popular addition to the medieval diet. By the 13th century the manor had been taken by the king. A neighbouring manor was taken over by the Abbot of Horton – hence ABBOTSKERSWELL. This, incidentally, was not the same abbot who built the nearby planned settlement of NEWTON ABBOT, who was from Torre Abbey in Torquay. This place was called Nyweton Abbatis in 1270.

⊞ OKEHAMPTON
The Domesday Book spelling Ochenemitona had previously been Ocmundtun (in 970) – the 'tun' (farmstead) on the river Okement. The derivation of the river name is lost in antiquity, but some scholars link it to an old Celtic root word, 'aku' meaning sharp or sudden, cognate with 'ocior', 'diog' or 'diauc' meaning swift.

⊞ PLYMOUTH
This name dates only from the 13th century, when it was spelled Plummuth. Before then the settlement was called Sutton (Sutona in the Domesday Book), for it was the south 'tun' (farmstead) owned by the priory at Plympton. Indeed, it was the village of Plympton which caused the river here to be called the Plym, the latter thus being a back formation. PLYMPTON was Plymentun in AD 904, a corruption of the Saxon 'plyman-tun': plum tree farm. Today Plymouth's original name survives in the name Sutton Pool, used for one of the town's harbours.

⊞ PRINCETOWN
A fairly recent name this, from the Prince Regent (later George IV) who – as Duke of Cornwall – held the 'Duchy' land of Dartmoor. The prison was built in 1808 to house French prisoners from the Napoleonic wars, and the town grew up around it.

⊞ TAVISTOCK
The prefix here is taken from the river Tavy, whose name – like the Tame, Tamar and Thames – goes way back to ancient Celtic times and a root 'tamio' – dark waters. The suffix could either be from 'stoc' (monastery, cell, secondary settlement) or 'stocc' (trunk, pile). The name has changed little since the Domesday Book version Tavestoc.

⊞ TIVERTON
Pre-Norman spellings – Twyfyrde and Twyfyrede – indicate a derivation meaning two fords – probably those across the rivers Exe and Lowman which meet here. The Saxons later added a 'tun' (farmstead) to give Tovretona in the Domesday Book.

⊞ TORQUAY
This is quite a recent name: it was Torrekay in 1591 and Torkay in 1668. It grew up around the quay built by the monks at Torre Abbey, the monastery founded in the 12th century at Tormoham, inland a little. That village was simply called Torre in the Domesday Book – the Saxon word for a hill.

▓ TOTNES

This name is not derived from 'totaern' (later 'toot') the Saxon for look-out post – although such might have been likely considering the landscape of the town – but from Totta's 'nes' (headland). This personal name is seen in the early spellings: Totanaes (AD 979) and Tottenas (1205).

Dorset

▓ BLANDFORD FORUM

Originally just called Bleneford (Domesday Book) or Bleinefort (1201) this town takes its name from the Saxon word 'blaege' meaning a gudgeon – a small freshwater fish now used by anglers as a bait but once eaten as part of a poor man's diet. In Norman times the town grew as a market centre, so an affix was used to distinguish it from other Blandfords nearby – first with 'Chipping' (Cheping Blaneford, 1288) and then with the Latin equivalent (Blaneford Forum, in 1291).

▓ BOURNEMOUTH

The present town grew as a Victorian seaside resort. Its name goes back only to medieval times – La Bournemowth in 1407 – and means literally stream mouth (from Saxon 'burna' and 'mutha'). The name of neighbouring CHRISTCHURCH is not much older, dating from the 12th century (when it was Cristescherche), the site of an Augustinian priory. The original name of that town was Twynham (called Tweoxneam in AD 901), this being a corruption of 'between eam' – between the streams. The rivers Stour and Avon flow either side.

▓ BRIDPORT

This was once the port (in this instance the gateway or market town) belonging to the borough of Bredy. The latter took its name from the river here, the 'Brit' or 'Bride', a word of Celtic origin meaning boiling or throbbing, so-called possibly because of its rapid current. The 1086 Domesday Book records Brideport, this changing to Bridiport by the 12th century.

▓ BROADWINDSOR

From Windesore in the Domesday Book two names had appeared by the 13th century: Magna Wyndesor and Parva Windlesor – in other words Great and Little Windsor, mother and daughter villages. The former received essentially its present name by the 14th century, the latter survives as a small hamlet a short distance to the north. It is thought Windsor could derive from the Saxon words 'windel' (windlass) and 'ora' (bank) – giving us the meaning landing place or river bank with a winding gear.

▓ CERNE ABBAS

The first part of this name comes from the local river – derived from the Celtic 'kar' (Welsh 'Cran') for rock, stone (hence strong river) – and the second part comes from the Abbey which was sited here in the 10th century. The Normans softened the pronunciation of the initial letter of the river name – as they did elsewhere with the same name, producing 'Char', as in Charmouth – and the Abbey was dissolved in the 16th century, but the name of this village has remained the same since the Domesday Book.

▓ CORFE CASTLE

Until the Norman castle was built this place was simply known as Corf (10th century) which was the Saxon word for a pass or cutting. The present village does indeed occupy a gap in the Purbeck Hills, a limestone ridge. North of Poole is CORFE MULLEN, so named from a mill that once stood there (from the Saxon 'mulin', or old French 'molin').

▓ DORCHESTER

The Roman name for this town was Durnonovaria, said to be a Latin version of the Celtic words 'dwrn-gwarae' meaning fist-play – perhaps indicating that boxing displays took place at the amphitheatre here. The Saxons later added 'caester' (Roman camp) to the name, producing Durnwaraceaster by the 9th century – the Roman fort of the Dorn dwellers. By the time of the Domesday Book this had been shortened to Dorecestre.

▓ LYME REGIS

Originally called Lim (in AD 774), Lym (in AD 938) and Lime (in the Domesday Book) this took its name directly from the river here. The word is of ancient origin, cognate with the Welsh 'llif' and the Cornish 'lif' – meaning flood stream. The 'Regis' addition (of the king) came in the 13th century when Edward I declared the town a free borough.

▓ MELBURY BUBB

This euphonic name was simply Melesberie in the Domesday Book – derived from 'mael' (coloured), 'middel' (middle) or 'melde' (a vegetable like beetroot) and 'burh' (fortified place) or 'beorg' (hill). In the early 13th century the manor was held by William Bubbe – leading to Bub Melebur in 1280 – whilst other Melbury villages acquired their own distinguishing affixes: Abbas (from an Abbey there), Osmond (from the church of St Osmond) and Sampford (from a family name).

▓ POOLE

Called Pole in 1194 and La Pole in 1235 this name simply derives from 'pol', the Saxon word for a pool. The harbour here has long been an important mooring site. BROWNSEA ISLAND was once called Branksea Island – corrupted from the earlier forms of Brunkes in 1235 and Brunkeseye in 1276. To the suffix 'eg' (island) was added a prefix derived either from Branoc, a personal name, or else from a Saxon word meaning brink – perhaps referring to the steep slopes of the island.

▓ SHAFTESBURY

The early versions of Sceaftesburi (AD 871) and Sceptesberie (1086) seem to indicate an origin from a personal name Sceaften, together with 'burh', Saxon for a fortified place. However, some people have suggested an alternative derivation – from the word 'sceaft' meaning a pole or shaft. It this were true, the pole might have stood on the hilltop here – as a boundary post or, more likely, a landmark – and the present name would be wholly descriptive.

▓ SWANAGE

The name evidently comes from 'swan-wic' but whether this referred to a swannery (swan farm) or to a herdsman's settlement ('swain's' dwelling) is not known. If the latter, then the herds might have been brought here in summer months, for seasonal grazing, by cattle farmers from further inland. In AD 877 the place was called Swanawic, in 1183 Swanewiz.

▓ TOLLER PORCORUM

In the Domesday Book the village was Tolre and it seems that this was originally the name for the river here (now called the Hooke). An old Celtic word 'tollthur' (meaning hollow stream or stream with potholes) could have been the origin. In the 13th century two separate villages were recorded: this one (named for its pig farms) and TOLLER FRATRUM (which belonged to the brothers of Forde Abbey, near Chard).

▓ TOLPUDDLE

Famous for its Martyrs who were deported to Australia in 1834 for opposing wage decreases, this village takes its name from the widow of Urc, Edward the Confessor's bodyguard, whose name was Tola. Her estate, here on the River Puddle, later passed to the Abbots at Abbotsbury, on the Dorset coast. The river name is of interest. From Saxon 'pidele' (for fen or fenland river) it has variously been called the Pidelan, Pudele and, in more recent times, Piddle and Puddle. The Victorians preferred the latter.

▓ WAREHAM

This town stands near the head waters of the river Frome and owes its name to the Saxon 'wer' or 'water-ham' (weir-village). The constriction in the stream could be natural, but since a fishery has been recorded here at least since the 14th century, then an artificial dam, creating a fish-farming lake, cannot be ruled out as the origin of the weir mentioned. In AD 784 the town was called Werham, and in the Domesday Book Warham.

WEYMOUTH

Clearly this was the 'mutha' (mouth) of the river Wey, formerly called the Waye. In the 10th century the town was called Waymouthe, in the 13th century Weymuthe. The river name as a derivation similar to that of the river Wye – from an ancient Celtic, Indo-European root meaning the moving one or the conveyor. Our modern word way comes from the same root.

Durham & Teeside Districts

BISHOP AUCKLAND

There are many Aucklands hereabouts, each with a distinguishing affix – 'West Auckland', 'Auckland St Andrew' and 'St Helen' (from their church dedications) and this one, the largest, which came under the jurisdiction of the Bishops of Durham in the 12th century. As to the main part of the name, this comes from a Danish word 'auki-land' meaning additional land. But the origin of the name goes back further than the Danes. It is thought that the Saxons used the name Alclyde or Alclyt as their version of an earlier, Celtic, name Alclut. This meant cliff on the clut. Whether the Clut, Clyt or Clyde was the former name of the river Gaunless, or was transferred here from Scotland is not known. Clyde is still the name of a river in Scotland and once existed as the old name for Dunbarton.

CONSETT

This is a tautological name as well as a hybrid one, with Celtic and Saxon elements both meaning hill. The prefix comes from the Celtic 'canuc' or 'cnocc' (as found also in Cannock) and the suffix from the Saxon 'heafod'. In the 12th century the place was called Covekesheued, in the 13th century Conekesheued. Consett stands on a prominent hill which, itself, was once called Coneke or Conke.

DARLINGTON

The early forms of the name, Dearthingtun (1050) and Dearningtun (1104), can easily be explained as deriving from 'tun', 'inga' and 'Deornoth': the farmstead belonging to the people of Deornoth (probably a tribal leader). The Normans changed the middle 'n' to an 'l' to facilitate pronunciation, just as the French did to the Latinised name 'Bononia', which became 'Boulogne'.

DURHAM

The central part of this city, where stands the Cathedral and Castle, is built within a meander of the river Wear, high up on a rocky outcrop. A fact reflected in the early name of the place, Dunholm, deriving from 'dun' (Saxon for hill) and 'holmr' or 'holm' (Norse for island). The early version became Dunhelm, Dunhelme and

Durealme in the 12th century, the first of which continued to be used officially by the University and the Bishop. The 'holm' suffix incidentally continues to be common in Denmark, as in 'Stockholm'.

▓ HARTLEPOOL
Where the old town stands today was formerly called Hart Island, otherwise Heruteu (in AD 730) and Herte (in 1242). This derived from the Saxon 'heorot-eg' (stag island). Below this upland area was a low-lying hollow or pool called 'Heoroteg Pol'. And so we had the beginnings of the modern name – which was Herterpol and Hertelpol in the 12th century.

▓ HETTON-LE-HOLE
Simply recorded as Heppendun in the 12th century, this name comes from the Saxon words 'heope' and 'dun' (hip and hill respectively) indicating an upland area where rosehips were found. In late medieval times the name Hetton-le-Hole was used for the place at the foot of the hill, distinguishing it from Hetton-le-Hill at the top. Nearby HOUGHTON-LE-SPRING also has a botanical connection, deriving from the Saxon words 'hoh-tun' (hillspur-farmstead) adjoined by 'spryng', which meant sapling or even a group of young trees.

▓ MIDDLESBROUGH
This was the middlemost 'burh' (fortified place, burg or manor) – the original spelling Midlesburg (in the 12th century) deriving from the Saxon superlative form of middel, midlest. By 1272 it had become the more mundane Middelburg. It is not known where the town was midway between, possibly the two monasteries at Durham and Whitby – St Cuthbert's and St Hilda's respectively.

▓ NEWTON AYCLIFFE
The New Town, designated in 1947, interestingly chose to call itself by the traditional name – Newton coming from the Saxon 'neowa-tun' (new farmstead). The original settlement here was called Heaclif in the 11th century and Acleia in the 12th century. These derived from 'ac-leah' (oak wood or clearing) or from 'ac-clif' (oak cliff or hill). 'Heah-acclif' would have been the high oak hill. The adjective 'Great' was added to one village to distinguish it from SCHOOL AYCLIFFE – which was given to a person called Scula (the skulking one) during the 10th century.

▓ REDCAR
The prefix here probably derives not from the Saxon 'read' (red) but from the Saxon 'hreod' (reed) – which would certainly match the suffix, which is from the old Norse word 'kiarr' (marsh). In the 12th century it was Redker, in the 13th century Rideker.

▣ SEDGEFIELD
The 11th century version of this name was Ceddesfeld which implies that the origin might be Cedd's 'feld' (clearing or field). It is thought by some historians that the personal name here could itself be derived from the Saxon word 'secg' meaning warrior. In 1190 the spelling was Segesfeld.

▣ SHILDON
This is purely a Saxon topological name, coming from the words 'scylf' and 'dun' meaning rock or ledge and hill respectively. This could either have referred to a rocky upland or else to a hill with a peak. In the 13th century the name was recorded as Sciluedon.

▣ SPENNYMOOR
It is thought that this name derives from a dialectic word 'spenning', 'spen' or 'spenne' (cognate with the Saxon 'spannan' meaning to clasp or fasten), which was used for a fence or hedge. If so, then the name meant moorland with fences. In the 14th century it was Spendingmore and Spennyngmore.

▣ STANHOPE
The name Stanhopa in 1183 was simply 'stan-hop' – stony valley, or stone-covered gorge. Such a name still applies, the settlement being sheltered under the steep slopes of the Pennine Hills.

▣ STOCKTON-ON-TEES
Like many other names with the stock or stoke element, this can have one of two origins. Either it was the 'tun' (homestead) belonging to a 'stoc' (a monastery or religious place) or else it was the tun made of 'stocc' (trunks or logs). In the 12th century the place was just called Stocton, the river name being added later. Incidentally, TEES derives from an old Celtic word 'tes' meaning heat or boiling – perhaps indicating that it must have been a surging or bubbling stream.

Essex

▣ BASILDON
Although this is a New Town, designated in 1949, its name goes back to Saxon times. In the Domesday Book (1086) it was Berlesduna, derived from Beorhtel's 'dun' (hill). The 'a' sound and spelling probably results from the Essex dialect.

▣ BILLERICAY
The origin of this name continues to be a mystery. It was Billerika and Billerica in the 14th century – the earliest records – but no-one seems to know why. One interesting theory, however, was proposed a few years ago – that it comes from the tropical fruit myrobalan or myrtolan which grows in the Far East and is used for

tanning and dyeing. This fruit was imported into England in the Middle Ages and there might have been a tannery or dyehouse here in Essex. And the etymological link? The scientific name for this fruit is 'terminalia bellerica'.

⬛ BRAINTREE
This name comes directly from Branuc's 'treow' (tree) which was either a boundary mark to an estate owned by a person called Branuc, or else a cross put up by him to serve as a focal point for meetings. Branchetreu in 1086 became Branketre in 1274. The river Brain has been named from the town.

⬛ CHELMSFORD
The Romans called this town Caesaromagus – Caesar's market (adapting the Celtic word 'magos' for a market). In Saxon times, however, it became Ceolmaer's ford, spelt Celmeresfort in the Domesday Book and Chelmeresford in 1190. The river Chelmer was named after the town. Its original name was Beaduwan, now preserved in the place-names Great and Little Baddow, south of Chelmsford.

⬛ CLACTON-ON-SEA
Claccingtun and Clachintuna, both of which were documented spellings in the 11th century, indicate an origin from 'Clacc', 'inga' and 'tun' – the farm of Clacc's people. The affix 'on-sea' was added when the place became a resort, to distinguish it from Great Clacton and Little Clacton.

⬛ COLCHESTER
The old Celtic name for this town was Camulodunon, derived from the war-god Camulos and the word 'dunum' meaning a fort. But the Saxons changed it to Colneceaster – the 'ceaster' (Roman fort) on the river Colne – this becoming Colcestra in the Domesday Book. The river name, related to Calne and Clun, comes from an ancient word for water.

⬛ HALSTEAD
The Domesday Book version of this name, Haltesteda, suggests an origin from the Saxon words 'hald' or 'hold' (protection, shelter) and 'stede' (place). The town, standing between the river Colne and a hillside, would have been protected from both sides.

⬛ HARLOW
The modern New Town goes back only to 1947 but its name goes back to here-hlaw, which became Herlawe in 1043 and Herlaua in the Domesday Book of 1086. The Saxon word 'here' (like the Scandinavian 'herr') meant army, multitude or host of people. The word 'hlaw' meant mount or hillock. Thus, Harlow was an important meeting place – for the people of Harlow Hundred in fact. The mound in question is probably that occupied by the old Roman temple at Harlow Old Town.

▦ INGATESTONE

This was Ginges Ad Petram in 1254 and Gynges Atteston in 1283. The first part comes from 'Giga's inga' – the people of Giga, perhaps a tribal leader. The second part – 'petra' being Latin for rock and 'stan' Saxon for stone – suggests there was once a large boulder here. A glacial deposit? A Roman milestone? A meeting stone? We do not know.

▦ MALDON

This was originally the 'dun' (hill) with a 'mael' (monument or cross), and as such the place was probably an important meeting point for the Saxons. Its early spellings include Melduna (in the Domesday Book) and Mealdona (in 1130). The settlement of Malden in Surrey has the same derivation.

▦ ONGAR, CHIPPING & HIGH

The Domesday Book version of this name, Angra, was almost exactly the Saxon word for grazing land. The affix Chipping is from 'ceping', the word for a market. In 1388 it was Chepyng Hangre. High Ongar stands above the Roding flood plain.

▦ SAFFRON WALDEN

From Waledana (1086) and Waldena (1141) – from 'denu' (valley) and 'walas' (foreigners, Britons or Welsh) – this became Safforne Walden in 1582. The saffron crocus was grown here in the Middle Ages, an important medicinal plant also used as a yellow-orange dye.

▦ SOUTHEND-ON-SEA

A fairly recent name this – Sowthende in 1481 – signifying that the place was once the southern end of PRITTLEWELL, formerly a village and now a suburb. An earlier name, Stratende (street end, so called because it marked the end of a Roman road) has been lost. The Domesday Book notes only Pritteuuella, derived from 'pritol' (babbling) and 'wella' (spring). Modern Southend grew as a seaside resort in the first half of the 19th century.

▦ STANSTEAD MOUNTFITCHET

This was called Stanesteda in the Domesday Book, coming directly from the Saxon words 'stan' (stone) and 'stede' (place). In the late 12th century the manor was taken by Richard de Muntfichet, a baron from Montfiquet in Normandy. Nearby GREAT and LITTLE DUNMOW are examples of mother-and-daughter villages, their common name coming from 'dun' (hill) and 'mawe' (meadow). In the 13th century they were called Magna and Parva Dunmawe.

▦ THAXTED

From 'thaec' (thatch) and 'stede' or 'stead' (place, site of building) this name became Tachesteda in the Domesday Book and Takesteda in 1176. Reeds were grown hereabouts especially to provide thatching material for use throughout East Anglia.

✹ WALTHAM ABBEY

Waltham is a common place-name and, interestingly, has changed little over the last thousand years. Sometimes it is spelt Waldham, occasionally Wealtham. It derives from 'weald' and 'ham' (forest and homestead). Indeed, so common is this name that it is usually accompanied by an additional element, in order to distinguish the different places: thus GREAT and LITTLE WALTHAM are found near Chelmsford. Here, the Abbey refers to the great church that was begun in the 11th century and is thought to be the last resting place of King Harold, brought here following his death at the Battle of Hastings. Nearby WALTHAM CROSS (Hertfordshire) is so called because it contains one of the Eleanor Crosses erected by Edward I in 1291. These marked the stopping-places of the coffin that took the body of his wife, Eleanor of Castile, to Westminster Abbey (from Harby, Nottinghamshire, where she had died).

✹ WALTON-ON-THE-NAZE

This was simply Waletuna in the 13th century, becoming Waleton in the 14th century. The suffix is clearly from the Saxon 'tun' (farmstead) but the origin of the prefix presents etymologists with a problem. It could derive from different roots: 'wala' (Britons or foreigners), 'weald' (forest or wood), 'weall' (wall) or even 'waelle' (stream). The addition of Naze appeared in the Middle Ages to distinguish this place from other Waltons. This word comes from 'naess' (ness, headland or ridge) which here refers to the sandspit. The same element is found in distant Epping Forest at NAZEING (the dwellers on the spur of land – 'naess inga'). This was Nasinges in the 13th century.

Gloucestershire

✹ CHARLTON KINGS

Before this manor came under the ownership of the King in the early Middle Ages – it was called Kynges Cherleton in 1270 – this place was known as Ceorlatun. It had originated as the 'tun' (farmstead or village) of 'ceorls'. These, otherwise known as churls or villeins, were free peasants – higher than servants and lower than yeomen in the social strata. It was not uncommon for groups of these people to set up villages together – outside the big towns – where they could farm their own lands.

✹ CHELTENHAM

The 9th century spelling, Cheltanhomme, indicates that the suffix may derive not from the usual 'ham' (homestead) but from the less common 'hamm' (meadow or pastured clearing). The prefix has three possible derivations: from a Saxon personal name; from the river here, the Chelt (although this could be a back-formation); or from an old Celtic root, 'celte' or 'celtae', meaning high place and as found in Chiltern Hills. In the Domesday Book (1086) the settlement was called Chinteneham.

Cirencester

The name mentioned by Ptolemy in the 2nd century – Korinion – was probably based on the name of the tribe Cornovii which lived throughout the West Country in pre-Roman times. It was this same tribe which gave its name to Cornwall – the home of the promontory dwellers. Under the Saxons this settlement became Cirrenceastre, with a softened prefix, and a suffix added to indicate that the place had once been a Roman camp.

Coleford

The earliest record of this place is only from the 16th century, when it was Colford: the charcoal ford – the ford over which charcoal was carried. Since early medieval times charcoal-burning has been an important industry in the Forest of Dean. Some historians believe that nearby CINDERFORD also derives from this activity. This was Sinderford in the 13th century, the prefix coming from a word meaning dross or waste material from burning.

Gloucester

This former Roman camp has a prefix derived from an old Celtic word 'glevum' (cognate with 'gloiu' and 'gloew') meaning bright or noble – perhaps indicating that the land here was favoured or fertile. In the 9th century it was Gleawecestre, changing to Glowecestre in the Domesday Book.

Lechlade

This was originally the 'lad' or 'gelad' (passage) over the river Leach, formerly known as the Lec or Leche. The passage could have been a path, stepping-stones or even a ferry, and the river Leche derived its name from a Celtic root meaning muddy one. Early spellings for this village include Lecelade (1086) and Lichelad (12th century).

Lydney

The Severn Estuary was once much wider than it is today and the land on either side more marshy. Some early Saxon settlements were built on islands in this watery landscape, Lydney being one of them. It was Lidaneg in the 11th century, a name coming from Lida's 'eg' (island). Lida was either a personal name or meant sailor. Neighbouring BLAKENEY was either 'Blaca's eg' or black island. This was Blakeneia in the 12th century.

Minchinhampton

The original name, Hantone in the Domesday Book, derived from the Saxon 'hea-tun' meaning high farmstead or village on a hill. By the 13th century, however, it had become Minchenhamtone, the prefix from 'mynecen' (nun) signifying that the estate had passed to the ownership of a nunnery based at Caen in Normandy.

✷ MORETON-IN-THE-MARSH

The addendum here is not a corruption of 'march' (border) – despite the village being close to where four counties meet – but a shortened form of 'hennemarsh' (a boggy waste where wildfowl live). Mortun, as documented in AD 714, was moor farmstead.

✷ NAILSWORTH

This was once Naegl's worth (enclosure). In 1196 it was Nailleswurd, in 1247 Naylesworth. Naegl is thought to be a personal name derived from the Saxon word for a nail. Perhaps that particular tribal leader was tall, thin and strong, or else sharp in the sense of being cunning.

✷ NEWENT

This is one of the few villages in Gloucestershire with a wholly Celtic name, coming from old Welsh meaning new place. In the Domesday Book it was Noent, a word that can be linked back to Gaulish Latin 'novientum' (old Latin 'nova venta' – new market town). Perhaps the Celts moved back to this spot after the invasion and settlement of the Saxon tribes.

✷ STROUD

This was known in the 13th century simply as La Strode, a name derived from the Saxon word 'strod' or 'stroth' meaning marshy land overgrown with brushwood – that is, scrubland. The area described lies to the south of the town, by the river Frome. The town of STROOD in Kent has a similar origin.

✷ TETBURY

Before this was called Tettan Byrg in the 9th century it was Tettan Monasterium (in AD 681), telling us that this was once the site of a religious foundation. In fact, the monastery or convent here was set up by Tette, the sister of King Ine of Wessex. The later suffix derived from 'burh' or 'burg' for a fortified place or manor. In the Domesday Book the place was Teteberie.

✷ TEWKESBURY

From the early forms – Teodechesberie in the Domesday Book and Theokesbiria in 1107 – it might be tempting to think that the prefix derives from the Saxon 'teo' for a boundary. In fact, however, it comes from the personal name Teodec. The suffix is from 'burh' or 'burg' for a fortified place.

Hampshire &
The Isle of Wight

⊞ ALRESFORD

Interestingly this name has remained unchanged since AD 701. The Saxon word 'alor' meant alder so this place was built at the ford by the alder tree. The river Alre was named after the settlement as a back formation and the separate villages of New and Old appeared in the Middle Ages.

⊞ ANDOVER

This place-name has developed from the name of the river here, now the Anton, but called the Ann or Andever throughout the Middle Ages. 'Ann' was probably a Saxon corruption of the old Celtic word 'onno' (ash tree), and 'dever' was a descendant of 'dubro' – Celtic for waters. Thus, we had the 'ash stream'. In AD 955 the settlement was called Andeferas, in the Domesday Book it was Andovere.

⊞ BASINGSTOKE

This was once called the 'stoc' (secondary settlement) belonging to the mother village of Basing – now ironically swallowed up by the modern development which bears its daughter village's name. Basing was derived from Basa's 'inga' (people) and its offshoot was Basingastoc in AD 990 and Basingestoches in the Domesday Book of 1086.

⊞ COWES

This is quite a new name: early records in the 16th century appear to name two sandbanks off the coast as Esturly and Westerly Cowe. Later these terms seem to have been transferred to the two forts either side of the Medina estuary. In due course the town which grew up around these forts took the same name. We do not know why a sandbank might have been called 'the Cow' in the first place. The Medina river was called Medine in the 12th century, derived from 'medme' or 'medema', Saxon for middle one. The river divides the Isle of Wight roughly in two.

⊞ FAREHAM

This was Fernham in the Domesday Book and simply derives from the Saxon words 'fearn' (fern) and 'ham' (enclosure or farmstead). This part of Hampshire was evidently infertile or, at least, little farmed. Not far away is HAMBLE LE RICE in which the addendum comes from the Saxon 'hris' meaning brushwood or scrubland. It was Amle in the 12th century, taken from the name of the river here: 'hamel' being Saxon for crooked.

⊞ GOSPORT

This name has changed little: it was Goseport in 1250, a name that simple meant a market town or harbour where geese were sold: goose-town. Across Portsmouth

Harbour is SOUTHSEA. This name only goes back to the 17th century. When the castle was built in 1540 it was called the South Castle of Portsmouth. By 1652 it was called Southsea Castle and the present town had begun to grow up around it.

▦ HAVANT

The earliest known spelling, Hamanfunta, shows the origin to be Hama's-funta. The prefix, of course, was a personal name; the suffix was a Saxon word (cognate with the Latin 'fontana' and the Celtic 'funton') meaning spring, stream or water spout. Our modern words fount and font come from this root. In the Domesday Book we find Havehunte.

▦ LYMINGTON

The river flowing through this town – now bearing the same name – was probably once called the Limen or Lemon which, like other names such as Lymn and Leam, would have derived from the Celtic word for an elm tree (in Welsh 'llwyf', in Irish 'lem'). To this the Saxons added 'inga' (the people) and 'tun' (farmstead). Thus we have the village of the elm river people. In 1186 this was written as Limington.

▦ MICHELDEVER

As with Andover the suffix here is a descendant of the old Celtic 'dubro' meaning waters or a river – an element also found in DOVER. The prefix could also be Celtic in origin – from 'micn' for bog or marshland – but is more likely to be derived from the Saxon 'micel' meaning great. It was Mycendefr in AD 862 and Miceldevre in 1086.

▦ PETERSFIELD

This settlement was originally built as a Norman 'new town' around the Church of St Peter. At that time (in the 12th century) it was called Petersfeld. The feld or 'open land' upon which that first village was constructed has partly survived as Petersfield Heath.

▦ PORTSMOUTH

Portesmutha was recorded as far back as AD 501 and Porceastra was the Saxon name meaning the 'ceaster' (Roman fort) of Port. From these it is thought that Port was actually the name of the harbour in Saxon times, being so important that 'The Port' needed no other name. PORTSEA is a corruption of 'Port-eg' (Port island) and PORTSDOWN was 'Port's dun' – the ridge or hill overlooking the Port.

▦ ROMSEY

Many place-names like this – Romsley in Shropshire and Ramsey in Huntingdonshire for example – derive from the Saxon 'hramsa' for wild garlic or ramson. This one does not, however. Instead it was Rum's 'eg' (island), named from the mound that the Abbey stands on, above the flood-plains of the river Test and its tributaries. The personal name Rum could be a shortened form of Rumwald – glorious ruler. In AD 966 the place was Romesye.

✺ RYDE

This largely Victorian resort grew up either side of a stream which, in the 13th century, was called La Ride but is now called Monktonmead Brook. Ride or rid was a dialect word meaning a small stream, cognate with the Saxon 'rith'.

✺ SHANKLIN

Called Sencliz in the Domesday Book and Schencling in the 14th century, this name derives from the Saxon words 'scenc' (cup) and 'hlinc' (hill). The explanation for this origin might be found in Shanklin Chine, where a waterfall flows down the ridges of a hillside. The Saxons might well have hung a water vessel from here, using the waterfall as a spout or drinking fountain. Nearby VENTNOR is a medieval place-name from a former estate owner by the name of Vintner or Vintener.

✺ SOUTHAMPTON

In Saxon times this was called, simply, Homtun, Hamtun or Hantune – from the words 'hamm' (meadow) and 'tun' (farmstead). Originally the place was sited on a coastal promontory between the rivers Itchet and Test. The present prefix appeared in medieval times to distinguish this town from Northampton, to which it was linked by an ancient routeway. In 1158 the town was Suhantune, in 1205 Suthhamtune.

✺ WINCHESTER

Before the Saxons added 'caester' (Roman camp), this place was called Ouenta by Ptolemy and Venta Belgarum by the Romans. Certainly the Belgae tribe lived here (the proud ones from the Celtic root 'belg', to swell) but what of the origin of Venta? Either it came from the Celtic 'ven' (cognate with the Welsh 'gwen' and Irish 'fine') meaning pleasing or kindred – hence indicating a 'favoured place'. Or it came from the Latin word 'vendere' meaning to sell – thus indicating a market. The 8th century version of the name was Uintancaester, the 9th century version Wintonia.

Herefordshire

✺ BROMYARD

From Bromgeard in AD 840 and Bromgerd in the Domesday Book of 1086 this name clearly has an origin in the Saxon words 'brom' (broom) and 'geard' (hedge, fenced enclosure). Broom was cut to provide fencing material and bendable timber for various household uses (including the making of besoms – hence the modern word broom) and 'geard' was a Saxon word which has given us our modern words yard and garden.

☒ EWYAS HAROLD

Towards the Welsh border place-names with Celtic elements become more common. Here the original village name (Euias or Ewias) derives from the old British words 'ewig' and 'dinas' meaning sheep and district respectively. The addendum came in the 12th century (Euuias Haraldi) when the manor was taken over by Harold, son of Earl Ralph, nephew of King Edward the Confessor.

☒ GOODRICH

In the 12th century this was called Castellum Godric – telling us that the settlement grew up originally around the Norman castle belonging to Godric. The Castle prefix was dropped during the Middle Ages.

☒ HAY-ON-WYE

This border town was called Haya in 1144 and La Haye in 1259, names descended from the Saxon 'gehaeg' meaning an enclosure. It is thought it once stood within a hunting estate, fenced off from the surrounding forest. The Hague, in the Netherlands, has the same derivation – it grew up around a woodland hunting lodge.

☒ HEREFORD

This name, interestingly, has remained unchanged since the 10th century. It is purely Saxon in character, deriving from 'here' (army, multitude, host) and ford. The old Roman road from Leintwardine to Monmouth crossed the River Wye at this point and this could well have led to the development of this name. To be called 'army-ford' it was probably a major crossing-point – perhaps wide and shallow enough for a marching column of men to pass across without breaking formation.

☒ HOPE UNDER DINMORE

This was just Hope in the Domesday Book, deriving from the Saxon word 'hop' meaning valley. By the 13th century it was Hope Sub Dinnemore, which located it below Dinmore Hill. This latter name is Celtic in origin, coming from 'din' and 'mawr' (hill and great respectively).

☒ LEDBURY

It might be tempting to assume – noting the high siting of this town above the river here – that this name comes from the Saxon 'hlid' meaning hill or slope. In fact it comes from the name of the river itself – the Leadon. So it was the 'burh or burg (fortified place) on the Leadon'. In the Domesday Book this was recorded as Liedeberge, changing to Ledebur in the 13th century. It has been suggested that the river name comes from 'hlyde' – a torrent.

☒ LEOMINSTER

The suffix here, and the prefix of the Welsh form of the name Llanllieni, suggests minster, church, monastery or chapel. The rest of the name in each case refers to a district – for the area around here was once known as Lene, Leon or Lien. Taken from the Celtic root – 'lei', 'lliant' or 'llion' for river or flood – this name meant district of the streams. The rivers Arrow and Lugg flow across here, and frequently overflow. In the Domesday Book the place was recognisably called Leominstre.

▦ LUGWARDINE

Elsewhere this might have been Lugworthy for the suffix comes from the Saxon 'worthign' (enclosure, yard) which normally became 'worthy'. But here the 'th' became 'd' as a result of the Normans' inability to pronounce 'th'. The prefix comes from the river Lugg. This name is thought to derive from an ancient root word 'leuk', cognate with the Celtic 'llug' and Greek 'leukos' meaning light or white. Thus the river was 'bright stream'. In the Domesday Book the village was called Lucvordine.

▦ PUTLEY

From Poteslepe in the Domesday Book to Putelega in 1180, this name is purely Saxon: from 'putta' (kite) and 'leah' (wood or glade). Although some etymologists think the prefix here could be a personal name (Putta, as found in the origin of Putney in London), the bird derivation is perhaps the more likely. Red kites were once very common all over Britain until being hunted almost to extinction in the 19th century. They have now, happily, made a comeback.

▦ ROSS-ON-WYE

Called Rosse in the Domesday Book and Ros in 1199, this name is directly connected with the Celtic word 'rhos' (old Celtis ros) meaning upland heath, moor or heather covered plain. The name of the river – which was added to the name of the town in recent times – is also Celtic in origin. Like the river Wey elsewhere, it is a corruption of 'weg' meaning carrier or transporter. Whether this referred to the carrying of stones and other stream material, or the Celts used these rivers for navigation, is not known.

▦ SYMONDS YAT

This beauty spot has a name little changed from its original form – Sigemund's Geat (gap, gate or – as in this case – a pass through the hills). Being close to the English-Welsh border this once must have been an important strategic point, and Sigemund might well have been a powerful local leader. Certainly his name indicates as much – meaning victory protector.

▦ WEOBLEY

This part of the country was once densely wooded and many of the place-names hereabouts indicate the fact. This one means Webba's 'leah' (clearing, woodland glade, forest grove) and was recorded as Wibelai in 1086 and Webberley in 1242. Close-by are many other leah suffix place-names – WORMSLEY, EARDISLEY, KINNERSLEY for example – together with more obviously woodland-connected names: BROXWOOD, KINGSWOOD, BAREWOOD and so on.

Hertfordshire

Baldock

This was established by the Knights Templars in the 12th century and named Baldac, the old French name for Baghdad. To the north is HINXWORTH deriving from 'hengesta-worth' (stallion enclosure) and STOTFOLD (Bedfordshire) deriving from 'stod-falod' (horse stud enclosure). This area was evidently associated with horse-rearing – giving the Knights a good reason for locating their settlement here.

Berkhamstead

In Saxon times the word 'ham' usually meant homestead or village and the word 'stede' meant place or site of a dwelling. When the two were used together – as found in this place-name – then the meaning took on greater importance, perhaps indicating a manor or an estate. The origin of the prefix here could either be 'beorc' or 'beorg', Saxon words for birch tree and hill respectively. Unfortunately neither the early versions of the name (Beorhthanstaedae in the 10th century and Berchehamstede in the 11th century) nor the town's situation can enlighten us. The settlement lies along a valley in the Chiltern Hills where birch woods have long been part of the natural vegetation.

Cheshunt

This could be an unusual example in which the Saxon element 'caester' (Roman camp) is found at the beginning and not at the end of a place-name. Certainly the Domesday Book version indicates as much – Cestrehunt. The suffix probably comes from 'hunta' (huntsman) but could come from 'funta' (spring or waterspout). Cheshunt stands on the Roman Ermine Street.

Harpenden

With an additional 'e' at the end, this name was the same in 1196. But etymologists differ about its origins. Some say it comes from the Saxon word 'hearpere' meaning harper – indicating an early resident or the melodious sound of the stream. Others say it comes from 'herepaeth' meaning army path, perhaps supported by the fact that the Roman Watling Street runs close by. Both sides, however, agree about the suffix; that it comes from 'denu' (valley).

Hatfield

This has the same origin as place-names like Hadfield and Heathfield – namely from the Saxon words 'haeth' (heather or shrub) and 'feld' (open land). In the 8th century this place was called Haethfelth, in the Domesday Book (1086) it was Hetfelle. In Saxon times this whole area, stretching eastwards into Essex, was open heathland with heather, bracken and birch trees.

Hemel Hempstead

The word 'hamstede' (from 'ham' – homestead, and 'stede' – place) was often used by the Saxons for a main farmstead or settlement as opposed to a small or secondary one. The first part of the name comes from the old name for the district, this part of Hertfordshire being called Haemele in the early 8th century. Some etymologists think this was derived from a long-lost Celtic root, others say it comes from the Saxon 'hamol' meaning maimed or broken. All about here the landscape is hilly, broken-up by many rivers. The Domesday Book records Hamelamstede, in 1173 it was Hemelhamsteda.

▨ HERTFORD

The pronunciation of this name tells us its origin: 'hart ford'. The Saxon word 'heorot' meant stag and this settlement grew up where such animals waded across the river Lee. It is an ancient place, the earliest records going back to the 7th century. In the 8th century it was Herutford, in the 12th century it was Heortford. The suburb of BENGEO, once a separate village, was called Beningho (13th century), this deriving from 'the ridge of the people of the river Beane' ('Beane-inga-hoh').

▨ HITCHIN

Before the Norman Conquest this was Hiccam, derived from the tribal name Hicce, a group of people evidently living here. Some etymologists think this could have been a Celtic tribe, linking its name with the old Welsh word 'sych' meaning a dry river. In 1197 the village was Hiche, in 1230 Hycche. Nearby ICKLEFORD was Ikelesforde in the 13th century, from the Saxon Icel's ford.

▨ HODDESDON

This was Hodd's 'dun' (hill) originally, and Hodesdone in the Domesday Book (1086). We do not know who Hodd was but the hill was probably Highfield Wood, west of the town.

▨ LETCHWORTH

This combines two Saxon words: 'loc' (sometimes 'loca' or 'lycce') and 'worth'. The first indicated a lock or bar used to safeguard an enclosure, the second was used for a clearing, homestead or village. In the Domesday Book the name was Leceworde.

▨ POTTERS BAR

This was called Potterys Barre in the 16th century and was situated at one of the entrances into the hunting park of Enfield Chase – the 'bar' being a gateway. There is some dispute as to whether it was owned by someone called Pottery, or was the centre of a local pottery-making industry. Another entrance into the Chase was at Southgate.

▨ ROYSTON

In the 12th century this was recorded as Crux Roaisie, which meant Roese's Cross. Apparently a cross had been erected by a certain Lady Roese or Roheis. A priory was then founded here. In the 13th century the name of the place became Croyroys and then Reyston. It is not clear whether the present suffix derives from 'tun' (farmstead) or from 'stan' (stone): the farm or stone at Roese's cross.

▓ ST ALBANS
Here the old names – Verulamium in Roman times and Waetlingaceaster in Saxon times – were superseded by the name of the saint to whom the ecclesiastical town was dedicated. A Benedictine Abbey was founded, it is said, on the spot where Alban had been martyred in the 3rd century. In AD 792 the town was called Aecclesia Sancti Albani, in the Domesday Book it was Villa S.Albani. The Roman name possibly derived from the Celtic 'uero' (broad or wide) and the Saxon name from the Waeclingas tribe, which also gave its name to WATLING STREET.

▓ STEVENAGE
The 1065 spelling, Stithenaece, suggests a prefix from a personal name Stitha or from 'stithan' (Saxon for strong or stiff) and a suffix from 'haecce' (Saxon for hatch or gate, possibly from Celtic root 'ac' for oak). Perhaps this was the site of a sturdy gateway across the major routeway northwards, subsequently the Great North Road.

▓ TRING
Oddly, it is the 13th century version, Trehangre, and not the earlier versions, Tredunga (1086) and Treange (1207), that best indicates the origin – from the Saxon 'treow' (tree) and 'hangra' (slope). Meaning 'overhanging slope where trees grow' the town still, today, is surrounded by beech woods.

▓ WARE
This name comes from the 'wer' or 'waer' (weir) which has long restricted the flow, here, of the river Lee. Either this was a natural blockage or else an artificial dam built to create a fishing enclosure. In the Domesday Book the settlement was called Wara.

▓ WATFORD
The present spelling first appeared in AD 944, although subsequently it was known as Wathford (in the 12th century). Either the prefix derives from the Saxon word 'wath' (hunting) or it comes from the Scandinavian 'vath' (ford). If the former the place grew up at a fording point used by huntsmen, if the latter the place has a tautological name – not uncommon in English place-names. The ford here was over the river Colne.

▓ WELWYN
All the early versions of this name – Weligun (10th century), Wilge, Welge and Welga (11th century) – are close to the original derivation. This was 'welewen', the dative plural of the Saxon word 'welig': at the willow trees.

Kent

⬚ ASHFORD

Whereas the Ashford in Middlesex probably derives from Eccel's ford this one comes from 'aesc-sceat-ford': ford by the ash copse. In the 11th century it was Essetesford and Aescedesford. This whole area was once well timbered – the word Weald coming from the Saxon 'wald' for a woodland.

⬚ CANTERBURY

There was a settlement here in pre-Roman days which the Celts called Darovernon, or Dorovernia – from 'duro' for town or fort, and 'verno' for swamp with alder trees. Then, under the Roman occupation, the place was renamed Durovernum Cantiacorum, the addendum meaning 'coastland' or 'district by the shore'. The Romans called Kent 'Cantium' from the old word for a rim or edge – hence our modern county name. Finally, the Saxons arrived. They called the people of Kent the Cantware ('waru', dwellers) and their main town Cantwaraburg – 'burg' or 'burh' being stronghold. The present name, of course, derives from this.

⬚ CHATHAM

The original suffix in this name, 'mearc' – as found in Cethaemamearc recorded in AD 995 – was the Saxon word for a boundary. The rest of the name, spelt Ceteham in the Domesday Book, comes from the Celtic word 'ceto' or 'kaito' for a forest (similar to the Welsh 'coed') and the Saxon 'ham' for a homestead. Perhaps the original settlement was situated at the edge or boundary of a woodland. Neighbouring GILLINGHAM derives from Gylla-inga-ham: the 'homestead of Gylla's people'.

⬚ DEAL

The present name is very close to the original: 'dael' which was the Saxon word for valley, hollow or, as probably used in this case, low-lying area. The town stands on a flat part of the coastline. In the Domesday Book the place was called Addelam, the prefix coming from the Saxon preposition 'at' – at Delam. In the 12th century the spelling was the more recognisable Dela.

⬚ DOVER

This name is purely Celtic in origin – from 'dubro' or 'dobra' meaning stream or waters. The name was formerly, of course, applied only to the river here (now the Dour) which was once wide and navigable for some distance inland. The town was variously called Dubris, Dofras and Dobrum by the Saxons.

⬚ FAVERSHAM

This was Fefresham in AD 811 and Favreshant in the Domesday Book. It comes from the Saxon words 'faefer' (smith) and 'ham' (homestead). The place was clearly a forge or metalworker's house. To the north lies the ISLE OF SHEPPEY which was sheep island ('sceap-eg'), recorded as Sceapig in AD 832. Interestingly, in the south of the county, north of Rye, is the ISLE OF OXNEY: ox island ('oxa-eg').

▓ FOLKESTONE

This was once the centre for the 'hundred' in this part of Kent, and as such was the place where meetings or 'moots' were held. These were probably, in early times, assemblies around a marked or significant boulder. Why might we think this? Because the name here could mean folk's stone ('folc-stan'). It might, alternatively, mean 'Falca's Stone', from a personal name and referring to his boundary stone. In the Domesday Book the town is Fulchestan.

▓ GRAVESEND

This name has nothing to do with burials. It derives from the Saxon word 'grafe' for a woodland grove or brushwood thicket. In the Domesday Book it was Gravesham – the 'ham' (homestead) in the grove – and in 1157 it was Gravessend – the end of the grove.

▓ HYTHE

This name is still almost purely Saxon, from the word 'hyth' meaning a landing place. The present spelling first appeared before the Norman Conquest although, strangely, the Domesday Book records Hede. In the Middle Ages this was a thriving port. Along the coast is DYMCHURCH, another ancient settlement. In Saxon times this was the 'church of the judge' (from 'dema' or 'diuma' and 'chirche'), the place obviously having some legal function. In the 13th century it was Demecherche.

▓ LYDD

Although clearly Saxon, this name presents etymologists with a problem. The early spellings of Hlidum (8th century) and Hlide (11th century) suggest one of two derivations. Either it comes from 'hlith' (slope) or else from 'hlid' (gate). Since the village stands in a marshy area neither seems likely. Perhaps the original settlement stood on a sandy ridge above the marsh or else it was seen as the gateway to the countryside inland. Nearby DUNGENESS is, of course, the 'naess' (headland) of Denge or Dunge Marsh. There was once a district called Denge north of Ashford to which this marsh may have been linked in ownership. The Saxon 'den-ge' meant the valley district.

▓ MAIDSTONE

It is probably not true that this name, and the name of the river Medway on which it stands, have common origins. The town's name derives from 'maegden stan' (maiden stone) whilst the river's name derives from 'medu wey' (mead-coloured water). The former is Saxon, the latter is Celtic. Why young girls should determine a place-name is not known – perhaps they assembled at certain places (in this case, a stone) for religious or ritual reasons.

❖ RAMSGATE

Before the Norman Conquest this was called Remisgate and Remmesgate, derived from 'hraefn' (Saxon for raven) and 'geat' (Saxon for gate or, as likely here, a gap in the cliffs). Hraefn might have referred to a tribal leader's name, a bird-shaped rock or even to the bird itself. Nearby MARGATE derives from 'mere-geat', the prefix meaning pool or, perhaps sea.

❖ ROCHESTER

The Venerable Bede called this town Hrofaescaestre in the 8th century – the 'ceaster' (Roman fort) of Hrofi. It is thought that Hrofi was a shortened and corrupted form of the original Roman name for this settlement, Durobrivis – this coming from the Celtic words 'duro' (stronghold) and 'briva' (bridge). In the Domesday Book the name is Rovecestre.

❖ SANDWICH

This was a wic built on a sandy place. 'Wic' had various meanings in Saxon times – dairy farm, village, salt workings, market town and, most likely in this instance, landing-stage. The sand probably referred to the soils rather than to the beach. In AD 851 the place was called Sondwic, in 1086 Sandwice.

❖ TENTERDEN

This was the 'denn' (swine pasture) of the Tenetwaru (Thanet dwellers). The place was held by Minster, in Thanet, and used for grazing pigs. In 1179 it was called Tentwardene.

❖ TONBRIDGE

Either this derives from 'tun-brycg' (farmstead-bridge) or from Tunna's brycg. From Tonebrige in the Domesday Book and Thunne Brigge in 1230, it became Tunbridge by the 17th century. Then, however, it reverted to the earlier 'o' spelling in order to differentiate itself from nearby TUNBRIDGE WELLS. The latter was quickly developing around the newly-discovered health springs and beginning to cause a confusion of names.

❖ WHITSTABLE

Either this name derives from Hwita's 'stapol' (post, staple) or from 'hwit' (white) stapol. In any case, the post itself might have been a boundary marker, a meeting or moot post, or a landing stage mooring post. The name was Witenstaple in the Domesday Book of 1086.

Lancashire
(including Manchester & Liverpool)

▦ ACCRINGTON

From Akarinton in 1194 and Akerynton in 1258 it seems that this name most likely derives from 'aecern-tun': acorn farm or farmstead where acorns grow. The town stands on the edge of Rossendale Forest and might once have been the centre of a pig-rearing district.

▦ BACUP

This either comes from 'baec-hop' meaning ridge-valley or else from 'baece-hop' meaning stream-valley. The 1324 spelling Bacop does not suggest which of these might be correct but an earlier version of the name – Fulebachope in about 1200 – could suggest the latter derivation. 'Ful' was the Saxon for dirty, foul or muddy. Hence, the name could have meant 'dirty river valley'.

▦ BLACKPOOL

Some little way inland from the modern seafront was a dark, peaty lake called Le Pul or Pull up to the 16th century and Blacke-Poole in the 17th century. In the late 18th century it was drained to create meadowland, in the 19th century it was built over. But the name stuck. Meanwhile, up the coast, a certain local industrialist founded a new town (in 1836) as a trade and market centre. His name was Sir Peter Fleetwood and the seaside town still bears his surname.

▦ BOLTON

This name derives from two Saxon words, 'bothl' (sometimes spelled 'botl' or 'bold') meaning dwelling and 'tun' meaning farmstead. Two such apparently similar word meanings, put together, probably indicated a main residential settlement as opposed to an outlying farm. In the Domesday Book the place was called Bodeltun, and in the 12th century Botheltun.

▦ BOOTLE

Although called Boltelai in the Domesday Book, the present pronunciation is directly linked to the original form – 'botl', the Saxon word for dwelling or building. But this was not just any building. Botl was used for a special, unusually large or important building. What this actually was is still to be discovered.

▦ BURNLEY

It was the river here that gave this town its name – the 'leah (clearing or meadow) on the Brune'. In the 12th century it was Brunlaia and Brunley. The name of the river probably comes not from 'burna' (stream) but from the Saxon word 'brun' for brown – it was a muddy river. The other river here, the Calder is of Celtic origin – from 'caled' (violent) and 'dubro' (water).

▦ CLITHEROE

Etymologists once thought this came from Old Scandinavian 'klithra' meaning a song-thrush, but they now link it with the much older Celtic word 'clyder' or 'clither'. This meant heap of stones, which aptly describes the hillslope upon which Clitheroe Castle now stands. To this root later settlers added the Norse word 'haugr' or the Saxon word 'hoh' – meaning hill or spur. In the 12th century there were two versions of the name Cliderhou and Clitherow.

▦ DARWEN

This town takes its name directly from the river here, called the Derewent in 1208. Like other rivers called Derwent this came from the old Celtic 'derva' meaning oak: Derventio – 'the river where oak trees grow'. Downstream from Darwen is the town which was called Blacheburne in the Domesday Book and now BLACKBURN. This comes from the Saxon 'blaec-burna' – the dark-coloured stream. The river that meets the Darwen here is now called the Blackwater, as if to prove the place-name origin.

▦ FORMBY

This name is from purely Norse roots – either the 'by' (homestead, village) belonging to Forn (a Scandinavian personal name) or the 'by' which was 'forn' (old). In the Domesday Book it was Fornebei, in 1177 Fornebia. SOUTHPORT, along the coast, is a self-explanatory and recent name for an industrial town developed over the last 200 years.

▦ GARSTANG

This is a Viking name, deriving from the old Norse words 'geirr' (a spear) and 'stong' (a pole). Some historians believe a boundary mark could be the meaning here although the site of a fortification cannot be ruled out: the site being distinguished by a warlike post or monument. The name was Gairstang in the 12th century. A few miles to the north is GALGATE and it would be tempting to think this derives from 'galga' (Viking for gallows). However, records show this to be a later name: Galewethegate in the Middle Ages (the Galway Road). It stands on the old drove road from Scotland. The suffix is the Scandinavian 'gate' (road).

▦ LANCASTER

Spelled Loncaster in the Domesday Book and Lanecastrum in 1094 this was the 'ceaster' (Roman fort) on the river Lune. It is thought that this river name comes from the old Celtic word 'slan' meaning healthy or sound – perhaps because the waters here were found to be health-giving.

▦ LEYLAND

Originally this name would have been 'laege-land' – fallow or unploughed land, no doubt because the meadows either side of the river Lostock hereabouts were used for cattle grazing rather than for crops. In 1086 (in the Domesday Book) the place was called Lailand, a century later Leilandia.

▦ LITHERLAND
The old Norse word 'hlitharland', using the genitive form of the word 'hlith' (slope) meant land on a slope – a good description of the site of what became the village of Liderlant in the 11th century and Litherlande in the 13th century. The separate villages of Down Litherland and Uplitherland developed in the Middle Ages.

▦ LIVERPOOL
This comes from 'livered-pol', that is, a pool clogged with mud or weeds. The first element derived from the Saxon word 'lifrig', meaning clotted or coagulated (and hence the word liver for the organ of our body). The pool probably referred to a tidal creek now reclaimed. In 1194 the town was Liuerpul, in 1222 Litherpol. Any 'Liver Bird' story is just a legend.

▦ MANCHESTER
All the old forms of this name, from the Roman Mamucium to the Saxon Mameceaster (in AD 923) and Mamecestre (in the 1086 Domesday Book) include a prefix derived from the Celtic word 'mam' or 'mamme' meaning breast or mother (giving us the modern word mammary). Perhaps the first settlement built here was sited on, or near, a rounded, or bosom-shaped hill. The suffix, of course, comes from the Roman 'ceaster' for Roman fort.

▦ MORECAMBE
This name was invented in the late 18th century when the place began to be developed as a seaside resort. It deliberately reflected the name of the bay as mentioned by Ptolemy, the 2nd century Greek geographer – Morikambe. The original name was Poulton-Le-Sands.

▦ NELSON
This town grew up during the early part of the 19th century as the cotton industry expanded. It is so called because of the public house which formed its focal point – the Lord Nelson Inn, named in honour of the victor of Trafalgar in 1805. By contrast, nearby COLNE is a place-name of ancient origin. It comes from the Celtic river name 'Calne' or 'Calaun' meaning roaring stream.

▦ OLDHAM
This was not an 'old ham' (homestead) as might have been expected but an 'old holm'. The Saxon word 'holm' (Norse word 'holmr') was a small island, an area of dry land within a marsh, or a promontory surrounded by streams. Here, the latter was most likely, Oldham being sited on a spur at the edge of Saddleworth Moor. It is not known why the adjective 'old' was used – perhaps it referred to an Iron Age fort nearby. In the 13th century the town was Aldholm and Aldhulm.

▨ PRESTON
This town, Prescot and Prestatyn in Wales all have the same root – 'preosta' (priest). Here the 'tun' suffix (Prestune in the Domesday Book) gives us 'priest's farmstead'.

▨ RAMSBOTTOM
It has been suggested that the prefix here derives from the Saxon 'ramm' (ram) and referred either to the animal itself or to a ram-shaped rock. However, the alternative derivation – from the Saxon 'hramsa' (wild garlic or ramson) – is perhaps more likely, bearing in mind the fact that the suffix comes from 'bothm' meaning a valley. In 1324 the town was called Romesbothum.

▨ ROCHDALE
On the face of it this name seems to derive from the river – meaning, simply, the 'dale of the river Roch'. But the truth is more complicated. The river, once called the Rached, actually took its name from the settlement, which was listed in the 12th century as Rachedham. Earlier, in the Domesday Book (1086) this was Recedham. Whilst the suffix obviously came from 'ham' (homestead), the prefix had two alternative derivations. Either it came from the Saxon 'reced' (hall, manor house) or from the Celtic words 'rac' (against) and 'coet' or 'coed' (wood). The present suffix, from the Norse 'dalr' for a valley, first appeared in medieval times.

▨ STALYBRIDGE
During the Middle Ages this place was variously called Stavel, Stauelegh, Staveley and Stayley, all of which derived from the Saxon words 'staef' (stave or staff) and 'leah' (wood or clearing). Here was a woodland where staves were cut. The present suffix appeared later, after the bridge had been built to link two villages either side of the river Tame.

▨ STOCKPORT
Here the prefix comes from the Saxon word 'stoc' (place, dependent settlement, monastery or cell) and the suffix from the Saxon 'port' (in this instance meaning market town rather than harbour). It was Stokeport and Stokeporte in the 12th century. Curiously, one 13th century document refers to Stockford but this name did not survive. As yet, no evidence has been found of a Saxon monastery, so the name probably meant, simply, 'market place belonging to a dependent settlement'.

▨ STRETFORD
As with the place-name Stratford this comes directly from the Saxon 'straet-ford'. Here the Roman road (street) from Chester to Manchester crossed the river Mersey. The site of the old ford is where, appropriately, Crossford Bridge now stands. The present spelling of Stretford was first recorded in 1285.

▦ Warrington

This was called Walintune in the Domesday Book, suggesting a Saxon origin: Waer (a personal name), 'inga' (people) and 'tun' (farmstead) – hence the settlement of Waer's tribe. Downstream along the Mersey is WIDNES, which simply comes from 'wide ness' or 'wide promontory'. It was Wydnes in the 13th century.

▦ Whalley

Called Hwaelleage in AD 798 and Whalegh in 1246, the suffix here clearly comes from 'leah', Saxon for grove, wood or pasture. But there is a debate about the origin of the prefix – either from 'hwael' or from 'hwealf', Saxon words for hill and vault or arch respectively.

▦ Wigan

This was spelt the same in records of 1199 and is thought to be Celtic in origin, being the name of a Welsh person or tribe. There is a Wigan in Anglesey. This Lancastrian settlement might have been inhabited by people from that part of Wales. In 1245 it was Wigayn. Interestingly INCE-IN-MAKERFIELD, nearby, also has a Celtic name, deriving from 'ynys' (island) and 'magwyr' (ruin), to which was added the Saxon 'feld' (enclosure). Thus it was the island in Makerfield (field by the ruin), the latter being an old district of Lancashire established in the Dark Ages. It was Ins in Makerfeld in the 14th century.

Leicestershire & Rutland

▦ Castle Donington

The Norman castle was built here in the early Middle Ages, giving us Castel Donyngton in about 1428. Before that the village was simply Dunintone (1086) and Doninton (1125). Whilst the suffix is unquestionably derived from 'tun' (farmstead), the prefix has one of two possible origins. Either it comes from 'Dunna-inga' (the people of Dunna, a tribal leader) or from 'dun-inga' (the people on the hill).

▦ Clipsham

The prefix here could come from a personal name Cype but might, alternatively, derive from the Saxon word 'cylp' (or Norse word 'kylp') meaning a small, sturdy man. The suffix 'ham' refers to the homestead in which he lived. The settlement was Kilpesham in 1203 and Clyppesham in 1428.

▦ Cottesmore

This name was Cotesmore in the Domesday Book of 1086 and Cottesmor in 1228. Previously imagined to derive from a personal name Cott, it is now thought more likely to have come from 'cot' or 'cote' meaning cottage or sheep shelter. The 'mor' was a Saxon word for moor, fen, upland waste or high heathland – for the sort of countryside, in fact, suitable for sheep grazing.

▨ FLECKNEY

Early spellings, such as Flechenie in the 11th century and Fleckeneya in the 13th century, suggest a possible origin from the Saxon words 'fleca' (hurdle) and 'eg' (island or dry land). Thus it was a mound or dry area of land surrounded by hurdles forming a wooden fence. Nearby are the KIBWORTH villages. From Cybba's 'worth' (farm), one of these was held by Walter de Bellocampo and is now called BEAUCHAMP and the other was held by Robert de Harewecurt and is now called HARCOURT.

▨ HINCKLEY

This name is descended from 'Hynca's leah', the former being a Saxon personal name, the latter being a Saxon word for 'woodland, grove or clearing. In the Domesday Book it was Hinchelie, in 1176 Hinkelai.

▨ HUSBANDS BOSWORTH

In the Domesday Book this was simply called Baresworde, becoming Boreswurth in 1230. Whilst the suffix is evidently from 'worth' (enclosure), the prefix has one of two origins – 'bar' (wild boar) or 'Bare' (a personal name). The descriptive adjective arrived in the Middle Ages, a word used in the sense of 'husbandry' (farming or land management). This addendum was to distinguish this village from that some distance away to the north-west, MARKET BOSWORTH. The latter derives from Bossa's worth and was Boseworde in the Domesday Book. It became an important market town. A little way to the south is the site of the Battle of Bosworth Field (1485) which saw the death of Richard III and the end of the Wars of the Roses.

▨ KETTON

This name is likely to have derived from the river Chater, which flows through here and was once called the Cetan. Some etymologists link this to the area of Kesteven in Lincolnshire. Perhaps people from that part of eastern England settled along the valley here. In the Domesday Book the place was called Chetene, in the 12th century Chetena and Ketene.

▨ LEICESTER

It has been suggested that this name comes from 'Legionis Castra' – the camp of the legion. It does not. The town was a Roman settlement but it was called Ratae Coritanorum, the fortifications of the Coritani tribe. The present name goes back to Saxon times. From Legorensis Civitas (in the 9th century) it became Ligera Ceaster (in the 10th century). The river here was then called the Legra, or Ligor, and the dwellers either side were the 'Ligoran' folk. And so, from 'the town (later, the 'Roman camp') of the Ligorans' we eventually got the Domesday Book spelling of Ledecestre.

✳ LOUGHBOROUGH
The suffix in the Domesday Book version (Lucteburne) derives surprisingly not from 'burna' (stream) but from the Saxon 'burh' or 'burg' (fortified place). Evidently the Norman scribe made a mistake. A later spelling was more accurate: Luchteburc. The prefix comes from the personal name Luhhede.

✳ LUFFENHAM, NORTH & SOUTH
Lufenham, alone, was mentioned in the Domesday Book and it was not until the early 13th century that records show Norlufeham and Suthluffenhama as separate villages. This name is of Saxon origin, a personal name (Luffa) followed by 'halh' (nook or recess) and 'ham' (homestead): Luffa's village in a remote valley or hidden corner. The villages today stand either side of the river Chater, an old Celtic name (from 'ceto-dubron') meaning forest stream.

✳ LUTTERWORTH
It has been suggested that the river here, the Swift, was once called the Lutter or Lutre. If so, then it was a name which meant pure stream (from the Saxon word 'hluttor' for clean). The settlement was subsequently named after this river, with the addition of the word 'wyrth' meaning homestead or village. The Domesday Book spelling, Lutresurde, became Lutterwurth in 1242.

✳ MELTON MOWBRAY
The spelling found in the Domesday Book, Medeltone, looks as though the origin is from the Saxon 'middel' (Old Norse 'methal') and 'tun' – the middle farmstead. However, failure by researchers to find any evidence of what this settlement was between – the middle of what – has led some people to propose an alternative derivation: from 'mael-tun' – mill farm. In the early 12th century the estate came into the ownership of Roger de Moubray (from Montbray in Normandy) thus giving the present affix.

✳ OAKHAM
This name derives not from 'ac' (Saxon for oak tree) but from the personal name Occa; not from 'ham' (Saxon for homestead) but from 'hamm' (Saxon for meadow or pasture enclosure). It was Ocham and Ocheham in the 11th century.

✳ QUORNDON
This village name – often written as 'Quorn' – derives not from 'quarrere' (quarry) but from 'cweorn', the Saxon word for millstone. Not that quarry would have been that erroneous in meaning, since this was probably a place where millstones were quarried. The suffix comes from 'dun' for hill. The name has not changed much over the years – it was Querendon in 1209 and Querondon in the 13th century.

✳ TICKENCOTE
The Saxon word 'ticce' or 'ticcen', for kid (a young goat) often became 'tichen' under Norman influence. It did here, for the Domesday Book version of this

place-name was Tichecote. The suffix 'cot' or 'cote' meant cottage, or – as it probably did with this name – animal shelter. The possibility that this settlement derives its name, instead, from 'Triccea's Cottage' has also been floated, but with less conviction.

UPPINGHAM

This name meant homestead or village of the hill people from 'ham' and 'yppingas'. The Saxon word 'yppe' meant look-out place as well as hill and Castle Hill just west of the town centre would have provided an excellent spot for such a place. The earliest recorded spelling of this name was in 1607 – Yppingeham

WANLIP

The old versions of this name – Anelepe, Anlepia and Anelep in the early Middle Ages – were very close to the word from which the name derives – 'anliepe'. This was Saxon for isolated. The original village stood alone in a broad swampland, to be reached only by way of a causeway, stepping stones or narrow footbridge.

Lincolnshire

BOSTON

The famous 'Stump' church here is St Botolph's and it is thought that this dedication could have given the town its name – 'Botolph's stone', possibly referring to a preaching cross, or even to a stone building or chapel. However, it could also be that the name has nothing to do with this particular 7th century saint, and that it derives from 'Botwulf's stan', the former being a tribal leader (nicknamed 'commanding wolf') and the latter being a boundary stone. Early versions of the name include Botuleustan and Botolfston (in the 12th century).

BRIGG

An early record of this name was in 1183 when it was called Glanford, descended from the Saxon words 'gleam' (revelry, merriment) and 'ford' – hence 'the ford where sports or games were held'. Later this became Glanford Brigg (in 1235), as a result of a bridge (Saxon, 'brycg') being built across the river Ancholme here. Subsequently the main part of the name was dropped.

GAINSBOROUGH

This place was originally built as a 'burh' (fortified place) by Sweyn Forkbeard in the early 11th century, to be used as a temporary headquarters. He was the King of Denmark and father to the famous Canute. The personal name which has given us the modern prefix was Gegn (possibly a shortened form of Gaenbeald), who might well have been one of Sweyn's local commanders. In the Domesday Book the town was listed as Gainesurg.

▦ GRANTHAM

In the 11th century this town had various spellings – Grandham, Granham and Graham as well as the present one. The name derives either from a personal name Granta, or from the Saxon word 'grand' (or Norse 'grandi') meaning gravel – since the settlement does stand on the sandy banks of the river Witham. The 'ham', of course, was Saxon for homestead or village.

▦ GRIMSBY

This was Grimesbi in the Domesday Book – 'by' (village) belonging to Grim. There is a theory that this personal name might have referred to Grimr another name for the ancient god of the dead Odin, otherwise known as Woden. In legend this god frequently disguised his appearance – thus producing the old Saxon word 'grima' meaning a mask. Neighbouring CLEETHORPES derives its name from the collective term 'the thorpes of Clee'. Clee (from the Saxon 'claeg' for clay) was a small place just inland from the Humber shore, and 'thorp' was the Saxon word for farmstead or outlying farm (similar to the Danish 'throp)'. Thus there was a group of farms hereabouts belonging to Clee village. Old Clee is now a Cleethorpes suburb.

▦ HORNCASTLE

Here the suffix does not come from 'castel' but from 'ceaster' (meaning a Roman fort, from the Latin 'castra'). In fact, the Roman name for this place was Banovallum, being on the river Bain, and some remains of its old walls can still be seen. The prefix comes from the Saxon 'horna' (tongue of land): the fort on a spur. The site is between two rivers. In the Domesday Book the spelling was Hornecastre.

▦ INGOLDMELLS

Originally this would have been Ingiald's sand-bank, the first part being a personal name and the suffix deriving from the Viking word 'melr'. Early spellings including Guldelsmere (Domesday Book) and Ingoldesmeles (1180). Interestingly the same personal name is found many miles away near Grantham: INGOLDSBY. This would have been Ingiald's by (village). This was Ingoldesbi in the Domesday Book.

▦ LINCOLN

Ptolemy, the 2nd century Greek geographer, called this place Lindon which was exactly the old Celtic word for a lake (cognate with the Welsh 'llyn'). The name probably referred to the widening of the river Withan here. Then the Romans built a settlement for retired soldiers and called it a colonia. And so the town became known as Lindocolina by the 8th century (as recorded by Bede). In the Domesday Book it was Lincolia, from which it has changed little.

▦ LOUTH

In AD 790 this was Hludensis Monasterium – for a monastery had been founded here – but later, in the Domesday Book, it was simply called Lude. This came from the river Lud, named 'the loud one' (from the Saxon word 'hlude').

MABLETHORPE
This was the 'thorp' or 'trop' (outlying farmstead) belonging to a person called Malbert, who probably came to England with the Conqueror. There are several such names hereabouts – Donisthorpe (Durand's thorp) and Herringthorpe (Heryng's thorp) for example.

MARKET RASEN
At the time of the Domesday Book in the 11th century there was just Rase or Rasa, a single village with a name derived from the Saxon 'raesn' for a plank – probably referring to a plank bridge. Later, however, three villages appeared: Est, Media and West Rasa were mentioned in the 13th century. These are now Market, Middle and West Rasen respectively. The river Rase was named from the villages, as a back formation.

PINCHBECK
Early spellings show Pincebec (Domesday Book) and Pinchebech (1183). The suffix comes from an original Saxon word 'baece' which was altered by the Vikings into 'bekkr' – both meaning stream. There is a debate, however, about the origin of the prefix. This comes either from 'pinca' or 'penk', Saxon words for finch and minnow respectively. Both are possible – the area was rich in wildlife, all the rivers here being much wider in the past than they are today.

SCUNTHORPE
This town grew rapidly in the 19th century when the nearby iron-ore deposits were exploited, but the name goes back to Danish times. It was called Escumetorp in 1086 (in the Domesday Book) and Scuntorp in 1245 – derived from Skuma's thorp – the outlying settlement belonging to Skuma.

SKEGNESS
Skegenesse (1166) and Skegenes (1256) derived from skeggi-nes. Either this was the ness (headland) belonging to a person called Skeggi, or it was the 'bearded headland' – possibly referring to a beard-shaped sandspit eroded by the tides.

SLEAFORD
This was the ford over the river Slea, called Slioford in AD 852, Eslaforde in the Domesday Book and Sliforde in about 1200. The river name here can be traced back to the Saxon words 'sliow', 'sleow', 'sliw' and 'slim', all used variously to mean muddy, slimy or trench-like – cognate with the word 'sloh' (slough).

SPALDING
This name comes from 'spald-ingas', the descendants or people of the Spaldas tribe, who once lived in this district. Their name, it is thought, derived from a local 'spald' (cleft, trench or ditch) – perhaps a reference to the old Roman canal called the Car Dyke. In the 12th century the town was called Spaldingis.

WASHINGBOROUGH

There are three district elements to this name, all of which are purely Saxon. 'Waesc' meant a whirlpool, 'inga' meant people and 'burh' meant fortified place. So this would have been the 'fort of the tribe at the whirlpool', the latter feature probably referring to the confluence of the river Witham and one of its tributaries. In the Domesday Book the name was Washingeburg.

Middlesex &
Greater London

BATTERSEA

This was recorded as Batriceseg in AD 693 and Patricesy in the Domesday Book, demonstrating how the letters 'b' and 'p' were often interchangeable in earlier times. With a suffix from 'eg', this name was thus Baduric's island or even Patric's island. Nearby CLAPHAM (Clopeham in the Domesday Book) derives from the Saxon words 'clop-ham' (hillock-homestead). The village evidently was sited on a small rise above the Thames floodplain.

CAMBERWELL

Here the origin for the suffix is clearly the Saxon 'wella' (spring or well) but the origin for the prefix is less obvious. Some etymologists think it comes from 'cran' (crane or heron), others suggest 'camb' (comb or crest) or 'cam' (a Celtic word for crooked). The settlement was Cambrewelle in the Domesday Book. Neighbouring PECKHAM derives from the Saxon 'peac-ham' (hilltop-homestead) and was Pecheham in the Domesday Book.

CHELSEA

From Cealchyp in AD 785 and Chelched in the Domesday Book, this name can be traced back to the Saxon words 'calc' or 'cealc' (chalk or limestone) and 'hythe' or 'hyth' (landing stage, wharf). Either there was a landing stage here built on an outcrop of chalk or the quay dealt in the limestone trade – lime being an important fertiliser.

CHISWICK

Although it is generally believed that this name comes from the Saxon 'cese-wic' (cheese farm), it has also been suggested that it might, alternatively, derive from 'ceosol' or 'cisel-wic' (sand or beach farm). The latter would refer to the gravel on the Thames riverbank. In the Domesday Book it was Ceswica.

CRICKLEWOOD

The earliest record for this name dates from 1294, when it was Le Crickeldwode, evidently the Norman French version of the original 'cruc-hyll-wudu'. The first two elements are an example of tautology, both meaning hill (the former being Celtic, the latter Saxon). The third element is Saxon for wood. Neighbouring HENDON comes from 'hind-dun' (high hill) and NEASDEN from 'nese-dun' (nose-shaped hill).

▓ ENFIELD

This comes from Enna's or Eana's Feld – 'the clearing belonging to Enna' – and not from the Saxon word 'ened' or 'aened' for a duck. In the Domesday Book it was called Enefelde. This area was well-wooded up to quite recent times, as indicated by such other names as Hadley Wood, Oakwood and Wood Green.

▓ FELTHAM

Before the Domesday Book, when it was Felteha, this had the same spelling as it does today (As recorded in a document of AD 969). Some say this is simply a form of 'feld-ham' (open land-homestead) but others think it derives from an old Saxon word 'felt' (as found in 'feltwurma', wild marjoram, and 'feltwyrt', wild mullein). Hence, this might have been a homestead where some kind of wild herb grew.

▓ FINCHLEY

The surname 'Finch' has been known in England since the 11th century and so this name could derive from the 'leah' (grove) belonging to a man called Finch. Otherwise it was 'finc leah' – the woodland where finches nested. These birds were eaten in early times. In the 13th century the area was called Finchlee or Fynchesl.

▓ HAMMERSMITH

First recorded in the 14th century as Hameresmythe, the origin here may be exactly as it sounds. Where the metal-worker's shop or forge stood has not been found however. Neighbouring FULHAM was Fulla's ham (meadow).

▓ HARROW

This is thought to have been the site of one of the most important pagan centres in Saxon England. The name comes from the word 'hearg', Saxon for heathen temple. Before the Domesday Book version (Herges) it was Hearge (in AD 825) but before that it was Gumeninga Hergae (in AD 767), which incorporated the Gumens tribe (Guma's people). The temple probably stood on top of the hill. The addendum 'on-the-Hill' appeared in the 14th century. HARROW WEALD (Waldis in Harwes in 1303) uses the root word 'wald', Saxon for forest.

▓ HAYES

This was Haese in AD 831 and Hesa in the Domesday Book – both clearly linked to the Saxon word 'hees', 'hese' or 'haes', variously used to mean brushwood, underwood or a young oak and beech woodland. But the early name of Lingahaese, found in AD 793, has a prefix which still baffles etymologists. Some say it was merely a corruption of 'hlinc', meaning a hill.

✳ HILLINGDON

The central, syllable here is misleading, for it does not come from the Saxon 'inga' (people of). It was merely introduced during the Middle Ages to help pronunciation. The early forms of the name were Hillendone (in the Domesday Book) and Hildedun (in about 1078), these coming from Hilda's dun (hill). Hilda was a man's name, possibly a shortened form of Hildric (war ruler) or Hildwulf (war wolf).

✳ HOLBORN

The Holeburne of the Domesday Book derived from the Saxon 'holh' (hollow) and 'burna' (brook). The original stream here, a river Fleet tributary, flowed through a narrow valley, now followed by Farringdon Street. The Holborn Viaduct crosses over it.

✳ KENSINGTON

This was Chenist or Chenesitun in the Domesday Book and Kensiton in about 1221, all descended from 'Cynesige-inga-tun': the farmstead of Cynesige's people. Nearby NOTTING HILL has a more recent origin, dating from the 14th century when it was Knottynghull and Knottyngwode. These were probably descended from a family called Knotting (perhaps from Knotting in Bedfordshire) which lived in the area.

✳ KILBURN

This was Keneburne in the 12th century – from 'cylen' (kiln) and 'burna' (stream). Whether this referred to a pottery kiln or to a lime kiln is not known. Nearby MAIDA VALE grew up originally around a tavern called 'The Hero of Maida' named after the 1806 Battle of Maida, in southern Italy, where the British beat the French during the Napoleonic Wars.

✳ MARYLEBONE

The village here was originally called Tyburn, from 'teo-burna' meaning boundary stream. But in the early 15th century the inhabitants asked their manorial owner, the Bishop of London, for permission to change the village name, such was Tyburn's bad reputation for thieves, crime and the famous gallows. Request granted, the village became Maryborne, after the local church. The 'Le' was added later.

✳ OSTERLEY

Here the prefix probably descends from the Saxon word 'ost' for a knot or knob, used in this case to mean a hillock, and the suffix is from 'leah', woodland clearing. The place was Osterlye in the 1294 and Osturle in 1375.

✳ PADDINGTON

This was the 'tun' (farmstead) of Padda's people, otherwise the family estate ('ingtun') of Padda or Paeda. It was Padintun in AD 959 and Padinton in 1168.

North-west of here is KENSAL GREEN (from Kings-holte-grene the green in the King's wood) close to which is WORMWOOD SCRUBBS, descended from the Saxon Wermeholte, being 'wyrm' (worm, serpent), 'holt' (wood) and an appendage from scrub (brushwood).

▒ PERIVALE
This name, called Pyryvale in 1508, replaced the earlier Greneforde. The district was once famous for its orchards and 'pirie', or 'pyrige,' was the Saxon word for a pear tree.

▒ PIMLICO
There is probably no truth in the story that this name is taken from a Red Indian tribe, living in the Appalachian Mountains of North America, which exported timber to London in the 17th century. More likely is that this district is named after Ben Pimlico, a local publican (originally from Hoxton) who once set up a tavern and brewery here. The area was called Pimlico in 1630.

▒ PINNER
Called Pinnora and Pinora in the 13th century, this name can be traced back to the Saxon words 'pinn' (peg, pin) and 'ora' (slope, edge, margin). The pin-shaped bank could have been the humped ridge which still crosses Pinner Park.

▒ RUISLIP
Called Rislepe in the Domesday Book, this either comes from 'rysc-hylpe' or from 'rysc-slaep'. Both were Saxon, the first meant rushy leap or crossing point, the second meant rushy slope – that is, a slippery slope with rushes.

▒ SOHO
In the Middle Ages this area was called St Giles Fields, being the open space around St Giles Hospital. But Henry VIII, in 1539, closed that hospital and turned the area into a Royal Hunting Park. The present name – first used in 1632 – derives from the traditional hunting cry So-Ho, used in hare hunting (like Tally-Ho in fox hunting).

▒ STANMORE
This name has changed little over the years, but has changed significantly. It was Stanmere in both AD 793 and in the 1086 Domesday Book. This tells us that it derives from 'stan-mere' (gravel lake or pond) and not from 'stan-more' (gravel waste or moorland). The area is low-lying and many pools still survive.

▒ STOKE NEWINGTON
This could have been the new village ('niewe tun') made out of logs ('stoccen'). It was called Stokene Neuton in 1294. Perhaps it was an 'overspill' settlement for neighbouring ISLINGTON – Gisla's dun (hill), which was Gislandune in the 10th century.

▨ TOTTENHAM

This derives either from the 'ham' (village) belonging to Totta or – more interestingly – from 'toot' or 'tot', the Saxon for a look-out post. The 'High Cross' here stands on the old Ermine Street. In 1086 it was Toteham.

▨ TWICKENHAM

The suffix here probably derives not from 'ham' (homestead) but from 'hamm' (meadow) for the place stands on the edge of the River Thames. The prefix could either have been Twicca, a personal name, or 'twicce' (twicene), a fork or confluence. This 'meadow by the river junction' was Tuican Ham in AD 704 and Twikeham in 1216.

▨ UXBRIDGE

There are many early spellings for this name. In the 13th century alone we find Uxebregg, Woxebruge and Wuxebrug; previously it was Oxebruge (12th century) and subsequently Wooxbryge (16th century). The present spelling was first used in 1398. All these are linked to the old Saxon tribe called the Wixan, which is thought to have lived, mainly, in the Midlands. Here members of that tribe settled close to a 'brycg' (bridge) over the river Colne.

▨ WALWORTH

This was Wealawyrth in the 11th century, probably coming from 'walh' (Briton or serf) and 'worth' (enclosure or homestead). When the Saxon invaders settled in England the native Celts did not all move to the western hills of Britain as supposed; many remained and became 'second-class citizens'. Neighbouring LAMBETH was Lamhytha in the 11th century, from 'lambru-hythe' (lambs-landing place).

▨ WEMBLEY

The original Wemba's leah (grove) became Wambeleg in 1249. Wemba might have been King Wamba, the Saxon monarch whose name came from the word for a womb, perhaps due to his unnatural birth.

Norfolk

▨ BLAKENEY

Before the 13th century this place was called Snitterley or - as the Domesday Book lists it – Snuterlea. This derived from Snytra's 'leah' (woodland clearing or grove). Since the 13th century, however, the present name has developed, first as Blakenye and then as Blakene. This was taken from the 'eg' (island) of higher land which rises above the marshes behind the seafront. Either this dry spot was owned by a person called Blaca or was called 'blaec' (black) because of its dark vegetation.

❋ CAISTER-ON-SEA

This name comes directly from the Saxon word 'ceaster', which itself was a corruption of the Latin 'castra' meaning Roman fort. Indeed, the name was actually spelt Castra in the Domesday Book, before becoming Castre in the 12th century. The addition of 'on-Sea' is fairly recent (as is the name Caister-next-Yarmouth) in order to distinguish this place from Caister St Edmunds, near Norwich, which once belonged to the Abbey at Bury St Edmunds. Incidentally, it is thought this latter village could have been the Roman camp of Venta Icenorum, named after the local Iceni tribe to which Queen Boudicca belonged.

❋ CROMER

The 13th century version of this name, Crowemere, gives a good indication of the origin – 'crawe-mere': the mere or lake where crows gathered. The area was once very marshy, with sandbanks and lagoons at the shoreline.

❋ DOWNHAM MARKET

Called simply Dunham under the Saxons – literally hill homestead – this settlement was turned into an important market town by the Normans. By 1110 it had become Forum de Dunham, by 1130 Mercatus de Dunham. The Latin was replaced by the English word 'market' sometime in the Middle Ages.

❋ EAST DEREHAM

This was simply called Derham in the Domesday Book of 1086, a name from 'deor' (deer) and 'hamm' (meadow or pasture). Large areas of Norfolk were used for stag hunting in Saxon times, and many names exist to indicate this. Here, the distinguishing adjectives 'East' and 'West' appeared in the 13th century.

❋ GREAT YARMOUTH

The river here has not always been called the Yare. The Greek geographer Ptolemy called it the Gariennos in the 2nd century, and it was the Gerne in the 12th century. This was from a Celtic root – 'ger' meaning roaring and cognate with the Welsh 'gair' for shout. Thus, the river name meant 'loud waters', possibly due to the sound of the waves. The town was sited at the 'muth' (mouth) of this river and so was called Gernemuta in the 13th century. The word 'Great', as well as 'Little' (applied to the place now called 'Southtown'), appeared in the Middle Ages.

❋ HETHERSETT

The Domesday Book spelling (Hederseta) suggests a derivation from 'heahdeor' (stag) and 'set' or 'geset' (fold, place where animals are kept). The Saxons certainly hunted deer and could possibly have reared them also. To the west is CARLETON FOREHOE which was the 'tun' (manor, homestead) of a 'ceorl' (free peasant or villein) next to the Forehoe Hills. Forehoe was the Saxon for four hills.

⌘ HUNSTANTON

The suffix 'tun' (farmstead) was added to a personal name like Hunstan to produce Hunstanestun in the 11th century. If, instead, it had been added to 'hunta' (huntsman) and 'stan' (stone) then the derivation of this settlement might have been linked, in meaning, to that of East Dereham. Perhaps Hunstan came from a hunting background.

⌘ KINGS LYNN

The word Lynn in this name (called Lena, Lun and Linna in the 11th and 12th centuries) is similar to the Welsh word 'llyn' and has the same derivation – from the Celtic 'lindon' or 'lyndo' meaning a lake or pool. Here it probably referred to one of the many ponds and meres which once characterised the marshlands around the Great Ouse river. Since more than one Lynn settlement appeared, distinguishing adjectives developed during the Middle Ages: 'North', 'South', 'West' and – in this case – 'Kings', so called because Henry VIII held the manor here in the 16th century.

⌘ METHWOLD

'Wald', which later developed as 'wold' (as in this case), 'walt' and 'weald', had various meanings in Saxon times – forest, sparse woodland, upland heath, even hill. Here in the Fens it probably meant open wasteland. The prefix comes from the Saxon 'middel', changed by the Danes to 'methal', meaning middle. Not far away is Northwold.

⌘ NORWICH

This was the north wic in comparison with Gipe's wic (Ipswich) some way to the south. The word 'wic' was used by the Saxons to mean village, dairy farm, market town or landing place. As with Ipswich the last named could be the derivation here, since the town stands on the river Wensum and Yare and was once a river-port. In about AD 930 it was Northwic, in the Domesday Book Noruic.

⌘ SHERINGHAM

Silingeham (in the Domesday Book) and Scheringham (in 1242) can be traced back to 'Scira-inga-ham': the homestead of Scira's people. The earlier version perhaps indicates that, at first, the Normans found the letter 'r' difficult to pronounce – thus supplementing an 'l'.

⌘ SPIXWORTH

Being spelt Spikesuurda in the Domesday Book and Spicheswrtha 200 years later, this name derives from Spic's worth. Either this was the homestead of someone called Spic or the place was a bacon farm – that is, a pig-rearing establishment. This area was evidently a region of animal husbandry: further north is HORSTEAD (Horsteda in the Domesday Book), a place where horses were kept.

TAVERHAM

This derives from the Saxon words 'teafor' and 'ham'. The former meant red pigment or vermilion and in this instance was probably used to mean red earth; or red-stained earth. Thus it was the red soil ham (farmstead). The spelling has changed little over the years, being Tauerham in the 12th century. Nearby is the interesting name of DRAYTON which comes from the 'tun' (manor) of the 'draeg' (portage: a place where boats or goods have to be dragged overland). This was Draituna in the Domesday Book.

THETFORD

The earliest spelling Theodford (in AD 870) was the exact Saxon form which meant 'ford of the people or masses'. Such a name probably indicated a wide and very important crossing point. It was Tedfort in the Domesday Book.

WELLS-NEXT-THE-SEA

The original form ('wella' for a stream) and the 1291 spelling (Wellis) are Saxon, but in 11th century documents we find Guelle and Guella. This shows that the Normans often supplemented 'gu' for 'w', which they found easier to pronounce. The springs along this coastline come out from the sand dunes.

WYMONDHAM

This is one of many Norfolk villages whose name consists of 'ham' (village) preceded by a person's name, in this instance Wigmund. Others include AYLSHAM, from Aegel, FAKENHAM from Facca, and WALSINGHAM from Waels. SWAFFHAM comes from a tribal name – the Swaefas.

Northamptonshire

BRACKLEY

This derives from a personal name, Bracca or Breahha, and the Saxon word 'leah' for woodland grove, glade or clearing. In the Domesday Book of 1086 it was recorded as Brachelai.

BRIGSTOCK

The prefix here clearly comes from 'brycg', Saxon for a bridge, but the origin of the suffix is more debatable. Either it comes from 'stoc', Saxon for a monastery, cell or holy place, or from 'stocc', Saxon for log, stock or pile. If the latter the whole name might refer to an old wooden bridge here, made of tree-trunks. In the 11th century the spellings included Bricstoc and Brichestoc.

CORBY

A purely Danish place-name this, deriving from Kori's 'by' (farmstead). We do not know who Kori was but he might have had an extensive district under his control, for there is a village in Lincolnshire, near Stamford, also called Corby. The name has changed little over the years – it was Corebi and Corbei in the 11th century and Coreby in the 12th century.

⊞ DAVENTRY
Despite popular imagination this name neither comes from 'dwy-afon-tre' (Celtic for house of two rivers) nor from Dane's tree (suggesting Norse origins). Whilst the tree might be correct – from 'treow' – the prefix is Saxon. It comes from Dafa or Daver, a personal name, a stream name, or a word meaning fitting. The tree might have been a religious marker, a wooden cross, or a boundary mark. The Domesday Book records the town as Daventrei.

⊞ FLORE
Spelled Flora in the Domesday Book and Floure in 1330, this derives either from the Latin 'flora' (flowers) or from the Saxon 'flor' (floor). The former might have indicated the fertile nature of the soils here, the latter could have referred to an old Roman tessellated pavement once uncovered nearby.

⊞ FOTHERINGAY
There are three possible origins to this name. Either it comes from 'Frod-inga-eg' (the island of Froda's people), or from 'forth-here-inga' (the people following an army leader) or else from 'fodring-eg' (foddering island). Certainly the village stands up above the meadows here, and has excellent grazing land, so the last option might be the most likely. In the Domesday Book the name was Fodringeia.

⊞ HIGHAM FERRERS
In the 11th century this was Hehham and Hecham, derived from the Saxon words 'heah' (high) and 'ham' (homestead). In the mid-12th century the manor passed to the Comes (Count) de Ferariis and by 1279 the place was called Heccham Ferrar. Neighbouring RUSHDEN probably comes from 'rysc-dun': rush hill.

⊞ IRTHLINGBOROUGH
This has changed little since AD 780 when it was Yrtlingaburg. This meant, literally, 'ploughman's burh' (fortified place). Perhaps there was an old fort here used for sheltering oxen and storing ploughshares.

⊞ KETTERING
The origin of this name continues to puzzle experts. Most likely it comes from a personal name, Cytra perhaps, and 'inga' meaning people. But an ancient Celtic root cannot be ruled out. In AD 956 it was Cytringan; in the Domesday Book Cateringe.

⊞ NORTHAMPTON
The spelling Hamtun in AD 917 was a word used by the Saxons to mean a main farm, or a chief manor in a district, cognate with the word 'haematun' which meant

home farmstead. By the 11th century, however, this had become Northhamtun and Northantone, the prefix used to distinguish the town from Southampton, to which it was linked by an old routeway.

▥ OUNDLE

All the old versions – Undolum (8th century), Undelum (10th century) and Undele (11th century) – were taken from the name of the tribe that once lived in this area. The word 'dal' was Saxon for a share, portion or division of land, so the Undals were either those people dispossessed of their territory or else those who took over districts not given to other tribes – that is, the undivided lands. From 'dal' we get the modern word dole.

▥ RAUNDS

This comes not from the old East Anglian dialectic word 'rond' (marshy river bank) but from the plural of the Saxon word 'rand' (border, edge, margin). The town was built close to where three counties met – Northamptonshire, Huntingdonshire and Bedfordshire. In the 10th century it was Randan, in the Domesday Book Rande.

▥ ROTHWELL

The earliest spellings – Rothewelle and Rodewelle – suggest a derivation from 'rothu' or 'rod' (meaning clearing) and 'wella' or 'wiell' (meaning spring). The suggestion that it comes, instead, from red-spring ('read-wella') is not supported by etymology, despite the reddish colour of the local limestone.

▥ SILVERSTONE

The Domesday Book spelling, Silvestone, suggests a simple derivation from Siulf's tun: the homestead of someone with the shortened form of the Saxon name Sigewulfe. The 1484 spelling, Sylson, is similar to the local pronunciation of the name today. Some historians have suggested that the prefix derives from 'silvre' (silvery or sunny) but there is little etymological evidence for this. Nearby SYRESHAM is named from another Saxon tribal leader – Sigehere's ham (village). This was Sigresham in the Domesday Book.

▥ STOKE BRUERNE

This was Stoche (in 1086) and Stokes (in 1220) but became Stokebruere in the 13th century to distinguish this place from other Stoke villages. The manor came under the ownership of William Briwerre. Stoke is a common element in Saxon place-names, deriving either from 'stoc' (religious place) or 'stocc' (trunk or log). Since this settlement was on the edge of Whittlewood Forest the latter meaning is more likely. STOKE ALBANY was a manor held by William de Albini in the 12th century and was probably a religious site since it stood near Pipewell Abbey. STOKE DOYLE was held by John de Oyly in the 13th century. This was in a wooded area near the once religious town of Oundle so the stoke here could have either derivation.

THRAPSTON

There were many early spellings here, including Trapestone (1086), Trapston (1202) and Tharpston (1533). It is probable that it was the 'tun' (farmstead) belonging to a person called Trapsta or Draefst – the letters 't' and 'd' being almost interchangeable in Saxon and Viking times. The village of ISLIP, across the river Nene, was called Hyslepe in the Domesday Book, deriving possibly from 'hyse' (warrior) and 'slaep' (slippery place). The present spelling could have arisen because this part of the Nene was once called the Ise.

WELLINGBOROUGH

The original Wendel's 'burg' ('burh' or fortified place) became Wendleberie and Wedlingeberie in the 11th century. The central syllable comes from the Saxon 'inga' meaning the people of.

Northumberland & Tyneside & Wearside

ALNWICK

This was the 'wic' (dwelling) on the Aln, the latter being a Celtic river name possibly derived from the old word 'gwyn' meaning white. The name was Alnewich in 1178. Downstream is ALNMOUTH (Alnemuth in 1201) which is self-explanatory. Nearby DENWICK is from 'denu-wic' (valley-dwelling). This was Denewyc in the 13th century.

AMBLE

In 1204 the spelling was Ambell, probably coming from Anna's bill (promontory). Anna may sound female but the 'a' ending in Saxon times was often found in male names, as in Kings Offa and Penda. 'Bill' for headland is found elsewhere, such as the south coast of England at Selsey and Portland.

BAMBURGH

This 'burg' or 'burh' (fortified place) was built in the 6th century by King Ida and acquired its name from Queen Bebba, who was the wife of Aethelfrith, King of Northumbria from AD 593 to AD 617. In the Domesday Book (1086) it was Baenburg.

BERWICK-UPON-TWEED

This site was occupied in Saxon times by a 'berewic' or barley farm. By the 12th century this had grown into a small town called Berewich. The river on which it stands was called Touesis by the Greek geographer Ptolemy in the 2nd century, Tuidi in the 8th century and Tuede in the 9th century. From a Celtic root word 'teva' (to swell) this name meant swelling river. The word 'berewic', incidentally, did not always mean a barley farm. It was often used also to mean an outlying or secondary farmstead, as in the case of Borwick in Lancashire.

▓ BLAYDON

There are three possible origins to this name. Either it comes from the river Blaydon Burn, which itself could have a Celtic root whose meaning has been lost. Or it comes from the Saxon 'blaw-dun', the hill where a blue pigment like woad was obtained. Or it comes from 'blaec-dun', black hill. Perhaps the last option, the simplest, is the most likely. In 1340 the place was called Bladon.

▓ CRAMLINGON

Interestingly, the middle element here probably does not come from 'inga' (people) as normally found. The 13th century spelling Cramelington might suggest the derivation is 'cran-wella-tun' (crane's spring homestead). Nearby BEDLINGTON has the more obvious origin, from 'Bedla-inga-tun' (the farm of Bedla's people). It was Bedlingtun in the 9th century.

▓ FELLING

This name has changed little, being Fellyng in the 13th century. It comes from either 'felling' (clearing) or 'faelging' (newly cultivated land) – thus meaning an area recently felled. Nearby HEBBURN was Heberne in the Middle Ages, from 'hea-byrgen' (high-burial mound).

▓ GATESHEAD

Ninth century records show a spelling of Raegeheafde, this becoming Gateshaped in the 12th century. Clearly it meant goats hill, the prefix coming from the Viking 'geit' or Saxon 'gat' (wild goat) and 'heafod' (Saxon for summit). Some historians, possibly taking their lead from the Venerable Bede, suggest that this was the site of a pagan festival involving the decapitation of goats and other animals. This has not been proved, however. Bede's own town JARROW has a name from the Saxon tribe the Gyrwe, which itself derived from the word 'gyr' meaning mud or fen. The main centre for the Gyrwe tribe in the Dark Ages was in the Fens near Peterborough, so one part of that group may have migrated to the North-East. The place was Jarum in the 12th century.

▓ HALTWHISTLE

This settlement stands near the confluence of the rivers Cow and South Tyne, a fact which has provided the second half of its name, which comes from 'twisla' meaning fork or river junction. The first half is a corruption either of 'haut' (old French for high) or – more likely – of 'heafod' (Saxon for hill). In the 13th century the place was called Hawtewysill.

▓ HEXHAM

The length of this name has been much reduced over the centuries – from Hagustaldes Ea and Hagustaldes Ham in the 7th century, and Hextoldesham in the

12th century. In the older versions 'ea' meant stream and 'ham' meant homestead, but the main part of the name came from 'gehaeg-stealdan' meaning, literally, enclosure-occupation. In Saxon times a 'hagusteald' was a word used for a warrior or bachelor, and specifically for a younger son who, not inheriting his father's estate, was allowed to set up his own farming settlement outside the village.

▦ LINDISFARNE

This, an alternative name for Holy Island, is derived from 'Lindis' and 'faran'. The former was an old name for northern Lincolnshire (Lindsey) and the latter was Saxon for travellers (cognate with the modern German word 'fahren'). Whether the people of Lindsey set up a colony on Holy Island, or travelled there for religious reasons, or even just used it as a base for fishing expeditions, is not known.

▦ MORPETH

The problem faced with this name is not how it arose but why. It derives from 'morth-paeth' meaning murder-path. Perhaps the village grew up next to a road that was dangerous to travel along (for natural or for human reasons); maybe the road was used as a route to a gallows tree; perhaps it was more of a 'dead' path either in the sense that coffins were carried along it to burial, or in the sense that it had disappeared as a trackway. In the 13th century it was called Morthpath. A derivation from moor path has been discounted by etymologists.

▦ NEWCASTLE-UPON-TYNE

This town grew up around an 11th century Norman castle. Its early names included Novum Castellum (in 1130), Novum Castellum Super Tinam (in 1168) and Novum Castrum (in 1254), all of which, like its present name, are self-explanatory. On this site, however, once stood the old Roman fort of Pons Aelii (Hadrian's Bridge) which was close to Hadrian's Wall at its eastern end. That name referred to the Emporor's family name – his full title being Publius Aelius Adrianus.

▦ SEATON DELAVAL

Setuna in the 13th century was simply derived from 'sea-tun' (farmstead on the sea). To distinguish it from other places with a similar name, this one added the name of the De La Val family, which owned the estate, whilst another, held by the monks at Tynemouth Abbey, became Monkseaton. In the 18th century a barrier was built across the mouth of a river to regulate flow and encourage natural dredging. The scheme did not work but the name of the place where it took place survived: Seaton Sluice.

▦ SOUTH SHIELDS

Just called Scheles in 1235 this name was taken from the Saxon word for a temporary building, shed, shieling or – as in this case – a fisherman's hut. On the other side of the Tyne estuary Chelis appeared in 1268, becoming Northscheles in 1275. Subsequently this town received its 'south' appendage in order to distinguish itself.

▦ SUNDERLAND

This name has not changed since 1168. It comes from the Saxon word 'sundor-land' – meaning land which had been separated from a main estate; that is sundered land. We cannot be sure where the main estate was in this case, but it could have been the large district ruled by the Bishops of Durham.

▦ WOOLER

This name derives not from wool (despite the local agricultural economy) but from 'wella' (stream or spring) and 'ofer' (edge or height). Thus, the name means river-bank. It was Wullour in 1187 and Wullouer in 1212.

Nottinghamshire

▦ ARNOLD

It is hard to believe that the name of this suburb comes from a meaning 'remote valley with eagles'. But it does: from 'earn' (eagle) and 'halh' (corner, angle, secret place or remote valley). In the Domesday Book it was listed as Ernehale and in 1169 Aernhala.

▦ BEESTON

The Trent Valley must have been wetter than it is today when this settlement was founded. For it comes from 'beos-tun'. 'Beos' was a Saxon word for bent grass, reed or rush – the kind of vegetation that grew in damp meadows and marshes. The 'tun' or farmstead here was either built to exploit these rich pastures for cattle grazing, or to cut and sell the reeds to thatchers. South of Nottingham is BUNNY whose name is similarly derived – from 'bune-eg' (reed island). Bune was also the name of the river there. In the Domesday Book Beeston was Bestune and Bunny was Bonei.

▦ BLIDWORTH

This can be traced back, through Blethewurda in 1164 and Blideworde in the Domesday Book, to Blithere's worth (enclosure, clearing or homestead), Blithere would probably have been a tribal leader.

▦ BOUGHTON

This is a common place-name all over the Midlands. Sometimes it derives from 'bucc-tun' (buck-farmstead, the farm where male deer are found) and sometimes from Bucca's tun (the farmstead belonging to a person called Bucca or Buchere). In this case the latter is the more likely. It was Buchetone in the Domesday Book.

▦ EDWINSTOWE

This clearly comes from Edwin's stow: the chapel of St Edwin was mentioned as being here in 1205. The suffix is from the Saxon 'stow' which usually meant holy place, hermitage, or sometimes church. In the Domesday Book the place was

Edenesou, Eden being a shortened form of Edwin. St Edwin was the first Christian King of Northumbria (7th century) and was largely responsible for converting much of northern England and southern Scotland. He also gave his name to EDINBURGH.

HUCKNALL

This name once applied to the district, originally known as Hucca's halh (corner of land or remote valley). It covered either side of the river Leen and crossed into Derbyshire. In consequence, there is more than one village called Hucknall. One has the affix TORKARD, taken from Geoffrey Torchard, a Norman noble who held the estate in the 12th century. Across into Derbyshire is AULT HUCKNALL, the affix there being a corruption of the French-Norman word 'haut' (high). In between these two is HUTHWAITE ('hoh-thveit' – spur-hill clearing), otherwise known as Hucknall-under-Huthwaite.

MANSFIELD

A local hill near here was once called Mammesheud – Mam Hill – and the settlement below it was named Mammes Feld (open land, clearing or field). In due course, the latter became Mamesfeld (in the Domesday Book) and the modern Mansfield. The former has an interesting derivation. It comes from Celtic 'mamm', Welsh 'mam' or Saxon 'mamme', all of which meant mother or teat. The hill was so called because of its rounded bosom-like shape.

NEWARK

The 11th century versions, Newercha and Newerch, were noticeably close to the original 'neowe' (new) and 'weorc' (building or work). The place was constructed as a new work by comparison with the existing Aldewerke (old work) which was a medieval name for the Roman fort Margidunum at Castle Hill, East Bridgeford.

NOTTINGHAM

In AD 868 this was called Snotengaham, and in the Domesday Book Snotingeham. This derived from 'Snot-inga-ham': the village of Snot's people. Close by was another settlement whose name derived from 'Snot-inga-tun': the farm of Snot's people. Yet whilst the one became Nottingham, the other became Sneinton. The Normans dropped the 's' only from the former.

OLLERTON

The Domesday Book spelling Alretone shows that this name derives from 'alor' (alder) and 'tun' (farmstead). In 1288 it was Olreton. Another tree name can be found to the south: MAPLEBECK which comes from maple brook. This was Mapelbec in the 11th century. It stands on the edge of Sherwood Forest.

RADCLIFFE ON TRENT

This was Radclive in the Domesday Book and Radeclyf Super Trent in 1291, the name deriving from 'reade clif' (red cliff). Further north is RETFORD (Redforde in the Domesday Book) which was red ford. Nottinghamshire has an interesting geology, successive bands of sedimentary rock running north to south: sandstone, clays, limestones. These two villages stand on the keuper marl plateau, which gives a red clay soil.

▦ SCROOBY

A purely Norse name this, coming from Skroppa (a Danish personal name) and 'by' (a farmstead or village). In the Domesday Book of 1086 it was Scrobi. Before then, in AD 958, it was Scroppen Thorp, 'thorp' being Scandinavian for an outlying farm or settlement.

▦ SOUTHWELL

This was the south spring (Saxon 'sud wella') and referred to the Lady Well at the minster church, a religious site long before the construction of the present building in Norman times. The place was called Suthwellan in the 10th century. It was called 'south' to distinguish it from NORWELL (north spring) some distance to the north-east. This was Nortwelle in the 11th century.

▦ TUXFORD

This was Tuxfarne in the Domesday Book but had received its present spelling by the 14th century. The prefix comes from an early Saxon word 'tux' or 'tusk' meaning tuft of rushes. Either the original ford crossed a reedy stretch of river or else the crossing itself used tufts of grass as a route over the waters. The MARKHAM villages to the north are named from 'mearc-ham' (boundary-homestead). This probably referred to a manor, parish or hundred boundary.

▦ WORKSOP

The prefix here derives from 'weorc', but whether this was a personal name, or referred to a building is not known. The suffix is from the Saxon word 'hop' meaning a small narrow valley. In the Domesday Book the place was called Werchesope.

Oxfordshire

▦ ABINGDON

The original settlement, called Aebbandun in the 8th century, was sited on the ridge close to Boars Hill. The name was taken from Aebba's dun (hill), Aebba being a woman's personal name, and became Abbandun by AD 931. In AD 968 King Edgar gave a charter to a group of monks who subsequently built a monastery on the site. In the Domesday Book the place was called Abbendone. During the Middle Ages, however, the entire settlement moved down to the Thames-side meadows, to occupy a site formerly called Seouechesham – Soefeca's ham (homestead).

▓ BANBURY

This was called Banesberie in the Domesday Book of 1086 and Banebiria in 1146. It derives from Bana's 'burh' or 'burg', the fortified place of a tribal leader called Bana. However, the stronghold in question is probably not Banbury itself, but one of the Iron Age forts nearby, Grimsbury for instance, north-east of the town.

▓ BENSON

This is also known as Bensington, which is actually quite close to the original name: Baenesingtun in the 6th century. It was the 'tun' (village) belonging to the 'inga' (people) of Benesa (probably a tribal leader). Close by are the interesting names BERRICK (SALOME and PRIOR) and BRITWELL (SALOME and PRIORY). The former derives from 'berwic' (corn farm) and the latter from 'bric-wella' (bright spring). In the Middle Ages there was a large, land-owning family called Suleham (hence Salome) and other lands were held by the prior of Christchurch, Canterbury.

▓ BICESTER

From the suffix it can be deduced that here is the site of an old Roman camp, which the Saxons called a 'ceaster'. The town stands on the Roman road of Akerman Street. The prefix comes from 'byrgen' meaning a mound – probably referring to a nearby Iron Age burial site. Early spellings of the name include Bernecestre (11th century) and Burnecestre (13th century).

▓ BLACK BOURTON

Bourton – from 'burh' and 'tun' (fortified homestead) – is a fairly common place-name and so most settlements which bear it have affixes attached to distinguish themselves. There is Bourton-on-the-Hill, Bourton-in-the-Water, Bourton Constable, Great Bourton, Little Bourton and this one. It is so called because it was once part of an estate owned by the Black Canons of Osney Abbey.

▓ CHINNOR

This was Chenore in the Domesday Book and Chennora in 1193. It derives from a personal name (Ceonna, perhaps) and the Saxon word 'ora' meaning edge. The village stands on the edge of the Chiltern Hills. The same suffix is found at nearby LEWKNOR, this being Leofeca's edge. This was Leofecanoran in the 10th century. These villages are along the springline of the chalk escarpment.

▓ GORING

The Domesday Book spelling of this name, Garinges, clearly shows a derivation from Gara inga (Gara's people). The place could have been a tribal centre, well-positioned as it is upon a Thames crossing point. On the other side of the river is STREATLEY, which was Stretlee in the 7th century. This was the 'leah' (grove) near the 'straet' (street, here meaning a Roman road). Not far to the north is the village of DORCHESTER. This stands on the site of a major Roman town called

Dorocina, from which name the Saxons christened the place Dorceceaster. The original prefix comes from old Celtic 'dorce', 'derk' or 'derch', a river name element meaning bright.

▣ GREAT TEW

This name was just Tiwan or Teowe during the 11th century. It has various possible origins. Either it comes from 'tig' meaning a meeting place; or from 'teohh' meaning race or troop; or from 'taewe' meaning good health or excellent; or finally from 'tiew' meaning a row or ridge. Each is possible: the village was a moot centre for tribes, is situated on fertile soil and is close to a long narrow hillock. In the 12th century documents recorded Tiwa Magna and Parva Tiwe (now Great and Little Tew) together with Dunnestywa (now DUNS TEW) which was owned by a person called Dunn.

▣ HENLEY-ON-THAMES

From Heanlea in 1186 and Henleg in 1219 it became Hanleya in 1224. The Saxon words from which the name was taken were 'hea' (high) and 'leah' (clearing, enclosure or grove), whose dative forms produced 'hean-leage': at the high clearing. Interestingly the settlement is not high up but on the Thames riverbank so perhaps in this instance 'high' meant important (as it does in High Street). The 'on-Thames' affix appeared in the Middle Ages to distinguish this town from other Henleys – in Suffolk, Somerset and Warwickshire.

▣ OXFORD

Just as it sounds, this was once the ox-ford, the crossing point over the Thames used by oxen. In AD 912 it was Oxnaford, in the Domesday Book Oxeneford. The suburb of COWLEY, however, does not come from 'cu-leah' (cow pasture). Instead, this comes either from 'Cufa's leah' or 'cufl-leah' – a pasture belonging to Cufa or a pasture where logs or stumps were cut. It was Couele in 1004 and Covelie in the Domesday Book.

▣ WALLINGFORD

This was Waelingford in AD 821 and Walingeford in the Domesday Book. The prefix here could come from a personal name – making the whole mean 'ford of Wealh's inga (people)' – but is more likely to come from the Saxon word 'walh', or 'wealh', for foreigner, serf or Briton – making the whole mean ford of the British people (ford of the Welsh). Perhaps the village was inhabited by Celts, surrounded by Saxons. Nearby DIDCOT, however, definitely does come from a personal name – Dudda's cot (cottage or shelter). This was Dudecota in 1206.

▣ WANTAGE

This name comes from the river, originally called Wanotingc Broc (brook) from the Saxon word 'wanotian' meaning diminishing or intermittent. In AD 880 the village was called Waneting and in the Domesday Book Wanetinz. In Saxon times 'ing' endings were pronounced 'inge' – hence the evolution of the present spelling.

✵ WITNEY

A derivation from Witta's eg (island) may at first seem curious for a place situated on the southern edge of the Cotswold Hills. But the 'island' probably referred to an area of dry land above surrounding watermeadows, or else to an 'eyot' in the middle of the river Windrush. In AD 969 the place was Wyttannige, in the Domesday Book Witenie.

✵ WOODSTOCK

This was simply the 'stoc (place) in the wudu (wood)'. In 1123 it was called Wudestoke. Nearby is Blenheim Palace. This was built in the early 18th century for the Duke of Marlborough and named after his famous victory over the French and Bavarians in 1704.

Shropshire

✵ BISHOPS CASTLE

This settlement was founded in 1154 by the Bishop of Hereford, who hoped to supplement his income with earnings from the market here. It was called Bissopes Castell in 1269 and Castrum Episcopi in the 14th century. Nearby RICHARDS CASTLE, in Herefordshire, had been founded by Richard, son of a noble called Scrob, with the same purpose in mind. But there the scheme failed and the town never grew.

✵ BUILDWAS

This name may look and sound Welsh but it is, in fact, purely Saxon in origin. It comes from 'bylda' (builder or building) and 'waesse' (swamp). The first buildings were sited on the damp Severn meadows. The 11th century version of the name was Beldewes, the 12th century version Billewas.

✵ CLUN

The village here (Clune in the Domesday Book) takes its name from the river: Clun deriving from an old Celtic word 'colun', thought to mean roaring river. Other villages along this valley include CLUNBURY (from 'burh' meaning fortified place), CLUNGUNFORD (from the ownership of a person called Gunward in late Saxon times) and CLUNTON (from 'tun' meaning farmstead).

✵ DAWLEY

This was originally the 'leah' (woodland clearing) belonging to Dalla, a personal name possibly connected with the Saxon word 'deall' meaning proud or resplendent. In the Domesday Book it was Dalelie and in 1185 Dalilega. Other names nearby are more recent: COALBROOKDALE was Calderbrok in 1250 (cold brook) and OAKENGATES was Lee Okynyate in 1535 (the oak gate). IRONBRIDGE, of course, was so called from Abraham Derby's famous structure over the river Severn and TELFORD is the New Town name taken from Thomas Telford the civil engineer.

❋ ELLESMERE
This was Elli's mere (lake) originally, becoming Ellesmeles in the Domesday Book. In the same way, nearby COLEMERE was Cula's mere, which became Colesmere in the Domesday Book. We are here in Shropshire's own little Lake District, with nine meres set amidst pretty countryside.

❋ HODNET
The spelling recorded in the 11th century, Hodenet, was a Saxon corruption of the older Celtic words 'hod' or 'hoth' (peaceful) and 'nant' (valley). In the Middle Ages this area probably had a strong Welsh influence. Nearby the village of PREES also has a Celtic name, this from 'pres' or 'prys' meaning brushwood.

❋ LUDLOW
Standing high up above the river Teme this town takes its name from 'hlud' or 'hlude' (loud) and 'hlaw' (hill). It was not, of course, the hill that was loud but the river below it. There are rapids here and, in periods of flood, the noise can be deafening. The settlement was developed as a 'bastide' or military town in the 12th century, when it was called Ludelaue and Ludelawa.

❋ OSWESTRY
According to legend, King Oswald of Northumbria – later to be canonised – died close by (at a place called Maserfelth) and was buried here beneath a tree. Certainly it is true that this place-name means St Oswald's tree (Saxon 'treow') and it is also true that tree in Saxon meant wooden cross as well. So perhaps there is some substance to the legend. In the 12th century the place was called Osewaldstreu; in the 13th century it was, interestingly, both Oswaldestre and Croesoswald (Cross Oswald).

❋ RUYTON XI TOWNS
The uniqueness of this name goes back only to the 18th century when the parish was divided into eleven townships. Before then it was just Ruyton. In the Domesday Book it was Ruitone, in 1276 Ruton. The derivation is from Saxon – 'ryge' (rye) and 'tun' (farm).

❋ SHREWSBURY
Before the Normans simplified it to Salopesberia and later, to Shrovesbury, this place-name was variously called Scrobbesbyrig, Scropesbyri and Sciropesberie during the 11th century. It was the 'burh' (fortified place) of a person called Scrob or Scrobb. This was a surname, or nickname, derived from the Saxon word for brushwood, perhaps indicating a gruff person. Gruff or not he was probably a member of the same family as the Richard who founded Richards Castle in Herefordshire (see above under 'Bishop's Castle').

❊ STRETTON

This was called just Stratun in the Domesday Book, from 'straet' (street) and 'tun' (farmstead). It was so called because it stood on a Roman road. But as the population of the valley grew, so different Stretton villages appeared. Alured Stretton in 1262 (from the personal name Aelfred or Aelfgyp) became ALL STRETTON; Parva Stretton in 1327 became LITTLE STRETTON; Chirchestretton in 1337 became CHURCH STRETTON.

❊ WELLINGTON

The prefix here could derive from a personal name Weola or from 'weoh', Saxon for heathen temple, church or holy place. The suffix derives from 'tun' (farmstead). As to the middle syllable: this could be from 'leah' (clearing, grove) or from 'inga' (the people of). We cannot say for sure and the early spellings help little – Walitone (1086) and Welintona (1220).

❊ WEM

Called Weme in the Domesday Book and Wemme in 1228 this name probably descends from the Saxon word 'wemm' or 'wamm' meaning a spot, stain or filthy mark, and often used for an area of marshy ground. The land is low-lying here and the word 'wem' meaning a stain was in common use up until the 16th century.

❊ WENLOCK

The first religious establishment here was founded in the 7th century and this, in due course, became Wimmicensis Eclesia, possibly from an old Celtic root. But this had become Wenloca by the 10th century and Wenloch by the time of the Domesday Book. Some people say this name meant white monastery (Welsh 'gwyn' and Saxon 'loc'). Some distance away 'Little Wenlock' was so named because it belonged to Wenlock Priory, after which Much was added here to distinguish it.

❊ WHITCHURCH

This is a corruption of 'hwit-cirice', Saxon for white church and probably referring to the fact that the church here was stone-built (limestone being a pale colour) as opposed to wooden, in which case it would have been dark. At one time, in the 12th century, it was known as Album Monasterium, it being the site of a monastery, and earlier still (in Roman times) it was Mediolanum. The latter name meant middle of the plain and derived from the same linguistic root which produced the name 'Milan' in northern Italy.

Somerset
(including Bath & Bristol)

▨ BATH

In Roman times this was called Aquae Calidae (hot waters) and subsequently, Aquae Sulis (the waters of Sul – a pagan goddess). But after the Saxons gained control of the city, in AD 577, these early names were lost. Thereafter, the place was called Akemanchester (possibly a corruption of Aquae-ceaster), Hat Bathu (hot baths) and – by the time of the Domesday Book in 1086 – Bade.

▨ BRIDGWATER

Interestingly, this does not come from 'bridge over the water' but from 'bridge belonging to Walter de Dowai' (a Norman baron). The bridge (Saxon word 'brycg') was over the river Parrett and, unusually, it was the owner's first name that was transferred to the place-name and not his surname. In the Domesday Book it was Brugie, in 1194 Brigewaltier.

▨ BRISTOL

The version of this name as recorded in 1063, Brycgstow, exactly matches the Saxon origin of the town, bridge-stow. The word 'stow' had various meanings in pre-Norman times – site, monastery, hermitage, church, meeting place, indeed, any place of holy or special significance. Here at Bristol it probably meant market or commercial place, referring to the port area and central bridging point. The Domesday Book spelling of Bristou changed to its present spelling as a result of Norman influence.

▨ CASTLE CARY

This little town takes its name from the castle, which was built by the Normans, and the river upon which it stands. A document of 1138 lists it as Castellum de Cari; in 1237 it was called Castelkary. The river name is derived from the Celtic word 'caric', which meant loving or pleasant stream.

▨ CHARD

Before being called Cerdre in the Domesday Book in 1086, this had been Ceardren and Cerdren – from the Saxon words 'ceart' (rough ground) and 'aern' or 'renn' (dwelling or house). The town stands on the edge of the Black Down Hills, an area of poor soils and upland pasture.

▨ CHEDDAR

Being spelled Ceodre in the 9th century and Cedre in the Domesday Book of 1086, this name comes from the Saxon word 'ceod' meaning a bag or pouch. This probably referred to the cave here, or alternatively, to the deep ravine now called the 'Gorge'.

✺ CLEVEDON

Called Clivedone in the Domesday Book and Cliuedon in 1172, this name derives directly from the Saxon words 'clif' (cliff or escarpment) and 'dun' (hill). Either it was sited on a hilly place with cliffs or it was named after the nearby cliff-like hill now called Dial Hill. The town developed as a fashionable Victorian resort.

✺ CREWKERNE

The prefix here derives, not from the Celtic 'cryw' (ford or stepping stones), but from the Celtic 'cruc', 'crug' or 'crouco' (hill). The nearby village CRICKET ST THOMAS has a name derived from the same root. The suffix comes from the Saxon 'aern' meaning house or storehouse. In the 9th century the place was called Crucern, in the 13th century Crukerne.

✺ EASTON-IN-GORDANO

The first element here is simply from 'east-tun' (east farm) and in the Domesday Book this village is just called Estone. The last element is more interesting, referring to the whole district. It either comes from the words 'gara-denu' (triangular valley) or else from 'gor-denu' (dirty valley) both being Saxon. Bearing in mind the topography of this area, and the widening of the Avon valley as it reaches the Severn estuary, the former meaning might be the more likely. In the 13th century the village was called Eston in Gordon.

✺ GLASTONBURY

The Glastonia of olden days was Glatingaea in AD 704 and Glaestingeberia in the Domesday Book. To the Celtic root 'glasto' (woad) the Saxons added 'inga' (people), 'eg' (island) and later 'burh' (fortified place). Woad – a plant of the cabbage family – grew all around here in pre-Norman times and provided an important source of dye colouring. The old Welsh name for Glastonbury, Ineswytrin, meant island of 'gutrin', an ancient Celtic word meaning glassy. The legendary Isle of Avalon, thought to be here, means island of apples, from the Celtic 'afal' for apple.

✺ ILMINSTER

This town was so named because the minster stands close to the river Isle. Although the present church is largely 15th century, there was certainly a great religious building here before the Norman Conquest since we know that the name was Illemynister in AD 995. The town stands on high ground overlooking the Somerset Levels to the north, which was once a large area of marshlands. Many of the local place-names indicate this early landscape: MARTOCK is from 'mere-stoc' (trunk by the lake), THORNEY is from 'thorn-eg' (thorn bush island), MUCHELNEY is from 'micel-eg' (large island).

✺ KEYNSHAM

The suffix here derives from 'hamm' (Saxon for meadow, or land in a river bend) and not from the more common 'ham' (Saxon for homestead). No doubt this refers to the loop of the river Avon within which the settlement was sited. The prefix is from the personal name Caega or Caegin, possibly a local tribal leader. In about 1000 the place was called Caegineshamme, in the Domesday Book, Cainesham.

▓ MANGOTSFIELD

From an original Mangod's Feld (field or open land) this became Manegodesfelle in 1086 (Domesday Book) and Mangodesfeld in 1231. Mangod is thought to have been a foreign (non-Saxon) personal name. Nearby YATE (Gloucestershire) is a corruption of the Saxon word 'geat' (gate) but it is not known whether this referred to the original entrance to Mangod's estate or to a gap in the hills.

▓ MINEHEAD

This name means head of Myne Hill, the origin being the Celtic or Welsh 'mynydd' and the Saxon 'heafod', both of which meant hill. In 1046 the place was called Mynheafdon, this changing to Menehewed by the 13th century.

▓ PORTISHEAD

Both this name, and nearby PORTBURY, include the Saxon word 'port' meaning a harbour – probably referring here to the sheltered bay between Battery Point and the mouth of the Avon. A ridge of land runs inland from here, thus giving us, originally, Port Haefod (the harbour by the hill or headland) and Port Burh (the harbour with a fortified place). The former became Portesheve and the latter Portberie in the Domesday Book.

▓ RADSTOCK

From the Saxon words 'rad' (road) and 'stoc' (place) the town acquired its name because it stands on the Roman Foss Way. In 1221 it was recorded as Radestok. Neighbouring MIDSOMER NORTON was the 'north town' where a Midsummer festival has been held annually since the Middle Ages on the day of St John, the town's patron saint.

▓ SHEPTON MALLET

Shepton is a common place-name in England, deriving from 'sceap-tun' meaning sheep farm. Here the name was Sepetone (in the Domesday Book) before the manor came into the ownership of Robert Malet in the early 12th century. Nearby the village of EVERCREECH (which was Evorcric in the 11th century) comes from 'eofor' (boar) and the old Celtic word 'cruc' (hill).

▓ SOMERTON

This was a 'sumor-tun' (summer farmstead) used by herdsmen when practising transhumance. Cattle were grazed on the drying-out Somerset Levels in summer and then taken back to the surrounding hills in winter. In the Domesday Book it was Summertone.

✳ TAUNTON

This name has changed very little – it was Tantun in AD 722. It was so called because it was the 'tun' (farmstead) on the River Tan (later, the Thon and today the Tone). This river name was from the Celtic root 'tanarus' – a roaring stream.

✳ THORNBURY

The meaning of this place-name is not difficult to guess: it was the 'burh' or 'burg' (fortified place) either where thorn trees grew, or which was protected by a thorn hedge. From Thornbyrig in AD 896 it became Turneberie in the 1086 Domesday Book.

✳ WATCHET

This name derives from two ancient Celtic words, 'gwa' (or 'gwo') meaning under and 'ceto' (or 'coed') meaning wood. Originally the slopes behind the settlement were densely wooded. In AD 981 it was Waeced, in 1086 Wacet.

✳ WELLS

A simple derivation this, coming from the Saxon 'wella' meaning spring. The 'large spring' mentioned in a document in AD 766 was probably St Andrew's Well, now in the garden of the Bishop's Palace. This whole area, on the edge of the limestone-made Mendip Hills, has numerous springs, as well as caves and gorges as found at nearby Cheddar. The town of STREET has an equally simple derivation – from Saxon 'straet'. It stands on the Roman road from Ilchester to the Bristol Channel.

✳ WESTON-SUPER-MARE

In the 13th century this was called simply Weston – a common Saxon place-name coming from 'west tun' (western farmstead). In the following century the present Latin addition (meaning on-sea) was first used to distinguish this settlement from Westonzoyland on the Somerset Levels. The suburb of WORLE derives its name from the Saxon 'wor-leah' meaning grouse wood. WORLEBURY was the 'burh' (hill fort) of Worle.

✳ WESTONZOYLAND

Weston (west-tun or farmstead) is a common place-name, so many villages or towns which possess it have an additional element. Weston-super-Mare, of course, is named from its coastal position. Here on the Somerset Levels, Zoyland is a corruption of 'sowi-land' – the land of streams. The introduction of the 'z' might have been due to the influence of Dutch workers who, in the late Middle Ages, helped to drain the fens around here. In the Domesday Book it was called, simply Sowi, in about 1245 Westsowi.

✳ WINCANTON

Called Wincaletone in the Domesday Book, this was originally the 'tun' (farmstead) on the river Wincawel (the White Cale, the upper reaches of the river Cale). 'Win' or 'gwyn' was the Celtic word for white or bright).

❊ YEOVIL

The river Yeo, which flows through this town, has the same origin of name as the river Ivel in Bedfordshire. Both came from the Celtic 'gablau' (Welsh 'gafl') meaning forked river. This Yeo was called the Gifl in the 10th century, when the town was given the same name. By the time of the Domesday Book it had become Givele.

Staffordshire

❊ BIDDULPH

The prefix here could have started out as the Saxon 'bi' (beside) and then changed to the Danish 'by' (homestead or village). Not that this affects the meaning of the main part of the name, which comes from the Saxon word 'dylf' or 'dulf' meaning diggings or workings. The reference, of course, was not to coal mines but to ancient quarries. The Domesday Book spelling of Bidolf in 1086 became Bydulf by 1291.

❊ BURTON-UPON-TRENT

Some 'Burton' settlements descend from 'brada-tun', Saxon for broad farmstead, whilst others come from 'burh-tun', Saxon for fortified or manor farmstead. Both are very common derivations but this one is probably the latter variety. It was Byrtun in 1002 and Bertone in the Domesday Book. The 13th century saw the first reference to the river upon which the town stands: Burton-super-Trente.

❊ CANNOCK

It is thought that Shoal Hill, north west of the present town, was once called Cunuc or Cnocc, from an ancient Celtic word for hill. If so then the word was transferred to the settlement at an early date, producing the name Canuc by the 10th century. This subsequently became Chenet (1086) and Cano (1157). The 'chase' refers to the ancient hunting forest that once covered a large part of this area.

❊ CHEADLE

This is a compound name, partly Celtic in origin and partly Saxon, and means something like chet wood or clearing. The former derives from Celtic 'ceto' (like Welsh 'coed') for wood, the latter from Saxon 'leah' (grove). Such apparent tautology is common in place-names. Early spellings include Celle (1086 Domesday Book), Chedelle (1197) and Chedle (1227).

❊ CROXALL

This name, meaning Croc's or Krok's Hall, could derive from the old Norse word 'krokr' meaning a hook, but is more likely to come from a personal name – the manor house belonging to someone called Crocc, Knuc or even Cnut. In AD 942 the place was Crokeshalle, in the Domesday Book Crocheshalle.

▦ ENVILLE

The 'Ville' here is a fairly recent corruption of field and not an indication – as it often is – of a model village or industrial town built in the 19th century. The name was originally Efnefeld (in the Domesday Book) and later Evenefeud (1240). It derives from the Saxon words 'efn' (even or smooth) and 'feld' (open land or field), although Efna as a personal name has not been ruled out by etymologists.

▦ GNOSALL

This name poses several problems for etymologists since there is no clear derivation. In the Domesday Book it was spelt Geneshale and in 1199 it was Gnodeshall. From these it may be surmised that the first element is a personal name, possibly a nickname since there was a Saxon word 'gneath' meaning mean or niggardly. However, this would assume the 'eath' sound changed to 'od' and that later this became 'os' with Norman French influence. The suffix is equally a problem, either coming from 'halh' (nook or recess) or 'heall' (hall or manor house). Nearby ECCLESHALL is only slightly easier to decipher: here the suffix is certainly from 'halh' but the prefix could either be derived from a personal name (Eccel) or else from an old Celtic word 'ecles' meaning church. Thus, it could be Eccel's nook or church in a recess. In the 11th century it was Ecleshelle.

▦ INGESTRE

This was probably the 'ingon', or 'ingum' (hilltop or peak) acquired through 'gestreon' (gain). The latter was often a word used by the Saxons to mean a property won by draining, reclamation or – as possibly here – by conquest. The place was called Ingestreon in the 11th century, Ingestret in the 13th century.

▦ LEEK

This name – spelled Lec in the Domesday Book and Lech in about 1100 – is directly linked to the old Saxon word 'lece' (or Old Norse 'laekr'), meaning stream, taken from 'laeccan' or 'leccan' – to drip or leak. The villages of Leake in Lincolnshire, Yorkshire and Nottinghamshire have the same origin.

▦ LICHFIELD

Formerly thought to be derived from Saxon 'lic' (corpse) and 'feld' (open land) this name has now been traced back to Celtic times. Its earliest known version, Letoceto in the 4th century, was evidently taken from 'leto-ceton', Celtic for grey wood (cognate with Welsh 'llwyd-coed'). The Saxons later turned this into Liccidd and then added feld. By 1130 it had become Lichesfeld.

▦ RUGELEY

The position of this settlement, close to the north-eastern edge of Cannock Chase, has led to the assumption that the prefix comes from 'hrycg', Saxon for ridge. If this is true, then the name means woodland clearing ('leah') on a ridge. It was Rugelie in the Domesday Book and Ruggelega in 1156.

✠ STAFFORD

This was the ford either next to the landing shore ('staeth') or made of stakes ('staefer'). Early versions of the name include Staeth and Staefford (10th century) and Stadford (11th century). The town is situated on the old limit to navigation on the river Sow, so perhaps the former derivation is more likely.

✠ STOKE-ON-TRENT

'Stoke' is such a common place-name that almost every settlement bearing it has a distinguishing addendum. In this case, the reference to the river appeared sometime during the Middle Ages. The main part of the name – Stoche in the Domesday Book – comes from the Saxon word 'stoc' (plural 'stocu'). This meant, variously, dependent settlement, holy site, monastery, cell or even, simply place. The river name is of Celtic origin, from 'tri-santon' meaning trespasser or flooding river.

✠ TAMWORTH

This was the old capital of Mercia so the origin 'worthig' probably referred to a fortified enclosure rather than to the more usual meaning of house in a clearing. It was sited on the river Tame. In AD 781 it was Tamouuorthig and in AD 922 Tameworthig.

✠ UTTOXETER

This was Wotocheshede in the Domesday Book and Wittokeshather in 1242. These spellings seem to disprove the theory, held by some historians, that the suffix here comes from 'ceaster' (Roman camp), as does a similar suffix in the names Exeter and Wroxeter. In this case the suffix comes from 'heather', Saxon for heathland. The first element derives from a personal name, Wittuc.

✠ WYRLEY

Originally only one village, Wereleia, in the Domesday Book, this became a mother-and-daughter pair by the 14th century: Great Wyrleye and Little Wyrle. The derivation is Saxon: 'wir' (bog myrtle) and 'leah' (glade). Neighbouring CHESLYN HAY comes from 'ciest' (a chest or coffin), 'hlinc' (hill) and 'hege' (enclosure) – possibly being an upland burial site. It was Chistlin in 1236 but Haye of Chistelyn in 1293.

Suffolk

✠ BECCLES

From the Becles of the Domesday Book (1086) this became Beacles (1095) and then Becclis (1158). It derives probably not from 'bece' (Saxon for beech tree) but from 'bec' or 'baece' (Saxon for stream or valley). The ending is from 'laes' meaning pasture or meadow. The town stands on the river Waveney.

▦ BUNGAY

This name derives from 'Buna-inga-eg': the island of Buna's people. The 'eg' probably refers to the loop in the river Waveney within which the original settlement was built. The Domesday Book records Bongeia, an 1175 document, Bungeia.

▦ BURY ST EDMUNDS

St Edmund – killed by the Vikings in AD 869 – was indeed buried here but the town is not so called because of that. Bury here derives from 'byrig', the dative form of 'burh' meaning a fortified place. After Edmund's interment the original name of the town Beadriceswyrth (Beaduric's enclosure) was changed first to Sanctae Eadmundes Stow (as recorded in the 10th century) and later to Sancte Eadmundes Byrig (as recorded in the 11th century). 'Stow' meant holy place. A monastery was founded (to protect the Saint's remains) sometime in the 10th century. Today the town is also known as St Edmundsbury.

▦ CLARE

Some place-name researchers link this name with the Saxon word 'claegen' meaning clayey, others think it derives from the older Celtic word 'claear', or 'clayar', meaning gentle, bright or mild. The former, of course, would have referred to the soils, the latter to the river. Domesday Book lists Clara, so either origin could be correct. In 1352 Lionel, third son of Edward III, married into the Clare family. Ten years later he was made a Duke by his father and took, as his title, the Latin form of the name Clare – Clarentia, thus creating the noble name 'Clarence'.

▦ FELIXSTOWE

This was called Filchestou in 1254 and Fylthstowe in 1359. Although the name appears to come from a 'stow' (holy place) belonging to a local landowner Felica, it is tempting to think that it derives, instead, from the name of East Anglia's first Bishop, Felix. Certainly the connection was seen during the Middle Ages, hence the present spelling of the town's name. The seat of St Felix's Bishopric was, in fact, along the coast at Dunwich.

▦ HAVERHILL

The prefix in this name probably comes, not from the Saxon 'haefer' (a billy-goat) but from the Saxon 'haeferi' (or Norse 'hafri') for oats. Thus, the place was the hill ('hyll') where oats were grown. It was Hauerella in the Domesday Book and Haverhell in 1158. The word for oats has survived into modern English with the word haversack – originally a farmers' bag used for carrying grain.

▦ IPSWICH

Early forms like Gipeswic (AD 993) and Gepeswiz (1086) tell us that the prefix derives either from a personal name Gyp or Gipe, or else from the Saxon 'gip' meaning a gap (from 'gipian' – to yawn). The latter would have referred to the broad Orwell estuary here. The ending comes from Saxon 'wic' for specialised farm, place, homestead or – bearing in mind the river location of the town – landing place.

▦ LEISTON
Whilst the suffix is clearly taken from 'tun' (farmstead), the prefix derives either from 'leah' (woodland clearing) or from 'lieg' or 'leg' (fire). Considering the position of the town, and its advantages as a site for a beacon to guide shipping, the latter is perhaps the more likely. Ledestuna in the Domesday Book became Legestona in 1168.

▦ LONG MELFORD
Simply called Melaforda in the Domesday Book this was, literally, mill-ford (from the Saxon 'mylen'). 'Long' was added in the Middle Ages, for the place is a linear village.

▦ LOWESTOFT
A very Danish name this, from Hlothver's toft – the homestead or dwelling belonging to a tribal leader by the name of Hlothuv or something similar. In the Domesday Book the place was listed as Lothuwistoft, in 1219 as Lowistoft.

▦ MILDENHALL
The suffix here is not from 'heall' (hall or manor house) but from 'halh' (corner, nook or hillside depression); and the prefix might come not from Milda (a personal name) or 'middel' (middle) but from 'milde' (mild or gentle). In the 11th century the place was Mildenhale and Mudenehalla.

▦ SOUTHWOLD
This was Sudwolda in the Domesday Book, evidently from the Saxon 'suth-wald' (south wood). The whole of Suffolk was densely forested until relatively recent times, much felling taking place from the 17th century onwards. Hence, there are many names here which include references to woods or trees: ASHFIELD (field with ash trees), ELMSWELL (spring where elms grow), WILBY (circle of willows from 'wilig-baeg') and so on. WOODBRIDGE, however, probably means wooden bridge rather than 'bridge in a wood'. This was Wudebrige in the 11th century.

▦ STOWMARKET
In the Domesday Book the village here was actually called Torneia, which can be interpreted as 'Thorney' (thorn island). The name Stou in that document referred only to the district or hundred, a name deriving from the Saxon word 'stow' (holy place or meeting place). However, in due course a market appeared and this settlement became known as Stowemarket (in 1269), it being the principal trading centre for the hundred.

▦ SUDBURY

Spelt Sudberi in the Domesday Book, this simply derives from the Saxon 'suth-burh' (south-fortified place). The prefix could refer to the fact that this town is close to the southern edge of the county. The nearby CORNARD villages have a name from 'corn-erth' (corn-land). It was Cornerda in the 11th century, becoming Corntherth Magna and Cornherth Parva in the 13th century.

Surrey

▦ BAGSHOT

Originally, it seems, this name applied to a woodland. The first element is thought to come for a word for a wild animal: Viking 'bagge' meant ram, Saxon 'bar' meant boar. So this prefix could derive from one of these. The second element comes from the Saxon 'sceat' for strip of land. Thus the oringinal wood could have been an area of trees where a particular wild animal roamed. The village which later appeared close by was given the same name, which became Bagsheta in the 12th century.

▦ CAMBERLEY

During the 1860s, when the Royal Military Academy moved to nearby Sandhurst, two residential developments took place. One of these new suburbs was called YORK TOWN (after the Duke who founded the Academy) and the other was called 'Cambridge Town' (after the Duke who was the British Army's Commander-in-Chief at the time). But whereas the former place-name survived, the latter was subsequently changed to Camberley to avoid confusion (by the postal services) with the City of Cambridge. The City of York was too far away to create problems for York town.

▦ CHEAM

The early spellings – Cegeham in AD 675, Ceiham in the 1086 Domesday Book – indicate a prefix derived from the Saxon word 'ceg' or 'cegel' for a low shrub or many-branched tree stump. The suffix could come from 'ham' (village) or 'hamm' (meadow).

▦ CROYDON

Etymologists think that an origin here from 'crawe' (Saxon for crow) is rather less likely than an origin from 'croh', 'crog' and 'crogen', all of which were used by the Saxons to mean the wild saffron crocus. There was once a 'denu' (valley) hereabouts where this plant grew, and was collected to be used for dyeing, cooking and medicinal purposes. Hence the name for this settlement became Crogedenu in the 9th century and Croindene in the Domesday Book.

▦ DORKING

This name comes from the 'ingas' (people) of the river Dork – presumably an old name for the river Mole – or, alternatively, the 'ingas of Deorc' (a personal name).

The settlement was Dorchinges in the 11th century and Dorkinges in the 12th century. There is some evidence that the name Dork (from Celtic 'derch' for bright) might have given its name to a local tribe here, known as the 'Dorce people'.

▦ ESHER

This name (called Aesaeron in 1005, Aissele in 1086) poses a problem to place-name researchers. Whilst the prefix evidently comes from 'aesc' (ash tree) the suffix could come from 'sceran' (to cut), 'scearu' (boundary) or 'scear' (ploughshare), all of which were common Saxon words.

▦ FARNHAM

From the AD 894 version of the name, Fearnhamme, it seems that the suffix comes not from 'ham' (homestead) but from 'hamm' (meadow). The settlement stands on the river Wey. In the Domesday Book it was Ferneham. The prefix is derived from 'fearn', fern, a plant burned by the Saxons to provide fertiliser.

▦ GUILDFORD

The problem posed by this place-name is not so much what it means but why it was so called. It derives from 'gylde-ford' – golden ford – but opinion varies as to the reason for such a name. Either it referred to the golden flowers (marigolds perhaps) which once grew over this part of the North Downs, or it described the colour of the riverbank gravels and local soils around the old crossing point. In the Domesday Book the place was Geldford.

▦ KINGSTON-UPON-THAMES

This was called King's 'tun' (farmstead) but it is not known which Saxon monarch once owned the manor to give it such a name. From Cyninges Tun (AD 838) it became Chingestune in the Domesday Book.

▦ LEATHERHEAD

The early forms of this name, Leodridan in the 9th century and Ledreda in the 12th century, have caused some debate amongst etymologists. Some think the derivation is Saxon, from 'leode' (people) and 'rida' (riding path or bridleway) but others argue for a much older origin, from Celtic 'leto' or 'llwyd' (grey) and 'ritu' (ford). The village grew at a crossing point on the river Mole and has long been a focal point for traffic, so both derivations could be possible: 'the public ford for horse traffic'.

▦ OXTED

Unlike most places with this prefix, this one derives not from the Saxon 'oxna' (oxen) but from the Saxon 'ac' (oak). With a suffix from 'stede', we have the meaning place where oaks grow. In the 12th century it was Akested. Nearby LIMPSFIELD comes from a combination of the Celtic 'lem' or 'llwyf' and the Saxon 'feld' meaning open land in an elm wood. Not far away is SEVENOAKS (Sevenac in 1200). This area has always been well forested.

⊞ REIGATE

Being Regata in 1185 and Regate in 1203, this derives from 'raege' (Saxon for a female roe-deer or doe) and 'geat' (Saxon for gap or gate). The place might once have been an entrance to a deer park or hunting forest.

⊞ RICHMOND

This was named in 1501 by Henry VII who rebuilt a fire-destroyed royal palace here and wanted a name to reflect its prestige. He accordingly chose the name from his previous title – 'Earl of Richmond'. The earlier name for the settlement – the more humble Sheen – had been Sceon in the 10th century, from an old Saxon word for a shed or animal shelter. No wonder Henry wanted a name change!

⊞ RUNNYMEDE

It was here, in 1215, that King John and his barons drew up Magna Carta. In those days it was called Ronimede or Runingmeth – derived from 'run' (secret meeting or assembly), 'eg' (island) and 'maed' (meadow). The place had already become a recognised meeting place – council island meadow.

⊞ STAINES

The dative form of the Saxon word 'stan' was 'stane', meaning at the stone. The boulder in question could have been a Roman milestone – there is a Roman road here and the site of the Roman camp Pontibus. Neighbouring HOUNSLOW was Hund's hlaw – the barrow or hillock owned by Hund or used by hounds.

⊞ WIMBLEDON

From the original Winebeald's dun (hill) this became Wunemannedune in the 10th century. But, by 1212, the Normans had simplified that name into Wimmeldun.

⊞ WOKING

Uuocchingas and Woccingas (in the 8th century), and Wochinges in the Domesday Book (1086) were corruptions of Wocca's ingas – the people or tribe led by a person called Wocca (otherwise, Wocc or Woco). Neighbouring BYFLEET was called Bifleote and Biflet in the 11th century. This was originally 'bi fleote' – by the fleet. The fleet or stream would have referred to the river Wey.

Sussex (East & West)

⊞ ARUNDEL

The river Arun – called the Aron in the 16th century – was named after the settlement and not the other way round. For the prefix of this town name derives from 'harhune', the Saxon word for hoarhound (a plant of the nettle family) which once grew in abundance hereabouts. The suffix is from 'dell', Saxon for a valley. In the 11th century the name was Harundel and Arundell.

▦ BEXHILL

The 'hill' in this name is misleading, for it appeared in relatively recent times. The original name was Bixlea (in AD 772) and Bexelei (in the 1086 Domesday Book) and as such derives from the same root as Bexley in Kent. This was the Saxon word 'byxe-leah' (box tree woodland or clearing). The suffix hill probably arose during the Middle Ages to help distinguish the two settlements.

▦ BOGNOR REGIS

This was Bucganora in AD 680 and Bugenor in 1275, names derived from Bucge (a Saxon female name) and 'ora' (shore or landing stage). The present town developed largely at the end of the 18th century due to the efforts of Richard Hotham, landowner and entrepreneur who wanted to build a rival resort to Brighton. For a while the town was actually called 'Hothampton' but this name did not survive Richard Hotham's death in 1790. The 'Regis' appendage was bestowed by George V after his convalescence nearby in 1929.

▦ BRIGHTON

Prior to the development of this town as a seaside resort in Regency England, and the building of the Brighton Pavilion in 1815–22, the name was Brightelmstone. In the Domesday Book it is Bristelmestune. This derived either from 'Beorhthelm's tun' (the farmstead belonging to a person whose name meant bright helmet) or from 'beorht-elmen-tun' (the farmstead by the bright elm trees).

▦ CHICHESTER

This was the 'ceaster' (Roman fort) of Cissa, who was the son of Aelle, the first King of the South Saxons. Earlier, in Roman times, the name was Noviomagus – meaning new market from the Latin 'novus' and Celtic 'magos'. In AD 895 it was Cisseceaster, in the Domesday Book it was Cicestre.

▦ CRAWLEY

This New Town, designated in 1947, has a name going back to Saxon times, when a settlement here was called 'crawe-leah' (crow wood or clearing). In 1203 it was Crauleia.

▦ CROWBOROUGH

The prefix here comes directly from the Saxon 'crawe' for a crow. But the suffix derives not from 'bearu' (grove, woodland) as one might have expected, but from 'beorg' (hillock). The place was Cranbergh in 1292 and Crowbergh in 1390. The CROWHURST in Surrey does indeed come from crow wood but not the one here in Sussex, which comes from 'croh' (corner) and 'hurst' (wooded hill or copse).

▦ EAST GRINSTEAD

Called just Grenesteda in 1121 this was simply the green place, with a probable reference to the verdant nature of its vegetation. A village some 20 miles away acquired the same name and so, in the 13th century, distinguishing adjectives were added to the two places. This settlement became Estgrenested and the other one Westgrenested.

▦ HAILSHAM
There are various options as to the origin of this name. The prefix could derive from Haegel (a personal name), 'haeg' (hay) or 'hamel' (maimed or crooked); the suffix could derive from 'ham' (homestead or village) or 'hamm' (meadow or pasture). Many researchers have opted for Haegel's homestead. In the Domesday Book it was Hamelesham, in 1198 Heilesham.

▦ HASTINGS
An ancient place-name this, little changed since Saxon times. It was Hastingas in AD 790 and Hastinges in the Domesday Book. As a tribal name – the 'ingas' (people) of Haesta – it probably referred originally to a district rather than to just a settlement. The name of the tribal leader was descended from 'haest' meaning violent, he was probably a forceful and quick-tempered man.

▦ HAYWARDS HEATH
This was originally just Heyworth (13th century), a name deriving from 'heg' (hay) or 'hege' (hedge) and 'worth' (enclosure). In those days the place was part of CUCKFIELD parish, whose name probably comes from a field either belonging to Cuca (a tribal leader) or else where couch-grass grew (from Saxon 'cwice'). Some etymologists link this name with cuckoo-field, but this derivation is of dubious validity. The 'Heath' was added to Hayward in the 17th century and the town grew substantially after the coming of the railways. BURGESS HILL also grew after the railway station was opened (in 1841), this name coming from the Burgeys family, landowners in the 14th century.

▦ HORSHAM
The spelling has remained the same since AD 947. It was the 'ham' (homestead) or 'hamm' (meadow) of the 'hors' (horse). Perhaps this was the site of a stud farm, or perhaps just a horse pasture.

▦ LEWES
Legend says that this name comes from Llwy, the Celtic god of light who is celebrated each year on November 5th instead of Guy Fawkes. Far more likely is that it derives from the plural form of the Saxon word 'hlaew' (hill) and refers either to the South Downs or to the numerous ancient burial mounds in the vicinity. The place was Laewe in the 10th century, Leuuas in the 11th century.

▦ MARESFIELD
This began as either 'mersc-feld' (marsh field) or 'mere-feld' (lake field). It was both Mersfield and Meresfeld in the 13th century.

▦ RYE

This name derives, interestingly, from a succession of writing errors. The Saxon phrase 'aet thaere iege' (at the island) became 'atter ie', which in turn became 'atterie'. This subsequently became wrongly divided into 'atte rie'. The town (Ria in 1130) was coastal before silting-up occurred. The English language has other examples of misplaced letters changing words: 'a napron' (from French 'naperon') became an apron and 'an eke-name' (an also name) became 'a nekename' (nickname).

▦ SELSEY

Despite this town's ancient links with St Wilfred and his monastery in the 7th century, its name comes not from 'selig-eg' (holy island) but from 'seoles-eg' (seal island). In the 8th century it was Siolesaei. The name probably referred originally to the whole area between Chichester and Pagham Harbour.

▦ SHOREHAM

This was Sorham and Soresham in the 11th century, derived from 'scora' (steep slope) and 'ham' (homestead). The original settlement, now Old Shoreham, is back from the coast but sited close to a steep river bank. The present seaside resort was called Nywe Shorham in the 13th century, becoming Shoreham-by-Sea in more recent times with the growth of tourism. Along the coast, PORTSLADE derives from 'portes-lad' (the stream by the harbour) and HOVE comes from 'hufe' (hood, shed or shelter).

▦ UCKFIELD

This was once Ucca's feld – an area of open land named after a tribal leader or else a person who lived here or owned it. In the 13th century the village was called Uckefeld. Nearby BUXTED (Boxsted in the 12th century) derives either from 'boc-stede' or 'box-stede': a place where beech or box trees grew.

▦ WORTHING

The English south coast has many place-names ending with 'ing', derived from the Saxon word 'ingas' meaning the people of. Usually such names have prefixes based on tribal or personal names, thus identifying which or whose people dwelt thereabouts. Here we have three such place-names close together. Worhing was Wurth's ingas, GORING was Gara's ingas, and LANCING was Wlenca's ingas. In the Domesday Book these were called Ordinges, Garinges and Lancinges respectively, the latter being a Norman corruption of the earlier Saxon version of Wlencingas. Evidently these tribal groups were small and their areas limited.

Warwickshire &
The West Midlands
Conurbation

✳ ALDRIDGE

The early forms, Alrewic in the Domesday Book and Alrewyz in 1236, can be traced back to the Saxon words 'alor' (alder tree) and 'wic' (dairy farm or market town). This whole area was once well timbered.

✳ BALSALL

This was Belesale in the 12th century, deriving from the personal name Baelli and the Saxon word 'halh' (recess, corner of land). Nearby is TEMPLE BALSALL, so named because here stood a preceptory or college of the Knights Templar, the religious order established to help recover the Holy Land for Christianity. Later the manor passed to the ownership of the Knights Hospitallers. BALSALL COMMON originally referred to the area of common land beyond the village fields.

✳ BILSTON

This was once the 'tun' (farmstead) of the Bilsaetan (the settlers or dwellers of Bil). Here the Bil was either a personal name, of a tribal leader for instance, or else the name of a district. It could descend from 'bill', the Saxon word for a sword. In AD 996 the place was Bilsetnatun, in the Domesday Book Billestune.

✳ BIRMINGHAM

This was the village ('ham') of Beorma's people ('inga'). It is thought the personal name Beorma could have been a shortened form of Beornmund. The place was Bermingeham in the 1086 Domesday Book and Brimingeham in 1169.

✳ BRINKLOW

The 1130 spelling of this name, Brichelawa, derived its suffix from 'hlaw' (Saxon for a burial mound or hillock) and its prefix either from 'brince' (Saxon for a steep slope) or from Brynca (a personal name). The 'hlaw' might have been used as a meeting place.

✳ CASTLE BROMWICH

The Bromwich of the Domesday Book was the 'wic' (farmstead) where 'brom' (broom) grew. There were many such names in Saxon times so most developed distinguishing additions. This one acquired its present name from the 12th century castle, whose motte-and-bailey remains can still be seen just north of the church. In 13th century documents Magna Bromwyce and Parva Bromwice were listed, the latter (Little Bromwich) is now called WARD END.

※ COVENTRY

Although there was a Saxon word 'cofa' (meaning cave or cove) the prefix in this name is more likely to have come from a personal name Cofa or Covar. This is because place-names ending with an element meaning tree (from 'treow') – as this one is – invariably have a personal name as a first element. Such a tree was usually a boundary mark or the focal point of a meeting place. In the 11th century the name was spelled Couaentree, Cofantrea and Coventrev. If Coventry were the exception, and derived its prefix from the word for cave, then it might have referred to an old pool (cove) in the river Sherbourne at this point.

※ DUDLEY

In the Domesday Book this was Dudelei, meaning Dudda's leah (grove). By the 13th century it had become Duddele and Doddeley. This place has been known as the capital of the Black Country, its coal and iron industries dating back to the 17th century.

※ EDGBASTON

The spelling recorded in the 13th century, Egeboldeston, gives an indication of the derivation: Ecgbald's tun (farmstead). This was possibly a tribal leader. Nearby SELLY OAK was originall Escelie (in the Domesday Book), which was a Norman-French spelling of the Saxon words 'scylf' (slope or ledge) and 'leah' (grove). The 'Oak' is a recent addition.

※ HALESOWEN

The prefix here comes from the plural form of the Saxon word 'halh' (nook, corner of land) – 'hales' or 'hallam' – whilst the suffix derives from Owain, the Welsh prince and son of David, who married a sister of Henry II and became Lord of Hales in 1204. In 1276 the place was called Hales Ouweyn.

※ HENLEY-IN-ARDEN

Like other 'Henley' village names this comes from 'hea' or 'hean' (high) and 'leah' (clearing or woodland grove). It was plain Henlea and Hanleye in the 12th century. The present affix first appeared in 1378 as Henleye in Ardern. It referred to the hunting forest here and derived from the word 'eardaern' meaning dwelling house.

※ KENILWORTH

The root of this place-name was Cynehild, a woman's personal name from Saxon times meaning royal battle, perhaps belonging to a female warrior. The suffix 'worth' here is the Saxon word for an enclosure or homestead in a clearing. From Chinewrde in 1086 (the Domesday Book) it became Kinildewurtha in 1173.

※ LEAMINGTON SPA

From the 17th century onwards the health springs here were developed, and in 1838 Queen Victoria granted the town the full honorific title of Royal

Leamingon Spa. Before then, however, it was plain Leamington – Lamintone in the Domesday Book. It was the 'tun' (farmstead) on the river Leam. Along the same waterway is LEAMINGTON HASTINGS (held by Aytropius Hastings in the 13th century) and LEAMINGTON PRIORS (held by Kenilworth Priory in the 12th century).

⬛ NUNEATON
The Etone of the Domesday Book (from 'ea-tun', river-farmstead) became Nonne Eton and Nun Eton in the 13th century after a Benedictine nunnery had been founded. Part of that priory is now incorporated into St Mary's church.

⬛ RUGBY
Rocheberie in the Domesday Book and Rokebi in 1200 indicate that an original Saxon ending from 'burh' or 'burg' (fortified place) was changed by the Danes into their own 'by' (homestead or village). The prefix derives not from 'hroc' (rook) or 'rugr' (rye) but, more probably from a personal name like Hroca.

⬛ SHIPSTON-ON-STOUR
This derives from the meaning farmstead ('tun') at the sheepwash. The words 'sceap', 'scept' and 'scip' were all used by the Saxons to mean sheep and 'waesce' was a washing place (from 'gewaesc' meaning to wash). The river Stour was probably where the sheep were washed. Early spellings of the name include Scepeuuaeisctune (AD 764) and Scepwaesctun (AD 964).

⬛ SOLIHULL
Called Sulihull in 1242 and Solyhulle in 1315, this place-name has various possible derivations. The prefix could come either from 'sulig' (pigsty) or from 'sylig' (muddy). The suffix could come either from 'holh' (hollow), or 'halh' (nook, recess), or 'hyll' (hill). If the latter then the hill could be that upon which St Alphege's church now stands. The soils hereabouts are certainly heavy and damp.

⬛ STRATFORD-UPON-AVON
Shakespeare's town stands where the old Roman road to Alcester once crossed the river Avon. The Saxons called it 'straet' (street) ford – this becoming Stradforde in the Domesday Book and Strafford-on-Avon in 1255. The original ford was, appropriately, at Bridgefoot.

⬛ SUTTON COLDFIELD
From Sutone in the Domesday Book this became Sutton in Colefeud in 1269. It was the 'suth' (south) 'tun' (farmstead) in a 'colfeld' (charcoal clearing). Charcoal was an important energy source throughout the Middle Ages.

❖ WALSALL

Here the prefix probably descends not from a personal name, Weal or Wale, but from the Saxon 'walh' meaning foreigner, serf or Briton. Thus, the place was the 'halh' (nook of land, little valley) where a group of Celts lived. In 1002 it was Walesho, in 1162 Waleshale.

❖ WARWICK

The prefix here is either from Waeringa (the people of Waer) or else from 'waering' (weir or dam). The town stands on the river Avon and so could well have the latter meaning. The suffix 'wic' meant special place, market town or dairy farm. In the 8th century it was Waerincgwican, in the Domesday Book it was Warwic.

❖ WEDNESBURY

This was Wadnesberie in the Domesday Book and comes from Woden's 'burg' (fortified place). It therefore has the same root as the word Wednesday, which was 'Wodnesdaeg' in Saxon times. Woden, or Odin, was one of the chief gods of the Dark Ages. Other deities also gave their names to our days of the week: Tiw (Tuesday), Thor (Thursday) and Frig (Friday).

❖ WOLVERHAMPTON

From Heantune in the 10th century ('heah-tun', high farmstead) this became Wolvrenehamptonia in 1074. The manor was given to Wulfrun in AD 985, a woman who, eleven years later, granted lands to the monastery here, sited where the church now stands.

Wiltshire

❖ AMESBURY

It is most likely that the origin of this name is Ambre's 'burg' (fortified place) since the earliest spelling, in the 9th century, was Ambresbyrig. However, some etymologists think the prefix could come from 'amore' meaning yellowhammer and some historians think the personal name was not Ambre but Ambrosius, the Welsh hero. This place is also linked to the Arthurian legend, Queen Guinevere retiring here after the death of her husband. Some distance to the north is AVEBURY, which was Afa's burg, the fortified place in this instance possibly not referring to the famous stone circle.

❖ BRADFORD-ON-AVON

This was the 'brad' (broad) ford across the river Avon and was called Bradeford in the Domesday Book. The river name here is from the Celtic 'afon' which simply meant river. Nearby STAVERTON, unlike other villages of similar name, probably does not derive from 'staefor-tun' (stake enclosure) but instead from 'stan-ford-tun' (stony ford farmstead). Like Bradford it stands on the river Avon. In the Domesday Book it was Stavretone.

❀ CALNE

This spelling has remained unchanged since AD 955. The name was originally applied to one of the rivers here, either to the Marden or to the Abberd Brook, and can be linked with the names of other English streams – notably the Colne, Calder and Clun. All these derive from an ancient Celtic root – something like 'calaun' or 'colun' (meaning noisy). We also have the Latin 'calare' (to call) and Welsh 'ceilog' (cock or cock's call). Thus the old river Calne probably meant roaring river.

❀ CHIPPENHAM

This is a market town but its name does not come from 'cieping' or 'chipping' (market) or from 'ham' (village). Instead it probably derives from Cippa (a personal name) and 'hamm' (a meadow). The original settlement was situated within a loop of the river Avon and upon fertile pastures. In AD 878 the place was called Cippanhamm; in the Domesday Book (1086) Chipeham.

❀ DEVIZES

A French name this, bestowed by the Normans upon a town which stood at the boundary between two Hundreds, those of Potterne and Cannings. Devises meant boundaries (Latin, 'divisae'), lines that literally, divide. In the 12th century the place was called Divisas and Divisis.

❀ FONTHILL

This name is largely Celtic in origin, being derived from an old river name, 'font', with the suffix 'ial' meaning fertile upland region. The Saxons, however, probably changed these elements later into 'funta' (water channel) and 'hyll' (hill). Thus Funtial (10th century) became Fontel (11th century). The village of FONTHILL BISHOP belonged to the Bishop of Winchester in the 10th century; FONTHILL GIFFORD was held by Berenger Gifard at the time of the Domesday Book. This is an upland area, with many streams and springs, with place-names to match: FOVANT (Fobba's 'funta' or spring), the TEFFONT villages ('teo-funta' or boundary spring), WYLYE ('gwili' or tricky river, being liable to flood), and FISHERTON (fisherman's 'tun' or farmstead).

❀ LACOCK

This name has changed little over the years, being Lacok in the 9th century and Lacoc in the 11th century. It probably comes form the Saxon word 'lacuc' (small stream), a diminutive form of 'lac' (river). The Abbey here dates from the 13th century when it was founded by Ella, Countess of Salisbury.

❀ MALMESBURY

According to the 12th century historian William of Malmesbury, a Scot by the name of Mailduf founded a monastery here and gave his name to the town. Accordingly the place was called Mailduif Urbs in the 8th century (as mentioned by Bede), Mealdelmes Byrig in 1016 and Malmesberie in the Domesday Book: Mailduf's 'burg' or 'burh' (fortified place).

✳ MARLBOROUGH

The suffix here comes not from 'burh' (fortified place) as might have been expected, but from 'beorg' (hill). The town lies at the foot of the Marlborough Downs. The prefix could derive from a personal name, Maerla or Marl but, more interestingly, could instead be a corruption of 'meargealla' or 'mergelle', meaning gentian – a plant used in Saxon times for medicinal purposes. The Domesday Book lists Merleberge.

✳ MELKSHAM

This was originally a 'hamm' (meadow or pasture field) which provided plenty of 'meoluc' (milk). It developed into an important dairying centre. In the Domesday Book it was called Melchesham, in 1198 Melkesham.

✳ PEWSEY

The Domesday Book of 1086 lists Pevesie. Two centuries before it had been Pefesigge, a century later it was to be Peuesia. And the derivation is thought to be Pefe's 'eg' (island). The first settlement here was built on a patch of dry land amidst the upper reaches of the river Avon, hence the reference to an island. According to some people Pefe, or Paf, was a Celt who also gave his name to PEVENSEY in Sussex and 'Penshurst' in Kent.

✳ SALISBURY

The present town was planned by Bishop Poore on a grid pattern and built on the sheltered Avon meadows in the 13th century. It was then call Nova Sarisberia, from which we get the modern name. The original town, on what is now Old Sarum, the Romans called Sorviodunum, from 'dunon' (fort) and 'sorvio' (meaning unknown). The mysterious latter word was made into Searu by the Saxons (linking it to their word for armour) and the suffix 'byrig' (fort) was added. Thus Searobyrig was created (in the 5th century). From this Sarisberie developed (as recorded in the Domesday Book). Sarum was a Latinised abbreviation of that name.

✳ SWINDON

Svindune in the Domesday Book and Swinedon in 1205 clearly show the origin here – 'swin-dun' (pig hill). However, it is not known whether the swine referred to were farm pigs or wild boar.

✳ WILTON

This was the 'tun' (farmstead) on the River Wylye. In the 9th century it was Uuiltun and Wiltun, in the 10th century it was Wiltune. The River Wylye was formerly known as the Wileo and Wilig – names probably derived from a Celtic root similar to Welsh 'gwil' meaning tricky. It is from that root we also get our modern words wily and guile. The WYLYE was probably a rambling, unpredictable river.

WOOTTON BASSETT
Called Wdetun AD 680 and Wodetone in the Domesday Book, this would have been the 'tun' (farmstead) next to the 'wudu' (wood). In the 13th century the manor was held by the Bassett family, producing Wotton Basset in 1271.

ZEALS
This name, called Sela and Sele in the Domesday Book, comes from the same root as Selwood Forest which is nearby – 'sealh', the Saxon word for a sallow or willow tree. The dative form of that word was 'seale' and the plural 'sealas'. The area north of the town is still well wooded.

Worcestershire

ALVECHURCH
Here the first element is unusual since it derives from a female personal name, probably something like Aelfgyth. So it was the 'cyrice' (church) built by or dedicated to a woman. In the 14th century it was Aefgyde Cyrcan.

BEWDLEY
This has exactly the same origin as 'Beaulieu' in Hampshire, namely from the Norman-French 'beau-lieu' meaning beautiful place. But whereas the one in the New Forest has remained unchanged since the village was founded, this one became Beuleu (in 1275) and Beudle (in 1335).

BIRTSMORTON
This was just Mortun in the early 13th century, derived from two Saxon words 'mor' (moorland, upland waste or fen) and 'tun' (farmstead or village). But, to distinguish it from another Morton nearby, it became Brittesmoretone, taking its affix from the Le Bret family which had acquired the estate in the 12th century. The other Morton village, meanwhile, became Castel Morton – now called CASTLE MORTON – from its Norman fort.

BROADWAS
This comes from the Saxon words 'brad' (broad or wide) and 'waesse' (fen or swampy area). It was Bradewesham in the Domesday Book, the 'ham' (farmstead) suffix being added for a while. The village stands on the river Teme where the flood-plain is very wide. Not far downstream is RUSHWICK, which is a corruption of the old Saxon word 'rixuc' for rushy brook or rushy place.

BROMSGROVE
Unlike other place-names with this prefix, the derivation here is not from the Saxon word for broom. Instead it comes from a personal name – something like Breme. The suffix comes from the Saxon 'graefe' for a grove or thicket. In the 9th century it was Bremesgraf, in the Domesday Book Bremesgrave.

✖ CROWLE

In the 5th century a stream is recorded here called Crohwaella, which probably meant winding stream. This name seems to have been shortened and the suffix 'leah' (grove) added. Thus, by the 9th century we find Croglea, this subsequently changing to Croelai by the time of the Domesday Book.

✖ DROITWICH

Salt has been extracted here since Celtic times – producing the Roman name of Salinae and the Saxon name of Saltwic (as recorded in AD 888). In the Domesday Book, however, it was just called Wich; by 1347 it had become Drightwich. 'Wic' was a Saxon word with various meanings but here probably meant specialist place or even saltworks. The present prefix could come either from 'drit' (dirt, mud) or from 'dryht' (troop, army), or else from 'dryht' (laudatory, grand, famous). Considering the town's reputation as a salt-producer the last suggestion seems the most likely.

✖ EVESHAM

From the early spellings – Eveshomme in AD 709, Eoueshamme in 1017 – it seems clear that the suffix comes from 'hamm' (meadow) rather than 'ham' (village). But the prefix derives from Eof (a personal name) rather than the more obvious 'eofer', or 'efer' (boar).

✖ INKBERROW

From the spelling in the 8th century, Intanbeorgas, and the Domesday Book version Inteberge, we can surmise that the derivation is from a personal name (Inta) and the Saxon word 'beorg' (hillock or burial mound). Nearby is HOLBERROW. The prefix here may come from 'holh', which usually meant hole but in this instance could have described the mound as breached or hollowed out.

✖ KIDDERMINISTER

In the 8th century there was a minster, or monastery, here standing on the site now occupied by All Saints Church. In the Domesday Book the village was called Chideminstre, in 1212 it was called Kidelministre. The prefix derives from a personal name – Cyda, Cydda or Cydela.

✖ MALVERN

There are a number of settlements hereabouts, all named after the Malvern Hills. Malvern comes from a Celtic root meaning bare hill: 'mel', 'mailo' and the Welsh 'moel'; 'fryn' and the Welsh 'bryn' respectively. GREAT and LITTLE MALVERN (known as Malferna in the Domesday Book) were mother and daughter villages; MALVERN LINK took its affix from the Saxon 'hlinc' meaning ridge; MALVERN WELLS was so called in the 18th century when it was developed as a spa town.

✇ Pershore

This was Perscoran in AD 972, Prescoran in about 1032 and Persore in the Domesday Book (1086). It derives from an old dialectic word 'persh' (meaning osier and, itself, coming from the Saxon 'persch' meaning twig) and from 'ora' (river bank), hence this place-name meant willow-bank.

✇ Redditch

Called Rededich and La Rededich in the 13th century, this can be traced back either to 'hreod-dic' (reed ditch) or to 'read-dic' (red ditch). But an earlier reference to Rubeo Fossato (in about 1200) seems to support the latter possibility. The soils here are indeed reddish in colour.

✇ Tenbury Wells

From Temedebyrig and Tamedeberie, both recorded in the 11th century, this was clearly the 'burh' or 'burg' (fortified place) on the River Teme. The latter is a name of Celtic origin similar in derivation to Tame, Taf and Thames, all of which come from Sanskrit 'tamas' – the dark river. Saline springs were discovered here in the middle of the 19th century leading to the town's development as a spa resort, hence the appendage 'Wells'.

✇ White Ladies Aston

Aston is a very common place-name, meaning 'east tun' (eastern farmstead). In fact, in the Domesday Book this village was simply called Estun. The present name first appeared as Whitladyaston in the 15th century, after the manor was taken over by the Cistercian nuns of Whitstones, in Claines, north of Worcester.

✇ Worcester

The Saxons called this the 'ceaster' (Roman camp) of the Weogoran tribe. Who the Weogorans were is not known but their name probably went back to early Celtic times and was linked to the same lingistic root as the Wyre Forest. From Wigorna Ceastre in AD 779, the name became Wigraceaster in AD 904 and Wirecestre in the Domesday Book.

Yorkshire
(including South Yorkshire conurbations)

✇ Barnsley

This was the 'leah' (woodland clearing) belonging to Beorn, a personal name meaning warrior and possibly short for Beornwulf (wolf-fighter). In the Domesday Book it was Berneslai.

⊞ BEVERLEY
From the spelling Beferic in about 1000 the origin appears to be 'beofor' (beaver) and 'lecc' (stream). The suffix was later corrupted into 'leah' (meaning grove) and then ley.

⊞ BLUBBERHOUSES
The old form, Bluberhusum in 1172, seems to suggest an origin in the Saxon words 'blubber' (foaming, boiling, bubbling) and 'hus' (house). If so, then the place was either sited next to a fast-flowing stream, or else had some connection with an early industrial process – salt extraction from evaporation perhaps.

⊞ BRADFORD
The derivation here is clearly from 'brad' (broad or wide) and 'ford', the Bradford Beck being a back formation. Bradeford appears in the Domesday Book of 1086.

⊞ BRIDLINGTON
Bretlinton in the Domesday Book probably had an origin from the Saxon 'Beorhtel-ingas-tun': the farmstead of Beorhtel's people. The personal name here could have come from 'beorht' meaning bright.

⊞ CATTERICK
The Latin Cataracta (cataract or waterfall) was changed by the Celts to a name based on 'catu' (war) and 'ratis' (rampart). The Saxons further changed it, to become Catrice by the 11th century.

⊞ DEWSBURY
Some etymologists suggest that the first element here could actually come from dew (Saxon 'deaw') and refer either to an old river name or else to a location that was prone to condensation or moisture, as a low-lying valley might be. However, a personal name is a more likely origin, Dewi, perhaps, or even David. The suffix comes from 'burh' (fortified place). In the Domesday Book it was Deusberia. Neighbouring BATLEY derives from Bata's 'leah' (glade) and OSSETT from Osla's 'geset' (fold or enclosure).

⊞ ELLAND
This name has not changed much over the centuries, being Elant in the 11th century. It comes from the Saxon word 'ealand' meaning island or land by a river. There are many place-names hereabouts connected with the river-cut landscape: BRIGHOUSE ('houses by the bridge' in this case over the river Calder); RIPPONDEN (the 'denu' or valley of the Ryburn, the village once being called Riburnedene); RISHWORTH (the 'worth' or enclosure where rushes grew).

⊞ FILEY

From the 10th to the 12th centuries the spelling here changed from Fiuelac to Fivelai to Fifle – all of which suggest a derivation from 'fif' and 'leah' meaning five clearings. Further north the name FYLINGDALES comes from a different root, from the 'inga' (people) of the personal name Fygla, to which the Viking 'dalr' (valley) was added. This was Figelinge in the 11th century.

⊞ GOOLE

This was Gowle in the 16th century, deriving from the Saxon word 'gool' (small stream, ditch, sluice) from which we get our modern word gulley. The river Ouse marshlands here have been continually drained over the centuries, giving rise to a network of waterways.

⊞ HALIFAX

Probably not from 'halig' (holy) 'feax' (hair) 'feld' (clearing), this name more likely comes from 'halh' (nook) and 'gefeax' or 'fax' (rough grassland or flax). The Feslei of Domesday Book became Haliflex by 1175.

⊞ HARROGATE

The suffix here is clearly from Old Norse 'gata' (road) but there are many origin options for the prefix: 'here' (army), 'hlaw' (mount), 'hoh' (ridge) and 'horg' (heap of stones). Sadly no early versions of the name survive.

⊞ HAWORTH

From Hauewrth and Hawurth, both recorded in the 13th century, we can deduce an origin here from the Saxon words 'haga' (hedge, fenced enclosure) and 'worth' (settlement). Today the place is famous for its links with the Brontë sisters.

⊞ HULL

This is actually called Kingston-upon-Hull, the latter being the river name (from a Celtic word meaning muddy). It was 'King's Town' because Edward I acquired the manor in 1292. An earlier name was Wike, from the Saxon 'wic' meaning dairy farm or secondary village.

⊞ ILKLEY

The Domesday Book version, Illicleia, suggests the suffix comes from 'leah' (glade). The first element is probably a personal name, Illica. Over the hill, KEIGHLEY has a similar origin (this being Cyhha's leah), as does the nearby town of GUISELEY (Gislica's leah). All the valleys hereabouts were once well forested.

⊞ KNARESBOROUGH

This either derives from Cenhearde's 'burg' (fortified place) or from 'knar' (rugged rock) burg. The Castle site is a rugged outcrop, so the latter is perhaps the more likely.

⊞ LEEDS

Loidis in the 8th century suggests an origin connected with Lindis (Lindsey) in Lincolnshire, and a Celtic root meaning district of rivers. The name was Ledes in the Domesday Book.

⊞ MALTON

This was Maltune in the Domesday Book, probably derived from the Saxon 'middel tun' (middle homestead or village) and altered by later Scandinavian settlers into Medaltun, this becoming Maaltun. There are many tun villages in this part of Yorkshire: NORTON (north village), SWINTON (swine or pig farm), HUTTON (from 'hoh'; spur or hill), HESLERTON (from 'haesel', hazel), LANGTON (from 'langa', long) and so on.

⊞ NORTHALLERTON

In the Domesday Book this was just called Aluertune, deriving from Aelfred's 'tun' (village). It was not until the late 13th century that it became North Alverton. This extra adjective was used to distinguish it from other Allertons in the county: ALLERTON near Bradford, ALLERTON MAULEVERER near Knaresborough, ALLERTON BYWATER near Castleford, CHAPEL ALLERTON near Leeds. It is not known whether or not all these places were named after the same Aelfred. Incidentally, Mauleverer was a Norman nickname and surname meaning poor harrier, and possibly refers to Richard Malus Leporarius who held that manor in the 12th century.

⊞ PICKERING

Picheringa, as recorded in the Domesday Book, was a name taken directly from the tribe, the Piceringas. This was from 'ingas' (the people of) and either 'picere' (the pointed hill) or 'picora' (the edge of the hill). Perhaps the latter is the more likely since the town stands just south of the North York Moors.

⊞ PONTEFRACT

The old Latin name Pontus Fractus gives us the meaning (broken bridge) and the old Norman-French version, Pontfreit in 1177, gives us the rough pronunciation ('pomfrit'). The place is famous for liquorice.

⊞ RIPON

The version of this name found in the 8th century, Hrypis, was the dative plural form of the Saxon word Hrype (otherwise Hreope), the name of a local tribe. By the 11th century it had become Rypum and Ripun.

⊞ SCARBOROUGH

According to legend this was the 'burh' (fortified place) built by Skarthi (a tribal leader whose name meant hare-lipped). However, the name could instead come from old Norse 'skarth-berg' (gap-hill) since the town does lie between two cliffs. In the 12th century it was Escardeburg.

▣ SHEFFIELD

This was the 'feld' (open land) on the river Sheaf. The latter was called the Scheve in the 12th century from the word 'sceath' meaning boundary. The river divides the old West Riding and Derbyshire.

▣ THIRSK

This is an unusual name since it comes from old Swedish – 'thraesk', 'thresk' or 'trask' meaning a lake or fenland. In the Domesday Book it was Tresch, in the 12th century Thresca. There are many rivers hereabouts and the land must once have been quite marshy.

▣ WAKEFIELD

The suffix here is clearly from 'feld' (open land) but the prefix has one of two possible origins. Either it comes, simply, from a personal name, Waca perhaps, or else from the Saxon 'wacu' (watch, wake, ceremonial gathering). The latter is the more plausible. 'Wakes', in the Northern sense of festivals, are still held here: twice a year there is a fair, wake-plays are still performed and the town still hosts the 'Towneley Plays'. In the Domesday Book the place was called Wachefeld, in 1219 Wakefeld.

▣ WHITBY

This could derive from 'hwit-by' (white village) but is more likely to come from a personal name – Hviti's by perhaps. It was Witebi in the Domesday Book and Quiteby in 1218.

▣ WOMBWELL

The Saxon word 'wamb', from which the prefix here is derived, meant either womb or hollow. So the whole name either indicates the site of a spring (Saxon, 'wella') possessing old pagan fertility powers, or else the site of a spring in a depression. In the Domesday Book it was Wanbuelle, in the 12th century Wambewelle.

▣ YORK

First of all the Romans called this place Eboracum, from the Celtic Eburus (connected with 'eburos' meaning yew tree). Then the Saxons called it Eoforwicceaster, meaning the 'Roman camp of the wild boar place'. By the 11th century this had been shortened to Eferwic and Euruic. Finally along came the Danes who made this version more Scandinavian: Jorvik. From this it was but a short step, through the Jeorc of 1205, to the present spelling.

Common Place-Name Elements

C – Celtic   S – Saxon   N – Norse or Danish   F – French

Element		Origin	Meaning
Beach, Bech, Batch	S	Baece	stream, valley
Berg, Berry, Barrow	S	Beorg	mound, hillock
Bold, Bottle	S	Bold, Botl	house, dwelling
Booth, Both	N	Both, Buth	temporary shelter
Breck, Brick	N	Brekka	hill, slope
Brig, Bridge	S	Brycg	bridge
Brom, Broom	S	Brom	broom, thorny bush
Brough, Broke	S	Broc	brook, stream
Burn, Bourne	S	Burna	spring, stream
Bury, Burgh, Borough	S	Burh, Burg	fortified place
By	N	By, Byr	farmstead, village
Camb, Com	S	Camb	ridge, crest
Carn	C	Carn	cairn, stone heap
Ches, Chis	S	Cisel, Ceosol	gravel, sand
Chester, Caster, Cester	S	Ceaster	Roman camp, old fort
Chir, Cheri	S	Cirice	church
Clough, Clof	S	Cloh	ravine, deep valley
Combe, Comp	S	Cumb	coomb, narrow valley
Cot, Coat, Coton	S	Cot, Cote	cottage, shelter, hut
Crich, Creech	C	Cruc	hill, barrow
Dal, Dale	S / N	Dael, / Dalr	valley, dale
Dean, Dene, Den	S	Denu	vale, valley
Den, Dean	S	Denn	woodland or swine pasture
Don, Dun, Down	S	Dun	hill, down, upland
Dun, Din, Don	C	Din, Dun	fort, hill fort
Ea, Ey, Eau	S	Ea	stream, river

Ey, Ea, Ye	S	Eg	island, dry mound
Ergh, Er	N	Erg	hill pasture, shieling
Field, Fel	S	Feld	clearing, open land, field
Fold, Fald	S	Falod	animal enclosure, fold
Font, Hunt	S	Funta	spring, water-spout
Ford, Forth	S	Ford	ford, crossing point
Frith, Firth	S	Fyrh	wood, woodland
Gate, Yat, Yate	S	Geat	pass, gap, hole
Gate, Gait	N	Gata	road, way, street
Grave, Greave	S	Graf	grove, copse, wood
Haigh, Hale	S	Halh	nook, hillside, recess
Ham	S	Ham	homestead, village
Ham, Homme	S	Hamm	meadow, pasture enclosure
Hanger, Honger	S	Hangra	slope, wooded slope
Haugh, Hay	S	Haeg, Haga	enclosure, fenced land
Head, Ide	S	Heafod	valley head, headland
Heath, Hed, Hat	S	Haeth	heath, heather
High, Hea, Hean	S	Heah	high, important
Hill, Hel, Hul	S	Hyll	hill, pointed mount
Holm, Holme	N	Holmr	small island, meadow
Hope, Hop	S	Hop	fen island, small valley
Hough, Hol, Hoe	S	Hoh, Hoe	hill spur, ridge
How, Hoe	N	Haugr	hill, burial mound
Hulme	N	Hulm	island, water meadow
Hurst, Hirst	S	Hyrst	wooded hill, copse
Hythe, Hive	S	Hyth	landing place, port
Ing, Ings	S	Inga(s)	people of, belonging to
Keld, Kel	N	Kelda	spring, water-spout
Kirk, Kir	N	Kirja	church, holy place
Lac, Lack, Lock	S	Lacu	stream, watercourse
Lan, Land	C	Lan, Lann	enclosure, yard
Latch, Lash, Leach	S	Laecc	stream, bog
Law, Low	S	Hlaw	hillock, burial mound
Lea, Ley, Leigh	S	Leah	glade, forest clearing
Lin, Linn, Lyn	C	Lindo	pool, lake

Lith, Leth	S/N	Hlith	hillside, slope
Lound, Lund, Land	N	Lundr	copse, sacred grove
Mar, Mer, More	S	Maerc	boundary, march
Mar, Mere, Mor	S	Mere	lake, pool
Mars, Mers	S	Mersc	marsh, swamp
Mead, Mede, Made	S	Maed	meadow
Med, Mid	S	Middel	middle
Mond, Mont	F	Mont	mound, hill
Mor, Mur, Moor	S	Mor	moor, waste, barren hill
Naze, Nes, Ness	{ S / N	Naess } / Nes }	headland, cape
Oare, Ore, Or	S	Ora	border, river bank
Over, Ore, Or	S	Ofer	slope, hill-edge, bank
Pen	C	Pen, Penn	hill, headland, peninsula
Pol	C	Pol, Poll	pond, pool, lake
Pool, Pol, Pole	S	Pol, Pull	pool, tidal stream
Port, Porth	S	Port	harbour, market town
Rick, Rigg	S	Ric	narrow strip of land
Ridge, Rigg	S	Hrycg	ridge
Rig, Rigg	N	Hryggr	ridge
Rise, Ris, Rice	S/N	Hris	brushwood
Rith, Reth	S	Rith	stream
Road, Rod, Ro	S	Rod, Roth	clearing, open woodland
Ros, Rhos, Rose	C	Ros, Rhos	headland, moor, heath
Scale, Skill	N	Skili	shieling, hillside hut
Scough, Scoe	N	Skogr	woodland
Seat, Side	N	Saetr	hill pasture, shieling
Set, Sett	S	Saete	dweller, inhabitant
Shaw	S	Sceaga	copse, grove, undergrowth
Shep, Ship	S	Sceap	sheep
Shott, Shat	S	Sceat	corner of land, small wood
Slade, Slate	S	Slaed	valley
Stead, Sted	S	Stede	place, religious site
Stoke, Stock	S	Stoc	religious place, moot site
Stoke, Stock	S	Stocc	trunk, log, wood-pile

Stone, Stan, Sten	S	Stan	stone
Stow, Stoe	S	Stow	holy place, meeting point
Strat, Stret	S	Straet	street, Roman road
Sty, Sti	S	Stig	path
Thorpe, Thorp	N	Thorp	secondary settlement, farm
Throp, Thrupp, Thorpe	S	Throp	hamlet, dependant farm
Thwaite	N	Thveit	clearing, meadow
Toft	N	Toft	homestead, site of dwelling
Ton, Tone, Town	S	Tun	enclosure, farmstead, manor
Tor, Ter	C/S	Torr	rocky peak, hilltop
Tre, Trey	C	Tre, Tref	homestead, hamlet
Trey, Trow, Try	S	Treow	tree, meeting marker-post
Ville	F	Ville	town, resort
Wade, Wad	S	Waed	ford, wading place
Walt, Weald, Wold	S	Wald	forest, high wood, upland
Wark, Walk	S	Weorc	work, fortification
Wash, Was	S	Waesse	wet place, swamp
Wath, With, Worth	N	Vath	ford
Well, Wil, Wal	S	W(a)ella	spring, stream, well
Weo, Wee, Wy	S	Weoh	holy place, heathen site
Wer, War, Ware	S	Wer	weir, dam
Wick, Wich	S	Wic	dwelling, dairy farm, village
With, Wath	N	Vithr	wood, forest
Withy, Weeth	S	Withig	willow, osier
Wood, Woot, Wid	S	Wudu	woodland, timber
Worth, Worthy	S	Worth(ig)	enclosure, farm, village

Index

Index

Abbess Roding 82
Abbotsbury 82
Abbotskerswell 162
Abbot Ways 50
Abingdon 210
Abram 20
Acaster Selby 82
Accrington 185
Akeman Street 45
Akroyden 109
Aldermaston 140
Aldridge 231
Alfreton 73
Alkham 79
All Cannings 97
Allerton Bywater 242
Allerton Mauleverer 242
All Stretton 215
Alnmouth 205
Alnwick 205
Alresford 174
Alsager 149
Alsop en le Dale 159
Alspath 103
Alston 22
Alvechurch 237
Amble 205
Ambleside 154
Amersham 142
Amesbury 234
Ampthill 138
Ancient trackways 41
Andover 174
Anglesey 60
Anstey 103
Arbury 95
Arnold 208
Arundel 227
Ascot 140
Ashbourne 158
Ashby-de-la-Zouch 99
Ashby Magna 97
Ashby Parva 97
Ashfield 224
Ashford 182
Ashton 67
Aspatria 154
Aston 22
Ault Hucknall 209
Avebury 234
Avon, river 59
Aylesbury 142

Aylsham 202
Ayot St Lawrence 82

Bacup 185
Baginton 158
Bagshot 225
Bakewell 21, 158
Baldock 83, 179
Balsall 231
Balsall Common 231
Bamburgh 205
Banbury 95, 211
Barewood 178
Barford 69
Barham 69
Barkfold 103, 158
Barking 21
Barnet 63
Barnsley 239
Barnstaple 160
Barnwell 76
Barrowden 83
Barrow-in-Furness 155
Basildon 168
Basingstoke 174
Bastide towns 101
Bath 26, 111, 216
Battersea 195
Batley 240
Baxterley 76
Beaconsfield 142
Beamish 99
Beauchamp 190
Beaulieu 237
Beaumont 99
Beccles 222
Bedford 138
Bedfordshire 138
Bedlington 206
Beeby 69
Beer Hackett 99
Beeston 208
Belgrave 83
Belper 99, 158
Bemersley 76
Bemerton 76
Benacre 91
Benfleet 104
Benson 211
Benwell 96
Berkshire 140
Beoley 69

Bere Regis
Bergholt 83, 95
Berkhamsted 179
Bernwood 83
Berrick: Salome & Prior
    211
Berwick 101
Berwick-upon-Tweed 205
Beverley 69, 240
Beversbrook 69
Bewaldeth 73
Bewcastle 155
Bewdley 237
Bexhill 228
Bicester 211
Biddulph 220
Biggleswade 104, 138
Billericay 168
Bilston 231
Birkenhead 149
Birmingham 231
Birtsmorton 237
Bishop Auckland 166
Bishop's Castle 96, 213
Bishops Stortford 82
Black Bourton 211
Blackburn 186
Black Country, the 38
Blackpool 185
Blakeney 61, 199
Blanchland 99
Blandford Forum 163
Blaydon 206
Blidworth 208
Blubberhouses 240
Blyth, river 59
Bodmin 151
Bognor Regis 112, 228
Bolsover 158
Bolton 185
Bootle 185
Borrowdale 155
Borwick 206
Boston 93, 192
Bosworth 69
Boughton 208
Bournemouth 163
Bournville 109
Bourton 95
Bowness 155
Brackley 67, 140, 202
Bracknell 140

Bradford 240
Bradford-on-Avon 234
Braintree 169
Bramber 38
Brandon 52
Brandwood 63
Bredon 95
Brentor 86
Brentwood 63
Bretby 71
Bretford 71, 103
Bretton 71
Bridgewater Canal 108
Bridgwater 103, 216
Bridlington 240
Bridport 163
Bridwell 77
Brigg 192
Brighouse 103, 240
Brighton 228
Brigsteer 73
Brigstock 202
Brimstage 104
Brinklow 231
Bristol 216
Britford 77
Britwell: Salome &
   Priory 211
Broadwas 237
Broadwindsor 163
Brockhall 69
Bromsgrove 237
Bromyard 90, 176
Brownsea Island 164
Broxted 69, 80
Broxwood 178
Buckden 69
Buckfast 50
Buckfastleigh 160
Buckingham 143
Buckinghamshire 142
Buckland 50
Bude 152
Budleigh Salterton 105,
   106
Bugley 79
Buildwas 213
Bulmer 68
Bungay 223
Bunny 208
Buntingford 103
Burgess Hill 229
Burial ways 52
Burnley 185
Burradon 95
Burrow Bridge 81
Burton 95
Burton-upon-Trent 220
Bury St Edmunds 73, 223

Buttermere 155, 156
Buxted 230
Buxton 111, 159
Byfleet 227
Bylaugh 83

Cadbury Castle 96
Caernarfon 101
Caister-on-Sea 200
Calne 235
Cam, river 59
Camberley 225
Camberwell 195
Camborne 152
Cambridge 103, 145
Cambridgeshire 145
Cannock 220
Canons Ashby 82
Canterbury 182
Cardington 138
Carlton Forehoe 200
Carlisle 29, 101, 155
Cartmel 156
Castle Acre 94
Castle Bolton 96
Castle Bromwich 231
Castle Cary 216
Castle Donington 189
Castle Morton 237
Castleton 96
Catterick 240
Cavendish 90
Celtic elements 55
Cerne Abbas 164
Chalfont St Giles 143
Chalfont St Peter 143
Chapel Allerton 242
Chapel Brampton 82
Chapel-en-le-Frith 158
Chapmanslade 104
Chard 216
Charlton 77
Charlton Kings 171
Chatham 182
Chatteris 145
Cheadle 220
Cheam 225
Cheddar 216
Chelmer, river 59
Chelmsford 59, 169
Chelsea 195
Cheltenham 111, 171
Chepstow 101
Cherry Hinton 145
Chesham 143
Cheshire 36, 149
Cheshunt 179
Cheslyn Hay 222
Chessell 83

Chester 149
Chesterfield 159
Chester-le-Street 37
Cheviot Hills 56
Chichester 228
Chiltern Hills 56
Chiltern Hundreds, The
   40
Chinnor 211
Chippenham 235
Chipping Barnet 104
Chipping Norton 104
Chipping Ongar 170
Chipping Sodbury 104
Chiswick 156, 195
Chrishall 82
Christchurch 82, 165
Christmas Common 10
Church Stretton 82, 215
Cirencester 172
Cissbury Ring 96
Clacton-on-Sea 169
Clapham 195
Clare 223
Cleethorpes 193
Clevedon 112, 217
Cley-next-the-Sea 61
Clipsham 189
Clitheroe 186
Clovelly 160
Clun 213
Clunbury 213
Clungunford 213
Clunton 213
Coalbrookdale 108, 213
Coalport 108
Coalville 108
Coastal areas 60
Cockermouth 156
Colchester 26, 169
Cold Ashby 58
Cold Eaton 58
Coleford 105, 106, 172
Colemere 214
Colne 187
Colne, river
Colsterworth 76, 106
Combe Martin 161
Congleton 149
Coniston 157
Consett 166
Cookham 140
Corfe Castle 164
Corfe Mullen 164
Corby 202
Cornard 225
Cornelly 82
Cornwall 29, 151
Cotswolds, the 56

Cottesmore 189
County Durham 37
County sub-divisions 37–40
Counties, consolidation of 36–37
Coventry 232
Cowden 106
Cowes 174
Cowley 66, 212
Crackpot Hall 34
Cramlington 206
Cranford 69
Craven Arms 109
Crawley 228
Cray, river 59
Crediton 161
Crewe 108, 149
Crewkerne 217
Cricket St Thomas 217
Cricklade 104
Cricklewood 195
Cromer 200
Crossthwaite 82
Crowborough 228
Crowhurst 228
Crowle 238
Crowmarsh Battle 82
Crowthorne 140
Croxall 220
Croydon 225
Cuckfield 229
Cullompton 161
Culmstock 161
Cumbria 29, 30, 154

Danby 71
Danelaw 33, 35
Darley 159
Darlington 166
Dartmoor 56
Dart, river 56
Darwen 186
Daventry 203
Dawley 213
Dawlish 161
Deal 182
Denby 71
Denver 103
Denwick 205
Derby 159
Derbyshire 158
Derwent, river 59
Devizes 99, 235
Devon 31, 160
Dewsbury 240
Dickley 95
Didcot 212
Diddington 22

Doddington 22
Dodington 22
Doncaster 95
Dorchester, Dorset 35
Dorchester, Oxon 211
Dorking 225
Dorset 163
Dotton 22
Dover 175, 182
Dowdyke 95
Downham Market 200
Dradnop 159
Drakehill 79
Drakelow 79
Drayton 202
Droitwich 49, 151, 238
Drove roads 49
Dudley 232
Dungeness 183
Dunstable 74, 138
Dunstew 212
Durham 166
Dwariden 79
Dymchurch 183

Eardisley 178
Earlestown 109
Easole 79
East Dereham 200
East Grinstead 228
Eastleigh 108
Easton-in-Gordano 217
Eastrea 95
East Stow 58
Eccles 80
Eccleshall 221
Edgbaston 232
Edinburgh 73, 209
Edith Weston 99
Edwinstowe 208
Eisey 79
Eland 95
Elland 240
Ellesmere 214
Ellesmere Port 149
Elmswell 224
Ely 12, 69, 81, 145
Enfield 91, 196
Englefield 71
English Riviera, The 38
Enham Alamein 98
Enville 221
Epping Forest 64, 66
Epping Upland 64
Epsom 111
Erith 104
Ermine Street 45, 46
Esher 226
Essex 31, 168

Evercreech 218
Evershed 80
Everton 69
Evesham 238
Ewyas Harold 177
Exeter 95, 161
Exmouth 104
Eyam 159
Eynesbury 147

Fakeham 202
Fareham 174
Farnham 226
Faversham 182
Felixstowe 223
Felling 206
Feltham 196
Ferrybridge 104
Finchingfield 69
Finchley 196
Filey 241
Fisherton 235
Five Towns, the 38
Fleckney 190, 200
Fleetwood 107
Flitton 138
Flitwick 138
Flore 203
Foleshill 95
Folkestone 183
Fordham 103
Fordington 103
Fordley 103
Forest of Dean, 64, 66
Formby 186
Fonthill 235
Fonthill Bishop 235
Fonthill Gifford 235
Fosse Way 46, 48
Fotheringay 203
Fountains Abbey 50
Fovant 235
Fowey 152
Fretherne 79
Frinton on Sea 112
Friston 71
Frogmore 69
Frome, river 59
Froyle 79
Fulham 196
Fylingdales 241

Gainsborough 192
Galgate 186
Galligill 84
Garden Cities 114, 115
Garstang 186
Gateford 103
Gateshead 206

Gillingham 182
Glastonbury 217
Glossop 159
Gloucester 172
Gloucestershire 171
Gnosall 221
Godmanchester 146
Godney 61
Godstow 82
Goodrich 177
Goole 241
Goonhilly 153
Goring 211, 230
Gorran Haven 153
Gorsley 67
Gosfield 69
Gosport 174
Gowbarrow 84
Grafton Regis 74
Grafty 90
Grand Union Canal 108
Grantchester 21, 145
Grantham 193
Grasmere 156
Gravesend 183
Great Baddow 169
Great Dunmow 170
Great Malvern 238
Great Missenden 97
Great Tew 212
Great Waltham 171
Great Yarmouth 200
Grimsby 193
Grosmont 99
Guildford 21, 226
Guiseley 241
Guyhirn 146

Hadleigh 20
Hadrian's Wall 96
Hailsham 229
Hainault 82
Halesowen 232
Halifax 241
Hallington 82
Halstead 169
Haltwistle 206
Hambledon 142
Hamble le Rice 174
Hammersmith 196
Hampshire 174
Harborough 95
Harcourt 190
Harlech 101
Harlow 114, 115, 169
Harpenden 179
Harperley 76
Harperwell 76
Harrogate 111, 241

Harrow 79, 196
Harrowden 79
Harrow Way, the 42
Harrow Weald 196
Hartland 69
Hartlepool 167
Haselbury 67
Haslingfield 72
Hassop 159
Hastings 72, 112, 229
Hatfield 91, 179
Hathersage 159
Havant 175
Haverhill 223
Havering-atte-Bower 20
Hawkchurch 82
Haworth 241
Hayes 196
Haynes 90
Hay-on-Wye 177
Haywards Heath 229
Hebburn 206
Hedingham 72
Helsby 150
Helston 152
Hemel Hempstead 179
Hendon 196
Henley-in-Arden 232
Henley-on-Thames 212
Henwick 82
Hepburn 83
Hereford 177
Herefordshire 176
Hertford 180
Hertfordshire 179
Heslerton 243
Heswall 150
Hethersett 200
Hetton-le-Hole 167
Hexham 76, 93, 206
Heyford 103
Higham Ferrers 203
High Ongar 170
High Wycombe 143
Hillingdon 197
Hilton 95
Hinckley 190
Hindhead 69
Hinxworth 179
Hitchin 71, 180
Hobmoor 79
Hoddesdon 180
Hodnet 214
Holberrow 238
Holborn 197
Holderness 76
Holland 37
Holyhead 82
Holywell 82

Honiton 69
Hope 159
Hope Under Dinmore
  177
Hopton 90
Horncastle 193
Horsham 229
Horstead 20
Houghton-le-Spring 167
Houghton Regis 74, 139
Hounslow 83, 227
Hove 230
Howton 99
Hoylake 150
Hucknall 209
Huish Episcopi 83
Hull 241
Humber, river 59
Hundreds 40
Hungerford 140
Hunstanton 201
Huntingdon 146
Huntington 76
Husbands Bosworth 190
Hutton 242
Huthwaite 209
Hythe 183

Ickleford 42, 180
Ickleton 42
Icknield Way 42
Ilfracombe 161
Ilkley 241
Ilminster 217
Ince-in-Makerfield 189
Ingatestone 170
Ingestre 221
Ingoldmells 193
Ingoldsby 193
Inkberrow 238
Internet, using the 13
Ipswich 223
Ironbridge 107, 108,
  213
Ironville 108
Irthlingborough 203
Isle of Dogs 62
Isle of Man 29, 30
Isle of Oxney 183
Isle of Portland 62
Isle of Purbeck 62
Isle of Thanet 62
Isle of Sheppey 182
Isle of Wight 62, 174
Isles of Scilly 62
Islington 198
Islip 205
Itchen, river 26, 59
Ivel, river 71

Ivinghoe 143
Iwerne Minster 82

Jamaica Inn 9
Jarrow 71, 206
Jugglers' Way 52
Jurassic Way 44

Keighley 241
Keld 34
Kempshot 76
Kempston 138
Kendal 156
Kenilworth 232
Kensal Green 198
Kensington 197
Kent 31, 182
Kesteven 37
Keswick 120, 156
Kettering 203
Ketton 190
Keynsham 217
Kibworth 190
Kidderminster 82, 238
Kilburn 197
Kimbolton 146
Kingskerwell 161
Kings Cliffe 74
Kings Lynn 74, 95, 201
Kingston-upon-Thames 226
Kingswood 178
Kinnersley 178
Kirkby Lonsdale 156
Kirkby Stephen 156
Knaresborough 241
Knavenhill 77
Knutsford 150

Lacock 235
Lambeth 199
Lambourn 141
Lancashire 36, 185
Lancaster 186
Lancing 230
Landbeach 148
Laneham 103
Langton 242
Lanivet 80
Lanteglos 80
Larkfield 69
Latchmere 69
Lathes 38
Launceston 100, 101, 152
Lazenby 76
Leake 221
Leamington Hastings 233
Leamington Priors 233

Leamington Spa 111, 232
Leatherhead 22, 226
Lechlade 172
Ledbury 177
Leeds 242
Leek 221
Leicester 190
Leicestershire 189
Leighton Bromswold 146
Leighton Buzzard 139
Leiston 224
Leominster 177
Letchworth 113, 180
Lewes 229
Lewknor 211
Leyland 186
Leyton 139
Lichfield 22, 221
Lime Ways 49
Limpstead 226
Lincoln 95, 193
Lincolnshire 37, 192
Lindsey 37
Lindisfarne 207
Linguistic developments 17
Linkenholt 91
Linslade 104, 143
Liskeard 152
Litchborough 84
Litherland 187
Little Dunmow 170
Little Hadham 97
Little Malvern 238
Little Missenden 97
Little Stretton 215
Little Waltham 171
Liverpool 187
Llandovery 80
London 26, 29, 195
Long Melford 224
Looe 153
Lostwithiel 152
Loughborough 191
Louth 193
Lower Caldecote 58
Lowestoft 224
Lowther 156
Ludlow 101, 214
Luffenham, North & South 191
Lugwardine 178
Luton 139
Lutterworth 191
Lyme Regis 74, 111, 164
Lymington 175
Lymm 150
Lympne 29

Lydd 183
Lydney 172

Mablethorpe 194
Macclesfield 150
Maida Vale 197
Maiden Castle 26, 96
Maidenhead 77, 141
Maidstone 183
Maidwell 77
Maldon 170
Malmesbury 235
Malton 242
Malvern 238
Malvern Link 238
Malvern Wells 238
Manchester 95, 187
Mangotsfield 218
Mansfield 209
Manshead 80
Maplebeck 209
Marazion 153
March 146
Maresfield 229
Margate 184
Market Bosworth 104, 190
Market Rasen 194
Markham 210
Marlborough 236
Marlow 144
Marlston 99
Marshfield 91
Marston Trussell 99
Martello Towers 108
Mantock 217
Marylebone 197
Maryport 107, 157
Matlock 160
Maund 35
Mawgan 82
Meadbourne 91
Melbury Bubb 164
Mells 106
Melksham 236
Melton Mowbray 99, 191
Mendip Hills 57
Mercia 31
'Merry Maidens', The 84
Mersey, river 59
Methwold 201
Metroland 39
Mevagissy 153
Micheldever 175
Mickleover 97
Middlesborough 95, 167
Middlesex 31, 195
Middlewich 151

Midgham 141
Midsomer Norton 218
Midwinter 91
Mildenhall 224
Military Roads 52
Millbourne 106
Millbrook 106
Milton Keynes 115, 144
Minchinhampton 172
Minehead 218
Mitcheldean 97
Molesworth 147
Monken Hadley 82
Morecambe 187
Moresby 158
Moreton-in-the-Marsh 173
Morpeth 83, 207
Mortgrove 83
Mousehole 153
Muchelney 217
Much Hadham 97
Muker 34
Mullion 153

Nailsworth 173
Names, Animal 68–69
Names, Christian 80–83
Names, Climatic 58
Names, Colonisation 97–99
Names, Death and Burial 83–84
Names, Directional 56–58
Names, Enclosure 90
Names, Estate 91–93
Names, Field 88–89
Names, Folk and Legend 84–86
Names, Folk and Tribal 70
Names, Football Club 126
Names, Forest 63–67
Names, Fortified Settlement 93–96
Names, Group 73–77
Names, House 123–124
Names, Industrial Revolution 106–111
Names, Market 104
Names, Medieval Trading 110
Names, Mineral 104–106
Names, Modern Regional 76–77
Names, Pagan 78–80
Names, Personal 72–73
Names, Pub 124–133

Names, Regional Image 38
Names, Resort 111–116
Names, Rivers and Estuaries 59–60
Names, Shopping Centre 110
Names, Street 117–123
Names, Theatre & Cinema 133–136
Names, Transport 102–104
Names, Tree & Plant 67
Names, Urban 112–116
Nantwich 150
Neasden 196
Nelson 187
New Brighton 112
New Forest 66
New Lanark 109
New Towns 114
New Tredegar 109
New Winchelsea 21
Newark 209
Newbury 141
Newcastle-upon-Tyne 207
Newent 173
Newhaven 99
Newlyn 153
Newmarket 99
Newport 99
Newport Pagnell 99, 144
Newquay 99
Newton Abbot 162
Newton Aycliffe 167
Non-Trading Routes 50–52
Norfolk 31, 199
Northallerton 242
Northampton 203
Northamptonshire 202
North Downs 57
Northfleet 104
Northumberland 205
Northumbria 31, 32
Northwich 22, 151
Northwick 22
Norton 242
Norwell 210
Norwich 22, 93, 121, 201
Nottingham 93, 209
Nottinghamshire 208
Notting Hill 197
Nuneaton 233
Nunney 82, 94

Oakengates 213
Oakford 67
Oakham 191

Offa's Dyke 32, 96
Okehampton 162
Oldbury Camp 96
Oldham 187
Old Sarum 25
Old Sodbury 97
Ollerton 209
Olney 142
Orchardleigh 91
Osset 240
Osterley 197
Oswaldtwistle 73
Oswestry 73, 214
Othenesburg 79
Oundle 71, 204
Ouse, river 59
Outwell 147
Owlpen 90
Oxford 212
Oxfordshire 210
Oxted 226

Paddington 197
Padstow 153
Pangbourne 141
Papworth Everard 99
Parracombe 161
Peacehaven 98, 112
Peckham 195
Peddars Way 46
Pembroke 101
Pendeford 73
Pennines, the 57
Penrith 157
Penshurst 236
Penwith 60
Penzance 95, 153
Perivale 198
Pershore 239
Peterborough 95, 147
Peterlee 114
Petersfield 175
Pevensey 236
Pewsey 236
Phepson 71
Pickering 242
Pilgrims' Way 42
Pilgrim Ways 50
Pimlico 198
Pinchbeck 194
Pinner 198
Plymouth 162
Plympton 162
Polperro 153
Pontefract 242
Poole 164
Poppyland 39
Portbury 218
Porthmadog 107

Portishead 218
Portland 104
Portmellon 153
Portsdown 175
Portsea 175
Portslade 230
Portsmouth 104, 175
Port Sunlight 109
Potteries, the 38
Potters Bar 180
Potton 139
Prees 214
Prescot 151
Prestatyn 151
Preston 188
Prestwich 82
Princes Risborough 144
Princetown 162
Prittlewell 170
Pub Names
 – Animal 130
 – Famous People 132
 – Heraldic 125
 – Miscellaneous 132
 – Royal 127
 – Trade 131
Puckeridge 79
Purbrook 79
Purfleet 21
Putley 178
Putney 90
Puxton 79

Quantock Hills 57
Quarndon 106
Quarrendon 106
Quorndon 106, 191

Radcliffe on Trent 209
Radstock 218
Ramsbottom 188
Ramsey 148, 175
Ramsgate 184
Rapes 38
Raunds 204
Ravenglass 157
Reading 72, 141
Reavely 76
Redcar 167
Redditch 239
Redruth 154
Regents Canal 108
Reigate 227
Rendlesham 12
Retford 209
Richards Castle 213
Richmond 99, 101, 227
Ridgemont 99
Ridgeway, The 42

Ripon 71, 242
Ripponden 240
Rishworth 240
Rivers & Estuaries 26, 59
Roads, Roman 26, 44–48
Roads, Toll 52–53
Robin Hood's Bay 85
Rochdale 188
Rochester 184
Roding 72
Rollright Stones 84
Romsey 175
Romsley 175
Ross-on-Wye 178
Rotherhithe 104
Rothwell 204
Routes, Non Trading
 50–52
Routes, Trading 48–50
Royal Military Canal 108
Royston 180
Rugby 233
Rugeley 221
Ruislip 198
Runcorn 151
Runnymede 91, 227
Ruscombe 142
Rushden 203
Rushwick 237
Rutland 189
Ruyton XI Towns 214
Rydal 157
Ryde 176
Rye 230

Saffron Walden 92, 170
St Albans 82, 181
St Austell 82, 154
St Breock 82
St Buryan 82
St Clear 82
St Erth 154
St Eval 82
St Helens 82
St Ives (Cambs) 147
St Ives (Cornwall) 82,
 154
St Just 154
St Mary Cray 82
St Michael's Mount 86
St Neots 147
Salisbury 236
Saltaire 109
Saltash 106
Salter 106
Salterford 106
Salthouse 106
Salthrop 106
Salt Ways 49

Sandbach 151
Sandwich 184
Sandy 139
Sattering 77
Sawtry 148
Saxham 71
Saxon Elements 55
Scandanavian Elements
 55
Scarborough 112, 242
School Aycliffe 167
Scotland 29
Scrooby 210
Scunthorpe 194
Seaton Delaval 207
Sedgefield 168
Sedgeley 76
Selly Oak 232
Selsey 230
Selworthy 90
Sevenhampton 85
Seven Kings 85
Sevenoaks 85, 226
Seven Sisters 85
Severn, river 60
Shacklow 79
Shaftesbury 165
Shallcross 82
Shanklin 175
Shap 157
Sheffield 9, 243
Shefford 103
Shepshed 80
Shepton Mallet 99, 218
Sheringham 201
Sherwood Forest 66, 85
Shildon 168
Shinfold 90
Shiplake 20
Shipston-on-Stour 233
Shires, development of
 33–35
Shoreham 230
Shotton Colliery 108
Shrewsbury 95, 214
Shropshire 213
Shugborough 79
Shuttleworth 90
Silverstone 204
Sittingbourne 72
Skegness 194
Sleaford 194
Slough 141
Smallburgh 95
Smugglers' Ways 49
Soham 148
Soho 198
'Sokes', the 37
Solihull 233

Somerset 216
Somerton 218
Southampton 35, 176
South Downs 57
Southend-on-Sea 112, 170
Southport 104, 186
Southsea 175
South Shields 207
Southwell 210
Southwold 224
Spalding 194
Speen 141
Spennymoor 168
Spixworth 201
Stafford 222
Staffordshire 220
Staines 227
Stalybridge 103, 188
Standlynch 91
Stane Street 45
Stanhope 168
Stanmore 198
Stanstead Mountfitchet 170
Stapleford 103
Statham 104
Staveley 66
Stevenage 114, 181
Stewkley 148
Stilton 46
Stocking Pelham 95
Stockport 188
Stockton-on-Tees 168
Stoke Albany 204
Stoke Bruerne 204
Stoke Doyle 204
Stoke by Nayland 82
Stoke Edith 99
Stokenchurch 95
Stoke Newington 198
Stoke-on-Trent 222
Stoke Poges 144
Stonehenge 80
Stotfold 139, 179
Stourbridge 104
Stourport 108
Stour, river 59
Stowmarket 104, 224
Stow-on-the-Wold 82
Stratford 103
Stratford-on-Avon 233
Streatley 211
Street 219
Stretford 188
Stretton 103, 215
Strood 173
Stroud 173
Stukeley 148

Stump Cross 82
Sudbury 224
Suffolk 31, 222
Sunderland 208
Surrey 31, 225
Sussex 31, 227
Sutton Coldfield 235
Swadlincote 160
Swaffham 71, 202
Swaledale 34
Swanage 112, 165
Swanmore 69
Swindon 108, 236
Swineshead 80
Swinford 104
Swinside 80
Swinton 242
Symonds Yat 178
Syresham 204

Tadmorton 69
Tamworth 222
Taplow 83
Taunton 93, 219
Taverham 202
Tavistock 162
Taw, river 59
Teddington 21, 22
Tees, river 168
Teesside 166
Teffont 235
Telford 107, 114, 213
Temple Balsall 231
Templecombe 83
Temple Normanton 83
Templeton 83
Tenbury Wells 239
Tenterden 184
Tetbury 173
Tewin 79
Tewkesbury 173
Thames, The 60
Thatcham 141
Thaxted 170
Theale 141
Thetford 202
Thirlspott 79
Thirwall 96
Thirsk 243
Thornbury 219
Thorney 148, 217
Thornhough 90
Thrapston 205
Thrushgill 79
Thunderley 79
Thundersfield 79
Tickencote 191
Tidmarsh 142
Tinhead 154

Tintagel 154
Tiverton 162
Toddington 139
Toller Fratrum 165
Toller Porcorum 165
Toll roads 52–53
Tolpuddle 165
Tonbridge 103, 111, 184
Topographical features 54–56
Torkard 209
Tormarton 95
Torquay 112, 162
Torver 157
Totham 95
Totnes 100, 163
Tottenham 199
Totternhoe 139
Tove, river 59
Trackways, ancient 41
Trading Routes 48–49
Trent, river 60
Trimdon Colliery 108
Tring 181
Tripsdale 84
Truro 154
Tuesley 79
Tunbridge Wells 111, 184
Turnpikes 52–53
Tuxford 210
Twickenham 199
Tynemouth 104
Tyne, river 79
Tyneside 205
Tysoe 79

Uckfield 230
Uffculme 161
Ulverston 158
Upland Areas 56
Upper Caldecote 58
Uppingham 192
Upshire 66
Upwell 147
Uttoxeter 222
Uxbridge 71, 199

Ventnor 176
Villages, Manorial 97
Villages, Mother & Daughter 97
Villages, New 99

Wakefield 243
Walbrook 71
Walcot 71
Wales 29
Wallasey 151

Wallbottle 96
Wallingford 72, 103, 212
Walltown 96
Walsall 234
Walsingham 202
Waltham Abbey 171
Waltham Cross 171
Walthamstow 21
Walton 71
Walton-on-the-Naze 171
Walworth 199
Wandle, river 59
Wanlip 192
Wansdyke 96
Wantage 212
Wapentakes 39
Ward End 231
Wards 39
Ware 181
Wareham 165
Warrington 189
Warwick 93, 234
Warwickshire 231
Wash, the 60
Washingborough 195
Watchet 219
Waterbeach 148
Watendlath 34
Waterlooville 109
Watford 181
Watling Street 45, 181
Wayford 103
Wayhill 103
Wayland's Smithy 85
Wearside 205
Weaverham 151
Wednesbury 79
Wednesfield 79, 234
Weedon 79
Weedon Bec 82
Wellingborough 205
Wellington 215
Wells 219
Wells-next-the-Sea 202
Welwyn 181
Welwyn Garden City
   113, 114

Wem 215
Wembley 199
Wendover 29, 144
Wenlock 215
Weobley
Weoley 79, 178
Wervin 151
Wessex 31, 32
West Midlands 231
Weston-super-Mare 219
Westonzoyland 219
Westow 77
West Stow 58
Westward Ho! 112
Weyhill 79
Weymouth 166
Wey, river 59
Whalley 189
Wharton 104
Wheathampstead 92
Wherstead 104
Whichwood 71
Whissonsett 77
Whistley 142
Whitby 243
Whitchurch 215
Whitehaven 158
White Ladies Aston 239
Whitechapel 82
Whitstable 184
Whittlesby 148
Whyly 79
Widnes 189
Wigan 189
Wigston Magna 97
Wigston Parva 97
Wilby 224
Williamston 99
Wilmslow 151
Wilton 236
Wiltshire 234
Wimbledon 227
Wincanton 219
Winchester 26, 95,
   176
Windsor 142
Winestead 77

Winscales 58
Winslow 142
Winterton 58
Wirksworth 160
Wirral 62, 149
Wisbech 148
Witney 213
Woburn 140
Wokefield 142
Woking 142, 227
Wokingham 142
Wolford 69
Wolsty 103
Wolverhampton 21, 38,
   234
Wolvey 69
Wombwell 243
Woodbridge 224
Woodnesborough 79
Woodstock 213
Wooler 208
Wootton Bassett 237
Worcester 95, 239
Worksop 210
Worle 219
Worlebury 219
Wormsley 178
Wormwood Scrubs 198
Worthing 230
Wrekin, the 35
Wymondham 202
Wye, river 59
Wylye 235, 236
Wyrley 222

Yardley 66
Yarnbury Camp 96
Yate 218
Yeo, river 59
Yeovil 220
York 243
York Town 225
Yorkshire 31, 37,
   239

Zeals 237
Zennor 82